MESSI

MESSI

MORE THAN A SUPERSTAR

Updated Edition

LUCA CAIOLI

An earlier edition of this book was published in 2008 by
10 Books and Columna, Spain and in 2009 by Planeta, Argentina

First published in the UK in 2010 by
Corinthian Books, an imprint of
Icon Books Ltd, Omnibus Business Centre,
39–41 North Road, London N7 9DP
email: info@iconbooks.com
www.iconbooks.com

This updated edition published in the UK in 2014 by Icon Books Ltd

Sold in the UK, Europe and Asia
by Faber & Faber Ltd, Bloomsbury House,
74–77 Great Russell Street, London WC1B 3DA or their agents

Distributed in the UK, Europe and Asia
by TBS Ltd, TBS Distribution Centre, Colchester Road
Frating Green, Colchester CO7 7DW

Distributed in Australia and New Zealand
by Allen & Unwin Pty Ltd,
PO Box 8500, 83 Alexander Street,
Crows Nest, NSW 2065

Distributed in South Africa
by Jonathan Ball,
Office B4, The District, 41 Sir Lowry Road,
Woodstock 7925

Distributed in India
by Penguin Books India,
11 Community Centre, Panchsheel Park,
New Delhi 110017

ISBN: 978-190685-081-4

Typeset in New Baskerville by Marie Doherty

Printed and bound in the UK by
Clays Ltd, St Ives Plc

Contents

Chapter 1

Rosario

Conversation with Celia and Marcela Cuccittini

'I buy the rump or a piece from the hindquarter. They're cuts of beef I've also seen in Barcelona but I don't know what they're called. I put a bit of salt on each piece, dip them in egg and coat them in breadcrumbs. I fry them until they're nice and golden-brown and I put them in an oven dish. I slice the onion finely and fry it over. When the onion turns white, I add chopped tomatoes, a little water, salt, oregano and a pinch of sugar. And I leave it on the heat for around twenty minutes. Once the sauce is done, I pour it on top of each piece of beef, making sure they're well covered. I take some cream cheese or hard cheese out of the fridge and lay it on top of the beef in thin slices. I leave them in the oven until the cheese melts. All that's left to do is fry the potatoes as a side dish and the *milanesa a la napolitana* [schnitzel napolitana] is ready to serve.'

With the passion and experience of a good cook, Celia describes her son Lionel Messi's favourite dish.

'When I go to Barcelona I have to make it two or three times a week. And with at least three medium-sized cuts of beef. I tousle his hair and tell him: "My schnitzel napolitana and my *mate* [traditional Argentine tea] are what make you score so many goals."' Lionel has simple gastronomic tastes: schnitzel, but not made with ham or horsemeat; chicken with a sauce made of pepper, onions, tomatoes and oregano. He doesn't care much for elaborate dishes, like the ones his brother Rodrigo makes, but then, as is well known, Rodrigo is a chef and his dream is to open his own restaurant one day. It is natural for him to experiment and try new recipes, although his younger brother doesn't always appreciate them. Does he have a sweet tooth? 'Yes, Leo loves chocolates and *alfajores* [traditional caramel-filled biscuits – a national delicacy]; when we go to Spain we have to take boxes and boxes so that he always has a good supply.' She tells the story about how, when he was little, when a coach promised him an *alfajor* for every goal he scored, he netted eight in a single match. Some feast.

Over a cup of coffee in La Tienda bar on San Martín de Rosario avenue, the mother of Barça's number 10 talks with great gusto about her world-famous son. Black hair, a delicate smile and certain facial features that remind one of Leo (although she laughs and says that he resembles his father completely), Celia María Cuccittini Oliveira de Messi has a soft, gentle voice. While she is speaking, she often glances at her sister Marcela, seated opposite. The youngest of the Cuccittini family, Marcela is also a mother of footballers: Maximiliano plays for Vitoria in Brazil; Emanuel plays for Olimpia in Paraguay; and Bruno attends the Renato Cesarini football school, which counts players such as Fernando Redondo and Santiago Solari among its alumni. Marcela Cuccittini de Biancucchi is Leo's godmother and his favourite aunt. When he returns to Rosario, he loves spending time at her house. 'We have to go and meet him or call him to see how he is, but, of course, my sister spoils him,' says Celia. 'And then there's Emanuel, they're inseparable.' From a very young age they were continually playing ball. 'There were five boys: my three, Matías, Rodrigo and Leo, and my sister's two, Maximiliano and Emanuel. On Sundays, when we would go to my mother's house, they all used to go out into the street to play before lunch,' recalls Celia. They were wild games, of football or foot-tennis and often Leo would end up returning to the house crying because he had lost or because the older ones had cheated.

'Just the other day, Maxi was reminding me about those games,' adds Marcela, 'and he was telling me that when they all meet back here in Rosario he wants to play Messis against Biancucchis, just like old times.'

And the memories bring us to the grandmother, Celia: her delicious food, the pastries, the Sunday family reunions and the passion for football. 'She was the one who accompanied the kids to their training sessions. She was the one who insisted that they let my Lionel play even though he wasn't old enough, even though he was the youngest and he was small. Because,' says Celia, 'he's always been small. They were afraid he'd get trodden on, that he'd get hurt, but she wasn't, she insisted: "Pass it to Lionel, pass it to the little guy, he's the one who scores goals." She was the one who convinced us to buy him football boots. It's a shame she can't see him today. She died when Leo was ten years old, but who knows if, from up there, she sees what he has become and is happy for that grandson of hers whom she loved so much.'

But how did Leo begin playing football? Who taught him? Where do all his many skills come from – is it a question of genes? 'I don't know, from his father, from his brothers, from his cousins. We have always loved football in our family. I am also a fan. My idol? Maradona. His career, his goals, I followed them with much passion. He was a barbarian on the pitch. When I met him, I told him: "I hope one day my son will be a great footballer and you can train him." And look what's happened … look how far he's come …'

A pause in the story: the mobile phone on the table starts to ring. Celia excuses herself and moves away to answer it. Meanwhile, Marcela returns to the topic of young Leo. 'He was incredible, before he was even five years old he could control the ball like nobody else. He loved it, he never stopped. He hit every shot against the front gate, so much so that often the neighbours would ask him to cool it a bit.'

Celia has finished her phone call, she sits down and nods in agreement. 'The worst punishment we could threaten him with was: you're not going to practice today. "No mummy, please, I'll be really good, don't worry, I promise … let me go and play," he begged and insisted until he convinced me. Leo wasn't a temperamental child and he wasn't lazy either, he's always been a good boy, quiet and shy, just as he is today.'

Really? 'Yes, really. He doesn't take any notice of the fame. When he comes back to Rosario he always wants to come and wander around this area, along San Martín avenue, with his cousin Emanuel. When we tell him it's not possible, that here the people of his hometown will get hysterical when they see him and not let him go two steps, he gets upset. He doesn't understand it, he gets annoyed. In Barcelona, he goes to the Corte Inglés department store in his trainers and sports gear. Ronaldinho often used to ruffle his hair and ask him if he was crazy going out dressed like that. He hasn't taken any notice of who he is. That's why being famous, signing autographs or taking photos with fans doesn't bother him. Some evenings, when he comes home after a long time and when I go to see him, I lay by his side on the bed. We chat, I ruffle his hair, I tell him things, and I say, half joking: "What all the girls wouldn't give to be next to you like this." He makes a weird face and says: "Don't be silly mum."'

On the walls of the bar hang the shirts of Argentine players. Leo's is there too, under a window, marked with the number 30 of Barcelona. 'They don't know I'm his mother, although we live in this town,' comments Celia, a woman who shies away from fame, very aware of the risks that come with celebrity, and having clear priorities for her life and those of her children. All well and good, but how does she feel being the mother of a star? 'Proud, very proud. Opening the newspaper and seeing – here just as much as in Spain – a piece about him or seeing his shirt number, or seeing the kids who wear it … it makes me swell with pride. That's why it hurts me to hear criticism about his playing or false information about his life. It affects you deep down in your soul and it pains you when someone calls you and says, have you seen this, have you seen that? Leo? He hardly reads what they write about him. If he notices it, it doesn't affect him that much. But that isn't to say that he hasn't been through some tough times. He has had his low moments, when he was injured, out for months, when things don't go the way he wants them to go. At times like that, I don't even think twice, I pack my bags and I go to Barcelona, to see what's happening, to be close to him, to look after him as much as I can. Leo has always been a boy who keeps all his problems inside, but at the same time, he's been very mature for his age. I remember, when we hinted at the possibility of him returning to Argentina, he said to me: "Mum, don't worry, I'm staying, you go, God will be with us." He is very strong willed.'

She returns to the topic of his success, of the people who go crazy for the 'Flea' on both sides of the Atlantic. 'The thing I like the most is that people love him,' says Celia. 'They love him, I think, because he is a simple, humble, good person. He always thinks of others and he makes sure that everyone around him is OK: his parents, his siblings, his nephews and nieces, his cousins. He's always thinking about his family. Of course, I'm his mother and a mother, when she speaks of her children, the apples of her eye, always says good things, but Leo has an enormous heart.'

How does a mother see her son's future? 'In terms of football, I hope he makes history like Pelé, like Maradona; I hope he goes far, very far. But above all, as a mother, I hope to God he will be happy, that he lives life, because he still hasn't really lived. He has dedicated himself to football, body and soul. He doesn't go out, he doesn't do many of the things that young people his age do. That's why I hope he has a wonderful life. He deserves it.'

Outside the large window, the sky has darkened. The traffic has become more chaotic: buses, rickety vans, cars leaving clouds of smoke behind them, a cart full of junk pulled by a skinny horse and a multitude of people who wend their way to the shops and the bus stops. Celia has to get home; María Sol, the youngest of the family, is waiting for her there. Marcela has to pick up Bruno from football school. It's raining and Celia insists on accompanying her guests back to the centre of town. She goes to fetch the car. At the door, a few last words with Marcela about a mother's fears – injuries, and the money that can go to one's head. 'For now, my kids, and Leo, haven't lost their sense of reality. I, my family, and my sister's family, we live in the same town in which we were born, in the same house as always, we haven't moved to a different region, we haven't wanted to leave our roots, and the kids are the same as always. I hope they never change. I hope what has happened to other footballers, who have lost themselves in all the fame, doesn't happen to them.'

A grey Volkswagen stops by the pavement. Celia drives rapidly through the streets in the southern part of Rosario. She passes Leo's old school and comments: 'He wasn't a good student. He was a little bit lazy.'

She turns right by Tiro Suizo, a sports club founded in 1889 by immigrants from the Tesino region. Two kids don't notice the car, they are too absorbed, scampering along with the ball between their feet.

'That's what Lionel was like,' says Celia.

Chapter 2

Garibaldi Hospital

24 June 1987

A cream-coloured block built in the nineteenth-century style occupies a rectangular plot at number 1249 Visasoro street. It is the Italian hospital dedicated to Giuseppe Garibaldi, who is also honoured with a statue in Rosario's Plaza de Italia. He is a popular figure, known as the 'Hero of the Two Worlds', because during his exile in South America he fought battles along the length of the Paraná river. In those parts his Red Shirts left their mark wherever they went: for example, in the names of the Rosario and Buenos Aires hospitals, which were founded by political exiles, supporters of Mazzini and Garibaldi, and their workers' unions. The Rosario hospital complex was inaugurated on 2 October 1892 in order to serve the Italian community, which at that time represented more than 70 per cent of the immigrants who had arrived from the other side of the Atlantic. Today it has one of the best maternity units in the city. It is here that the story of Lionel Messi, third child of the Messi-Cuccittini family, begins at six o'clock one winter morning.

His father, Jorge, is 29 years old and is the head of department at steelmaking company Acindar, in Villa Constitución, some 50 kilometres outside Rosario. Celia, 27, works in a magnet manufacturing workshop. They met as youngsters in the Las Heras neighbourhood, previously known as Estado de Israel and today known as the San Martín neighbourhood, in the southern area of the city, where the residents are humble and hardworking. Celia's father Antonio is a mechanic – he repairs fridges, air conditioning units and other electrical items. Her mother, also called Celia, has worked for many years as a cleaning lady. Jorge's father Eusebio makes his living in construction; his mother, Rosa María, is also a cleaning lady. Little more than 100 metres separate their homes. Like many other local families, they have Italian and Spanish ancestors. The surname Messi comes from the Italian town of Porto Recanati, in the province of Macerata, which saw the birth of the poet Giacomo Leopardi and the tenor Beniamino Gigli. It is from there that one Angelo Messi departed on one of the many boats bound for America at the end of the nineteenth century, in search of a better life in the new world, like so many other emigrants carrying third-class tickets. The Cuccittinis also have Italian roots, on their father's side. Despite these families originating from the humid pampas, they eventually came to settle in the city.

At 305 kilometres from the capital city of Buenos Aires, and with around a million inhabitants, the city of Rosario is the largest in the Santa Fe province, extending along the banks of the Paraná river. The Costanera promenade runs alongside the river until the Nuestra Señora del Rosario bridge, which crosses the waters and the islands in the river and connects the city with Victoria. The Paraná has always been an important highway in the river trade: from here, many agricultural products are exported to the whole of the Mercosur – like soya, which, in recent times, has brought wealth to this region and transformed the area's urban fabric. New buildings, skyscrapers and incredible villas are springing up in front of a beach of fine sand deposited by the river. And yet, Rosario remains the patriotic city *par excellence.* School groups dressed in white pose for photos at the base of the monument of the flag, built in the old Soviet style and inaugurated in 1957 to mark the place where General Manuel Belgrano ordered the raising of the national flag for the first time, on 27 February 1812.

Rosario is a city of the grandchildren of immigrants, of slums and country houses. But let us leave aside the stories of immigration, the mix of cultures, languages and traditions, which are plentiful in Argentina, and return to Jorge and Celia, who fell in love and began dating at such a young age.

On 17 June 1978 they marry in the Corazón de María church. The country is thoroughly absorbed in the World Cup – so much so that the newlyweds, honeymooning in Bariloche, still ensure that they catch the Argentina-Brazil match taking place in Rosario. The result is nil-nil. Eight days later, at River Plate's Monumental stadium in Buenos Aires, César Luis Menotti's Argentine national team, known in Argentina as the Albiceleste (literally meaning 'white and sky blue'), beats Holland 3-1 to win the World Cup. Collective mania ensues. Fillol, Olguín, Galván, Passarella, Tarantini, Ardiles, Gallego, Ortiz, Bertoni, Luque and Kempes seem to banish all memories of the Proceso de Reorganización Nacional (period of military rule) – the deceased dissidents, the more than 30,000 'disappeared' citizens, and the tortures and horrors of General Jorge Rafael Videla's ferocious and bloody military dictatorship, which was instigated on 24 March 1976 with the dismissal of Isabel Perón. On the streets of Buenos Aires you can still see the words 'Inmundo mundial' – dirty world (cup) – painted beneath the green of a football pitch and the inscription '1978'.

Two years after the *coup d'état*, the country is still under a reign of terror, but life goes on. Celia and Jorge become parents: Rodrigo Martín is born on 9 February 1980, and their second son, Matías Horacio, is born in one of the darkest hours of the country's history. The date is 25 June 1982, just eleven days after the end of the Falklands War. Argentina, defeated, counts her losses (649 dead) and her casualties (more than 1,000), as well as all the men who will never forget those two and a half months under fire. Young, inexperienced and ill-equipped, volunteers convinced to enlist by a cheap patriotism in order to re-conquer the Falklands archipelago, occupied by the British in a distant 1833. Operation Rosario, the name of the key Argentine invasion led by General Leopoldo Galtieri on 2 April 1982, was the umpteenth attempt at distraction orchestrated by the military junta, intended to divert attention from the disasters of the economic programme introduced in 1980 – policies that had led to 90 per cent inflation, recession in all areas of the economy, a rise in external debt for both private companies and the State, the devaluation of salaries, and in particular the progressive impoverishment of the middle class (a characteristic of the country's history which stands out as compared with other Latin American nations). The war should have made the country forget the dramas of the past and engulfed the people in a wave of patriotism, but Galtieri was not prepared for the Iron Lady, Margaret Thatcher, nor had he taken into account the British army.

In a few weeks British forces quash the Argentine army – a disaster that will lead to the fall of the military junta and the celebration of democracy within the year. But the restoration of the Malvinas – the Argentine name for the Falklands – to Argentina remains an ongoing demand: in Rosario, in the Parque Nacional de la Bandera ('national park of the flag'), a monument has been built in honour of 'the heroes that live on the Malvinas Islands', and the 1994 Constitution lists the territory's restitution as an objective that cannot be renounced. In 1983, however, election victory belongs to Raúl Alfonsín, one of the few politicians who had kept his distance from the military, maintaining that their only objective in going to war was to reinforce the dictatorship.

Four years later, when Celia is expecting her third child, the situation is still dramatic. In Semana Santa (Holy Week) of 1987, Argentina is on the brink of civil war. The *carapintadas* (literally, painted faces) – young army officers captained by Colonel Aldo Rico – have risen up against the government, demanding an end to the legal trials against human rights violations committed during the military regime. The military commanders are unwilling to obey the president. The people take to the streets to defend democracy. The CGT (Confederación General de Trabajo – the labour union) declares a general strike. On 30 April, Raúl Alfonsín addresses the crowd gathered in the Plaza de Mayo, saying: 'The house is in order, Happy Easter' – a phrase that will go down in history, because nothing could be further from the truth. With no power over the armed forces, the president has had to negotiate with the *carapintadas*, guaranteeing them an end to the military trials. The law of Obediencia Debida (due obedience) exculpates officers and their subordinates of the barbarities that were committed and deems them responsible only for having obeyed the orders of their superiors. It comes into force on 23 June 1987, the same day that Celia is admitted to the maternity ward at the Garibaldi hospital. Her other sons – Rodrigo, seven, and Matías, five – stay at home with their grandmother, while Jorge accompanies Celia to the hospital. After two boys he would have liked a girl, but the chromosomes dictate that they are to have another boy. The pregnancy has been uneventful, but during the final few hours complications arise. Gynaecologist Norberto Odetto diagnoses severe foetal distress and decides to induce labour in order to avoid any lasting effects on the baby. To this day, Jorge can recall the fear of those moments, the panic he felt when the doctor told him that he was going to use forceps, his plea that he do everything possible to avoid using those pincers, which, as is the case with many parents, concerned him greatly due to the horror stories he had heard regarding deformity and damage to one's baby. In the end the forceps were not needed. A few minutes before six in the morning, Lionel Andrés Messi is born, weighing three kilos and measuring 47 centimetres in length, as red as a tomato and with one ear completely folded over due to the force of labour – anomalies which, as with many other newborns, disappear within the first few hours. After the scare comes happiness: the new arrival is a little bit pink, but healthy.

Outside the confines of the hospital, however, the situation is much less calm. A bomb has exploded in the city and another in Villa Constitución, where Jorge works. Throughout Argentina the number of blasts – in response to the due obedience law – rises to fifteen. There are no victims, only material damage. The bombs reveal a country divided, overwhelmed by military power and entrenched in a grave economic crisis. The secretary of domestic commerce has just announced the enforcement of new prices for basic goods: milk and eggs are to rise by nine per cent, sugar and corn by twelve per cent, electricity by ten per cent and gas by eight per cent – difficult increases for a working-class family like the Messi-Cuccittinis, despite being able to rely on two salaries and a property to call their own. Aided by his father Eusebio, Jorge built the house over many weekends on a 300-square-metre plot of family land. A two-storey, brick building with a backyard where the children could play, and in the Las Heras neighbourhood. Lionel arrives here on 26 June, when mother and son are discharged from the Italian hospital.

Six months later, Lionel can be seen in a family album, chubby-cheeked and smiling, on his parents' bed, dressed in little blue trousers and a white t-shirt. At ten months he begins to chase after his older brothers. And he has his first accident. He goes out of the house – no one knows why – perhaps to play with the other children in the street, which is not yet tarred, and along which cars rarely pass. Along comes a bicycle and knocks him over. He cries desperately; everyone in the house comes running out into the street. It seems it was nothing, only a fright. But throughout the night he does not stop complaining and his left arm is swollen. They take him to hospital – broken ulna. He needs a plaster cast. Within a few weeks it has healed. His first birthday arrives and his aunts and uncles buy him a football shirt, already trying to convince him to support his future team – Newell's Old Boys. But it is still too soon. At three years old, Leo prefers picture cards and much smaller balls – marbles. He wins multitudes of them from his playmates and his bag is always full. At nursery or at school there is always time to play with round objects. For his fourth birthday, his parents give him a white ball with red diamonds. It is then, perhaps, that the fatal attraction begins. Until one day he surprises everyone. His father and brothers are playing in the street and Leo decides to join the game for the first time. On many other occasions he had preferred to keep winning marbles – but not this time. 'We were stunned when we saw what he could do,' says Jorge. 'He had never played before.'

Chapter 3

The smallest of them all

A summer afternoon in 1992

The Grandoli ground is almost bare. A lot of earth and only a few spots of green near the touchline. The goalposts are in a terrible state, as is the fence, as is the building that houses the showers and dressing rooms. The neighbourhood itself is not much better: makeshift carwashes at every junction along Gutiérrez avenue, used-tyre salesmen, signs declaring 'metals bought here' – in other words scrap metals; there is even a piece of cardboard advertising dog-grooming services. And in the background: the popular construction towers, which appear abandoned although they are not; low, little houses, which have lost their charm of yesteryear; vegetation growing between the cracks in the asphalt; rubbish cooking in the heat; men and old folk with nothing to do; kids on bikes that are too small for them. 'People have changed around here,' say the oldest of the old folk, adding: 'At night it's scary to walk these streets.' The delinquents have moved in.

At three in the afternoon there is hardly a soul about. The football pitch is deserted. The kids from the neighbouring schools, who come to play sports at the Abanderado Mariano Grandoli Physical Education Centre number eight (named after a volunteer in the 1865 war who gave his life for his country), have already left and the footballers don't arrive before five o'clock. The only person around is a teacher, in a white t-shirt, blue tracksuit and trainers. He points the way, 150 metres or so, towards the home of señor Aparicio, Lionel Messi's first coach.

Aparicio opens the door with wet hands – he is preparing a meal for his blind wife, Claudia, but he invites his guest to enter and make himself comfortable. Four armchairs, an enormous white dog and a certain musty odour occupy a sparse lounge dominated by an old television. Salvador Ricardo Aparicio is 78 years old, with four children, eight grandchildren and four great-grandchildren; he has a worn face, with the shadow of a moustache, his body twisted like barbed wire, his voice and hands shaky. He has worked his whole life on the railways. As a youngster he wore the number 4 shirt for Club Fortín and, more than 30 years ago, he coached children on Grandoli's 7.5 by 40 metre pitch.

He has nurtured hundreds and hundreds of children, including Rodrigo and Matías. The eldest Messi was a speedy and powerful centre forward; the second played in defence. Grandmother Celia accompanied them to training every Tuesday and Thursday. And one summer afternoon, Leo came with them.

'I needed one more to complete the '86 team [of children born in 1986]. I was waiting for the final player with the shirt in my hands while the others were warming up. But he didn't show up and there was this little kid kicking the ball against the stands. The cogs were turning and I said to myself, damn … I don't know if he knows how to play but … So I went to speak to the grandmother, who was really into football, and I said to her: "Lend him to me." She wanted to see him on the pitch. She had asked me many times to let him try out. On many occasions she would tell me about all the little guy's talents. The mother, or the aunt, I can't remember which, didn't want him to play: "He's so small, the others are all huge." To reassure her I told her: "I'll stand him over here, and if they attack him I'll stop the game and take him off."'

So goes señor Aparicio's story, but the Messi-Cuccittini family have a different version of events: 'It was Celia who forced Apa to put him on when he was one short. The coach didn't like the idea because he was so small. But his grandmother insisted, saying: "Put him on and you'll see how well the little boy plays." "OK," replied Apa, "but I'm putting him near the touchline so that when he cries you can take him off yourself."'

Regarding what happens next there are no disagreements. Let's return to the old coach's narrative: 'Well … I gave him the shirt and he put it on. The first ball came his way, he looked at it and … nothing.'

Don Apa, as he's known around here, gets up from his chair and mimics little Messi's surprised expression, then sits back down and explains: 'He's left-footed, that's why he didn't get to the ball.' He continues: 'The second it came to his left foot, he latched onto it, and went past one guy, then another and another. I was yelling at him: "Kick it, kick it." He was terrified someone would hurt him but he kept going and going. I don't remember if he scored the goal – I had never seen anything like it. I said to myself: "That one's never coming off." And I never took him off.'

Señor Aparicio disappears into the other room and returns with a plastic bag. He rummages through the memories of a lifetime. Finally he finds the photo he is looking for: a green pitch, a team of kids wearing red shirts and, standing just in front of a rather younger-looking Aparicio, the smallest of them all: the white trousers almost reaching his armpits, the shirt too large, the expression very serious, bowlegged. It's Lionel; he looks like a little bird, like a flea, as his brother Rodrigo used to call him.

'He was born in '87 and he played with the '86 team. He was the smallest in stature and the youngest, but he really stood out. And they punished him hard, but he was a distinctive player, with supernatural talent. He was born knowing how to play. When we would go to a game, people would pile in to see him. When he got the ball he destroyed it. He was unbelievable, they couldn't stop him. He scored four or five goals a game. He scored one, against the Club de Amanecer, which was the kind you see in adverts. I remember it well: he went past everyone, including the keeper. What was his playing style? The same as it is now – free. What was he like? He was a serious kid, he always stayed quietly by his grandmother's side. He never complained. If they hurt him he would cry sometimes but he would get up and keep running. That's why I argue with everyone, I defend him, when they say that he's too much of a soloist, or that he's nothing special, or that he's greedy.'

His wife calls him from the next room; señor Aparicio disappears and returns to recount more memories.

Like that video that he can't seem to find, with some of the child prodigy's games – 'I used to show it to the kids to teach them what you can do with a ball at your feet'. Or the first time Leo returned from Spain and he went to visit him. 'When they saw me it was madness. I went in the morning and when I returned it was one o'clock the next morning. We spent the whole time chatting about what football was like over there in Spain.' Or that time when the neighbourhood organised a party in Lionel's honour. They wanted to present him with a plaque at the Grandoli ground, but in the end Leo couldn't go. He called later to say 'Thanks, maybe next time.'

The old football teacher holds no bitterness; on the contrary, he speaks with much affection about the little boy he coached all those years ago.

'When I saw on TV the first goal he scored in a Barcelona shirt I started to cry. My daughter Genoveva, who was in the other room, asked: "What's wrong dad?" "Nothing," I said, "it's emotional."'

Aparicio pulls another gem from his plastic bag. Another photo of the little blond boy, shirt too big, legs too short; in his hand he is holding a trophy, the first he ever won. It's almost as big as he is.

Leo is not yet five years old. And in the Grandoli ground he is already starting to experience the taste of goals and success. In the second year, he is even lucky enough to have his old man as his coach. Jorge accepts the offer from the club's directors and takes charge of the '87 team. They play against Alfi, one of their many fixtures across the city. And they win everything: 'But everything, *everything*: the championship, the tournaments, the friendlies …' recalls Jorge Messi, with more of a paternal pride than that of a coach.

Apart from football, there is school. Leo goes to school number 66, General Las Heras, at 4800 Buenos Aires street. He is accompanied by either his mother Celia, his aunt Marcela, or by the neighbour Silvia Arellano, mother of Cintia, his best friend. They go on foot, making their way across the open country or skirting the edges of the football fields on the grounds of the army barracks of the Communications Batallion 121. In little more than ten minutes they are at the door.

Today, when approaching the entrance, the youngest class can be seen absorbed in drawing. Two of them are wearing Messi shirts. In the enormous covered pavilion, some kids in white kit are playing a match with incredible concentration. There are goals – what's missing is the ball – a bundle of brown paper held together with tape serving instead. They move at a giddying pace, without taking too much notice of the harsh grey gravel – slaloming, feinting, dribbling. Among the players is Bruno Biancucchi, Leo's cousin. Sweating profusely and red from the effort, his charcoal-black hair matted against his face, wearing a white-and-pink-striped earring, his companions soon mark him out as the best. The press has already dedicated a substantial number of articles to hailing him as Leo's successor. His coaches say that he weaves really well, that he has the same talent as his cousin. And, like him, he is shy. The only thing he says is that he envies his cousin's initiative and ability to score goals. Bruno is also a striker and he would like to wear a Barça shirt one day.

A circle of children has gathered. They all want to give their opinion about the boy who until a few years ago went to their school. For Pablo, age eleven, there is no doubt whatsoever: 'He has what it takes to be the best in the world. Better than Maradona. The thing I like best about him is his speed, he's incredible.' Something is worrying Agustín, age nine – something that concerns many of his fellow countrymen – 'Maradona started out at Argentino Juniors, Messi … at Barça'. Without question, too far away from here. Even the girls, who are more embarrassed, end up joining the group. And here, opinion is divided. Some think he's good-looking, others think he is too short.

It's break time, and under a crooked old piece of wood – an ancient tree – the little pupils chase one another around. Leo used to dodge round the enormous trunk running after paper or plastic balls. For him, the most wonderful memories of those years are precisely those games with whatever object found its way between his feet. He has no problem admitting that he didn't enjoy studying.

And Mónica Dómina, his teacher from first to third grade, confirms that fact: 'No, Leo didn't do so well in his studies, but his work was of an acceptable level. At the beginning he had difficulty reading, so I advised his mother to take him to a speech therapist. In the other subjects he managed to improve little by little, although he didn't obtain wonderful results. He was a quiet child, sweet and shy, one of the shyest students I have seen in my entire teaching career. If you didn't address him, he would sit silently at his desk, at the back of the classroom. The older children competed with him in order to play in Rosario's inter-school tournaments. He was good, of course – he used to win trophies and medals; but I never heard him boast about playing well and scoring goals.'

Chapter 4

The same as always

Conversation with Cintia Arellano

She has bright blue eyes, fine facial features and a slim figure. She lives at 510 Ibañez passage, a modest house, where she receives her visitor with a friendly smile. A black dog wags its tail and studies the new arrival before leaving the bare living room and going out into the courtyard that backs onto the Messi family courtyard. Cintia has always been Leo's friend. 'Our mothers were "womb sisters",' she says. Silvia Arellano became pregnant around the same time as Celia. 'We kept each other company,' Silvia explains. 'We would go shopping together and we chatted about the future of our children. It was my first. We were good friends.' She puts a glass of soda on the table and retires, leaving the story to her eldest daughter, who is 22 years old and who went to nursery, infant school and primary school with Lionel, always going to, and coming home from, school together, as well as to birthdays, parties and matches.

What was Leo like when he was little?

'He was a typically shy child and he talked very little. He only stood out when he played ball. I remember that at break time in the school playground the captains who had to pick the teams always ended up arguing because they all wanted Leo, because he scored so many goals. With him they were sure to win. Football has always been his passion.

He often used to miss birthday parties in order to go to a match or a practice.'

And what was he like at school?
'We called him Piqui because he was the tiniest of all of us. He didn't like languages or maths. He was good at PE and art.'

They say you used to help him …
'Yes, sometimes … In exams he used to sit behind me and if he was unsure about something he would ask me. When the teacher wasn't looking I would pass him my ruler or my rubber with the answers written on it. And in the afternoon we always used to do our homework together.'

Then later, in secondary school, your paths separated and Leo went to Barcelona …
'We all cried that summer afternoon when he and his family left for Spain. I couldn't believe it, I was losing my best friend. When we would speak on the phone we would get very emotional and it seemed to me that living over there in Europe was very hard for him. But when he returned we chatted and I realised that it was a very important experience for him, it helped him to mature a lot. It put a strain on his family, so much so that Celia and María Sol came back. He told me that he integrated because there were kids his age who played football. And for him that was fundamental. He wanted to be a footballer and he's made it.'

Cintia gets up, and returns with a folder full of photos and newspaper cuttings. There the two of them are as babies: Leo with a dummy and a blue bib; behind them, an enormous doll dressed as a bride; next to him, Cintia, in nappies and pigtails. And there, at infant school in 1992, in the class photo, all of them dressed in blue uniform.

Dressed up for the carnival, him in a policeman's helmet with a fake moustache, her made up, with huge glasses and a white dress. And then there are numerous newspaper cuttings: 'The new Maradona', 'Waiting for the Messiah', 'What planet have you come from', until we reach the headlines of July 2005, the victory in the FIFA Under 20 World Cup.

'I was the one who organised the party here in the neighbourhood. We went round all the neighbours and asked for money to buy confetti, firecrackers and paint. We wrote "Leo, the pride of the nation" in white letters on the ground, and we put up a banner in his street that said "Welcome champion". He was supposed to arrive at one in the morning, the whole neighbourhood was waiting for him, it was winter, it was bitterly cold and he didn't arrive. Some people got tired and went home. We stayed there waiting until five in the morning, when a white van turned into the street beeping its horn. At that moment all the television cameras were switched on. People started to scream, people were throwing firecrackers, playing the drums and yelling: "Leo's here, Leo's here." He was exhausted. He wasn't expecting such a reception, but it made him really happy.'

Yet more cuttings and more photos of Leo, as well as some tough pages full of criticism after the Argentina-Germany match at the 2006 World Cup, after that image of Leo sitting alone on the bench.

'They said that he was impulsive, that he didn't integrate into the group. They tore him to pieces. But it's not like that. Only someone who knows him knows what he feels. When he's not doing so well Leo is a little bit solitary, he retreats, he withdraws into himself. He was like that even with me sometimes. It was like drawing blood from a stone trying to find out what was going on inside. But no matter what, Leo always made me smile.'

And he hasn't changed?

'No, to me he's the same as always, shy and quiet. He's the same Leo I grew up with. The only difference is that before when he used to come here he would grab his bike and come through town; now he takes the car because people don't leave him in peace. He can't believe the madness he generates. The same people from his neighbourhood now take photos of him, the girls wait outside his front door to say hello to him. The boys want to be like him. It surprises and amazes me when I hear what they scream in Spain or when he plays with the national team. So when someone asks me about him, I usually prefer to keep quiet. I don't want them to think I'm gossiping or trying to get myself noticed. No, for me Leo is a humble, lifelong friend, who still has no idea that he is so famous.'

Chapter 5

Red and black

21 March 1994

Raúl: 'I've always been surrounded by good Argentines like Valdano, who gave me my debut at Real Madrid, or Redondo, or the team-mates with whom I have shared a dressing room. I have a great relationship with all of them. I wish I could go to Argentina sometime soon and enjoy some football over there. I want to see a Boca or a River match.'

'Or Newell's,' adds Lionel Messi in a low voice.

'The Flea' does not miss a single opportunity to reaffirm his red-and-black passion. To the extent that even at a publicity event in conversation with the former Real Madrid captain – now striker for Qatar Stars League club Al Sadd – he ends up bringing up the team he loves. It is to be expected – Newell's is a family love. His father Jorge played there from the age of thirteen until he began his military service. A midfielder with a great eye for the game, more defensive than attacking, although he never made it to professional level. Rodrigo joined their football school aged seven and Matías followed in his footsteps.

Leo arrives directly from Grandoli in early 1994. The club scouts know about him. They have asked his brothers to bring him along to find out if he really is extraordinary, which is how the youngest Messi brother ends up playing eight games in as many different formations in the minor leagues, during afternoons and evenings over the course of almost a month for the club. It is an intense test and he does not disappoint. The Newell's coaches think he is phenomenal and recommend him for the Escuela de Fútbol Malvinas (Malvinas School of Football), which nurtures particularly young players. He is not yet seven years old. The club's directors have to consult with the parents first, but given their family passion for football there is no problem.

'The father came to see me and said to me: "I'm going to take him to Newell's,"' recalls Salvador Aparicio, the old Grandoli coach. 'What could I say to him? Well ... take him then!'

And so, on 21 March 1994, Lionel Andrés Messi, ID number 992312, becomes a member of Club Atlético Newell's Old Boys.

Newell's and Rosario Central are the two rival clubs who divide the passion of the *Rosarinos* (people from Rosario). The Club Atlético Rosario Central was founded on 24 December 1889 as the Central Argentine Railway Athletic Club. It was founded by the English workers who were employed on the railway line. Its first president was Colin Bain Calder. Later, with the merging of the Ferrocarril Central Argentino and the Buenos Aires Railway companies in 1903, the club's name changed. From then on it was to be the Club Atlético Rosario Central. Its colours: blue and gold. Great players have worn that shirt, like Mario Kempes, Luciano Figueroa, José Chamot, Cristian González, Roberto Abbondanzieri, Roberto Bonano, César Delgado, Daniel Díaz, Daniel Pedro Killer, Juan Antonio Pizzi and César Luis Menotti, to name just a few. Two notable fans? Ernesto 'Che' Guevara, who was born in Rosario on 14 June 1928 and whose first home was an apartment at 480 Entre Ríos street. A few blocks away, there is a Ricardo Carpani mural in his memory, in the city's Plaza de la Cooperación. And the unforgettable Roberto 'El Negro' Fontanarrosa, one of Argentina's greatest football cartoonists and writers, among other things, who sadly passed away in 2007.

Newell's was founded on 3 November 1903 by the teachers, students and alumni of the Argentine Commercial Anglican school that Kent-born Isaac Newell founded in Rosario in 1884. According to legend, it was he who introduced the first leather ball and the official football rules into the Latin American country. The students at his school – among them his son Claudio, the club's promoter – began to play ball and created the club. From there the name Newell's Old Boys was born, in honour of the father and the school. Its colours: black and red.

One of the things that makes the hackles stand up on the back of the necks of their Rosario Central 'cousins' is having seen Diego Armando Maradona wearing the club's shirt, albeit only for five official matches and two friendlies. It was 1993 and the 'Golden Boy' was back from Europe, where he had begun in Barcelona, moved to Napoli and ended up finally at Sevilla. Aside from Diego there are many other illustrious names, from Gabriel Batistuta to Jorge Valdano, from Abel Balbo to Maxi Rodríguez, from Sergio Almirón to Mauricio Pochettino, from Juan Simón to Roberto Sensini, from Jorge Griffa to Walter Samuel, from Américo Gallego to 'Tata' Martino. The nickname given to the fans? The lepers. Strange, but true. A derogatory epithet that ends up becoming a strong and recognised symbol. This deserves an explanation, and indeed one is offered by a Newell's fan website which is dedicated to more than 100 years of footballing history.

> According to what our grandparents told us – which coincides with what is claimed to be popular legend

– many years ago the women's beneficiary committee of the Carrasco Hospital wanted to arrange a charity match in aid of 'Hansen's disease', commonly known as leprosy. The match was to be played between Rosario's two biggest teams, so the authorities of both clubs were approached for their approval in order for the match to go ahead. Newell's immediately accepted the invitation, but it was met with a flat rejection by the Central team, making this historical event the first sign of trouble with the Gold and Blues. So it was that Central became the city scoundrels, and this was the main reason for mocking on the part of the Red and Blacks, who gloated over their time-honoured rivals. The Central crowd argued that if Newell's were so interested in playing this particular game, it must be because they were lepers – and it was from here onwards that the Newell's fans became known as 'the lepers' and those of their Central rivals as 'the scoundrels'. Even though this has become the most widespread version of the story over the years, and perhaps is the only true version of the facts, it is worth pointing out that some of the older Rosario generation recount a different explanation of why, according to them, the Newell's fans were always known as the lepers, even before the founding of the club in the early twentieth century, when it was no more than a Rosario educational establishment. According to their version, the issue centres around the fact that in those days it was unusual for houses in the Rosario neighbourhoods to be separated by big dividing walls, which meant that people could talk to their neighbours simply by standing on tiptoe or by standing on a bench next to the aforementioned wall. On the other hand, in those days, this meant that leprosy devastated a substantial part of the population, and Rosario was no exception. This illness, which dates back to biblical times, has always been characterised by the fact that no matter who the sufferer was, they were quarantined out of sight and out of contact with others. Perhaps for this reason, when passing in the vicinity of Mr Isaac Newell's school and upon noting the enormous and apparently impenetrable wall that surrounded it, people were inclined to comment that all the leprosy victims must surely be quarantined out of sight behind it. And so, according to these particular folk, the Newell's Old Boys have been known ever since as the lepers.

It is a nickname that will also be associated with Lionel when Rosario's *La Capital* newspaper interviews him for the first time. But that is still six years away, six more minor leagues and almost 500 goals before Messi will be accorded the honour of appearing in the local press.

Faded red-and-black murals. 'The force of the lepers' written on a fist painted on the fence, the work of some hooligan fans. Above the railings is the banner: 'Escuela de Fútbol Malvinas Newell's Old Boys'. The pitch is in a sorry state, but the children playing there are unfazed. The club's coaches have come to hold trials so they have to do well at all costs. Next to the dressing rooms, a rusty bed lies abandoned in a corner. On the other side, along the Vera Mujica avenue, there are another two pitches in the same state of abandon. Someone comments that the income made from season tickets and ticket sales, and in particular from the sale of so many players to foreign clubs, has not been invested here, in the school where the younger generations are trained. It's patently obvious. Although the truth is that it was not much different when Lionel played his first season in his red-and-black shirt. Perhaps back then there was simply more enthusiasm – more people who worked hard and less money going into the directors' pockets. But let us leave that to one side and talk about that year that started so well and ended with a 3-0 defeat against Tiro Suizo. The boys lost the title, but they learned from their mistakes, given that in the following four seasons they suffered one defeat, this time at the hands of their training mates, the Newell's C team. Thanks to that unstoppable run, the team ended up earning the club the glorious name *la Máquina del '87* – the '87 Machine. The greatest source of satisfaction for Leo was a dolphin, the trophy won at the Cantolao international tournament held in Lima, Peru, in 1996. More than 25 teams from Argentina, Chile, Ecuador and Colombia participated. But in the end it was Newell's who emerged triumphant. And little Messi captured the attention of the media with, among other things, his tricks with the ball. During training and before matches, he would play 'keepy-uppy' for his own amusement. It is a skill of his that even the club's most senior directors appreciate, to the point that he is soon asked on various occasions to entertain the public during the half-time break of the first team's matches. They would announce Messi's name over the speakers and he would go down through the stands doing tricks and then position himself in the centre of the pitch, where he would perform wonders with the ball. It is a half-time that many lepers still remember – their first image of the boy who would one day become Leo Messi.

'He was something special,' recalls Ernesto Vecchio, Messi's second coach at Newell's, from among old American cars in his mechanic's workshop. 'He had wisdom, he could sprint, his passes were spot on, he played for his team-mates, but he was capable of going past half the opposing team. Once on the Malvinas first pitch, the goalie passed him the ball in defence and he ran the length of the pitch and went on to score an incredible goal. He didn't need to be taught a thing. What can you teach to a Maradona or a Pelé? There are only very tiny things for a coach to correct.'

There are so many memories of those two years, from age nine to eleven, when Vecchio coached Leo. Like the Balcarce tournament, for example, where the Newell's '87 team knocked out teams like Boca, Independiente and San Lorenzo. Lautaro Formica, a defender in that particular team, maintains that they had nothing to do because 'the ball never came back in our direction. I remember that Rodas and Messi created havoc between them. Once Messi had the ball, the opposition would get out of the way. Sometimes those of us at the back got quite bored.'

Gustavo Ariel Rodas, aka Billy, the other star of that team, is the antithesis of Leo. Or, to put it another way, the proof that possessing a natural talent does not guarantee success. Billy, an attacking midfielder from the '86 team with extraordinary technical abilities, is also from Rosario but was born in a shanty town. At fourteen he was a substitute in the Newell's first team and he had his first child. Before his sixteenth birthday he debuted in the first division and everyone predicted a bright future. Today, at 22 and with two children to call his own, he is lost to oblivion. 'It happens to many players who come from the slums, from poverty,' explains Vecchio. 'Football helps them escape their misery, but afterwards, if it doesn't suit them, they return to the slum, they fall into alcohol, drug use, desperation. Education is the definitive difference. In Leo's case, he has a father and mother who have supported him and helped him become what he is today. I believe very strongly in family environment as one of the factors in a footballer's success.' Ernesto Vecchio still has time for one more anecdote, the most juicy of all: 'We were playing against Torito, a club from our league. Leo was sick and I didn't want to make him play. I kept him on the bench. There were only a few minutes left before the final whistle and we were losing 1-0, so I went over to Leo and I said: "Do you fancy playing?" He said yes. He warmed up and just before he went on I yelled to him: "Win me the match!" And he did – in five minutes he netted two goals and turned the score around.' Nothing out of the ordinary seeing as, between championships, tournaments and friendlies, the Flea scored around 100 goals a season.

In 2000, the tenth league is the last that thirteen-year-old Leo plays in with the '87 Machine, under the direction of Adrián Coria. They win it at the Bella Vista ground, where the first team trains. And it is then that, on 3 September, just two weeks before his departure for Barcelona, *La Capital* prints the first interview, a double-page spread: 'Lionel Andrés Messi, a little leper who's a real handful.' The introduction goes something like this: 'He is a tenth-division player and he is the team's playmaker. As a boy he is not only one of the most promising junior lepers, but he also has a huge future ahead of him, because, despite his height, he can go past one, past two, beat all the defenders and score goals, but above all, he has fun with the ball.'

And next, a barrage of questions. Here are just a few of his answers:

Idols: my father and my godfather Claudio
Favourite players: my brother and my cousin
Favourite team: Newell's
Hobby: listening to music
Favourite book: the Bible
Favourite film: *Baby's Day Out*
Possible career: PE teacher
Objectives: to finish secondary school
Aims: to make it into the first team

Happiest moment: when we became champions of the tenth league
Saddest moment: when my grandmother passed away
A dream: to play in the Newell's first team
A memory: when my grandmother first took me to play football
Humility: is something a human being should never lose
What Newell's means: everything, the best.

Chapter 6

He was a Gardel

Conversation with Adrián Coria

The television is on. On the table, the computer is running. Adrián Coria, ex-Newell's player and ex-coach of the lepers' youth teams, is on vacation and working from home. But it is always a pleasure to reminisce about one of his ex-players.

Let's begin with your first impressions when you saw him play.
'At that time there was a lot of talk about Leandro Depetris, a little blond boy who went to Milan aged eleven. Everyone was saying wonderful things about him. I disagreed. I always used to say to a friend of mine: "Leo will be ten times better than Depetris. When he grows up he'll be greater than Maradona – and I'm a huge fan of Diego."'

How could you be so certain about predicting such a great future for a twelve-year-old boy?
'When you saw him you would think: this kid can't play ball. He's a dwarf, he's too fragile, too small. But immediately you'd realise that he was born different, that he was a phenomenon and that he was going to be something impressive. Why? Because he was explosive, he had a command that I had never seen on a football pitch. He's Formula One, a Ferrari. He anticipated the next step, he had moves – one-on-one he'd make mincemeat of you. He dominated the ball, always on the ground, always glued to his foot. He left

behind all the big boys who still didn't have good control of movement and coordination. He was 1.2m tall. He dazzled against central defenders of 1.8m. He made a huge difference. And he had a strong temperament – he was competitive, he liked to win. I have never seem him resign himself to any result. He wanted to win every game.'

What position did he play?
'Behind the strikers. I used a 4-3-1-2 formation; with me, Lionel always played freely or in the hole. During a match it was impressive to watch him pick off his opponents. The others wanted to take him down, they knew of his abilities and they tried to stop him. He'd get kicked at from all sides. But him … nothing. He never complained. On the contrary, it seemed that fouls spurred him on, the more they went for him, the more he stood up to them. He would go after the ball and within a few moments he was already in front of goal. He won matches all on his own, so much so that they used to say to me: "You don't direct this team when Leo's on the pitch."'

Any goal or match that stands out in particular?
'There were goals of all different types. Matches? With him we won them all. He was a Gardel [in other words, a legend, like the famous tango singer Carlos Gardel].'

Did he listen to the advice of the coach?
'Yes, he was respectful. He paid attention. He never said "I'm playing", he never said "I'm the best". His team-mates adored him. The only thing was … he didn't like exercises. He loved the ball. That's why I once had to send him off during training. I'm not an ogre or a sergeant major, but I've always liked people to take things seriously. We were doing a lap, and he kept playing around with the ball. I called to him once, twice, but it was like he took no notice … Finally

I said to him: "Give me the ball, get changed and go home." Ten minutes later I saw him with his bag on his shoulder, glued to the wire fence, watching the pitch. I felt bad and it saddened me to see him like that. "You left without saying goodbye," I yelled over to him. He came over to say goodbye and I sent him back to the changing room so that he could rejoin the practice. He was a shy kid with a tough character, but that was the only time I had to say something to him.'

What did you think when he went to Spain?
'That Newell's didn't take a chance on him, they didn't make enough of a financial effort, they didn't want to spend money on a thirteen-year-old kid. I think they didn't realise the value of what was right in front of them.'

And now, what do you think of him?
'It seems to me that he has grown an enormous amount in Europe – in terms of football. But he still hasn't reached his full potential.'

Fame, celebrity, money ... can they detract from the game?
'I think fame has helped him grow, because he knows how to use his head. And he hasn't changed. He is still the same humble boy. I ran into him recently. We were just finishing our training, they were starting. He saw me. He left the warm-up. He came over to say hello and gave me his shirt. My players couldn't believe it and they asked me if they could meet him, or if I could ask him for another shirt.

'That's just one example. It had been a while since I had seen him ... but he seemed to me to be the same kid who trained at Bella Vista.'

Chapter 7

Size: small

31 January 1997

Doctor Diego Schwarsztein remembers precisely the date of the first appointment: 31 January, his birthday. That was the day he met Lionel. He was nine and a half, and his parents, concerned about their third son's limited growth, had brought him to the doctor's consultation room at the Clinic for Glands and Internal Medicine, number 1764 Córdoba street, in central Rosario.

'It was a consultation about small stature, of which I do many each day,' recalls the doctor. Leo measured 1.27m; he was not a star, he was not a renowned footballer, nor even a professional, he was just playing junior football at Newell's. 'And I have always been a lepers fan [to prove it, there is a picture of his son underneath the glass on his desk, at a match where the Red and Blacks scored a goal against Boca]. This helped me to establish a good rapport with the patient. We used to talk about football, the only topic of conversation that would conquer the little boy's shyness.'

Numerous appointments, more than a year of investigation, complex tests, biochemical analyses and clinics. 'Because only tests can determine if we're dealing with a hormonal problem or if it's simply a case of finding ourselves up against what is usually known as a "late bloomer" – a child whose growth rhythm differs from that of his contemporaries, who develops later.'

To clarify, the doctor points out the significant dates and time periods in a clinical history, indicating the normal periods which are necessary in these cases in order to reach a diagnosis: growth hormone deficiency.

The explanation: 'The glands aren't making any growth hormone,' says Schwarsztein. 'To make a readily understood comparison, it's a case analogous to that of a diabetic, whose pancreas does not produce insulin. In this case, we're dealing with the substance needed in order to grow. The difference is that diabetics represent seven per cent of the world's population, whereas Messi's case is not very common: it affects one in every 20 million, according to statistics. And it's worth noting that it's not hereditary. Just look at Leo's brothers, or María Sol, his little sister, who is decidedly tall.' How did Leo deal with this news? 'I remember,' says the doctor, 'that he had a very healthy relationship with his illness; he dealt with all the tests – even the most invasive ones – and the therapy, without too much trouble. His family helped him a lot with that – a first-class family.'

Once the problem was identified, the endocrinologist began a programme of growth hormone treatment. One subcutaneous injection every day for anywhere between three and six years, until the patient has developed sufficiently.

How can the development be evaluated? How can one measure the potential for growth? With an x-ray of the hand. The doctor shows them at different stages of development: age nine, ten, eleven, up to eighteen years old. He points out the blank spaces between one bone and another and explains that when these disappear it means that the patient has reached their potential – they will not grow any more. Then he adds: 'Nothing allows us to overcome genetics, but if difficulties arise we can help it along. I should emphasise that those who genuinely have growth hormone deficiency have it for life. That's why it is necessary to intervene.'

In the case of Messi, this definitely was not some kind of experiment. He was not, as someone has written, a lab rat. The doctor loses his patience and says emphatically: 'It was never an experiment. For many years growth hormone has been used in such cases, more than 30 years in fact. It used to be extracted from cadavers, but there was a risk of CJD. Since the mid-1980s it has been produced through genetic engineering. The long-term side effects are not confirmed. But we haven't had any problems in any of our cases so far – like in Messi's case, where it is imperative that we replace what is lacking.'

So, why are growth hormones such a taboo subject, and why is it one of the most commonly used products when it comes to drug taking among sportsmen?

'Administered to an adult without a deficiency, in other words to a person with a normal level of secretion, growth hormone serves as an anabolic steroid to increase muscle mass and decrease fat tissue. It increases physical output and performance,' explains the doctor. But the risks to one's health are extremely high: it can trigger anything from liquid retention to hyperthyroidism, from high blood sugar levels to cranial hypertension, and there is also a risk of tumours.

Despite having dealt with suspicions and fears, in both Argentina and Spain, there remains an issue about which much has been written – although generally without rhyme or reason – namely the cost of treatment, which was the equivalent of around £10,000 a year. It is a considerable sum, which may well have pushed the Messi family to depart for Spain, since Barcelona was the only club willing to take care of the expenses.

'It always caught my eye, the story in the media that the father took the footballer away because they wouldn't pay for the treatment here. It's not definite that they didn't want to pay here. The father's social security took care of the treatment, along with the Acindar Foundation. It's not certain that they had to leave the country for that reason. Because here, if the parents have social security or medical insurance the treatment is approved by the Programa Médico Obligatorio [Compulsory Medical Programme] and if they don't have cover, there is the National Advisory Committee for Children with Growth Hormone Deficiency which has administered free treatment since 1991.'

It's a version that contrasts with that of the Messi family. According to Jorge, the father, the medical insurance and the Acindar social security stopped paying the total cost of the treatment after two years. Seeing the child's promise, the Newell's authorities initially agreed to cover part of the costs (every other injection). But little by little, the payments began to arrive late. 'We went so many times to ask for the money, that in the end my wife said to me: "I'm not going to ask any more." And that's what happened,' says Jorge, who did everything he could to find a solution to the problem.

'River had opened an office in Rosario. It was a chance for the boy, and also a way of putting the pressure on Newell's. We went to Buenos Aires for a trial. Leo trained in Belgrano and during the first match, when they brought him onto the pitch, they realised what he was worth, that he wasn't just some little kid. "We want him," they told me,' recalls Jorge Messi, '"but only if you bring us the paperwork, if you can get Newell's to agree to let him go." In other words, they didn't want to get into trouble with Newell's. So nothing was done about it. Newell's found out about it and they asked me not to take him away. They made other promises. Then along came Barcelona ...'

With the matter more or less cleared up, there is one

fact about which the Messis and Schwarsztein agree: 'The hormone deficiency and its treatment are nothing more than an anecdote – what really matter are the boy's footballing skills.' And here, getting up from his chair and pacing around his study, the doctor unleashes a series of reflections of a man passionate about football. He speaks with great fervour about the quick sprint; about control of the ball; about speed; about 'Leo's limits, which nobody can pinpoint; the *porteños* [Buenos Aires locals] who are jealous of a player who has hardly set foot in the capital, because here, in order to be successful, it's imperative that you play for one of the big Buenos Aires teams. Look at Batistuta – he was from Newell's, but he only became famous in Argentina when he went to Boca.'

Let us leave football aside for a moment and take a step back. The growth hormone treatment might be anecdotal but look at how a recent article has appeared in *La Capital* entitled 'They want Messi's drug for their children'. The body of the article reads as follows: 'Ever since the therapy given to Messi became public knowledge, for many people the growth hormone has been transformed into the "magic drug" that makes little children grow. Small stature is a huge concern for parents, especially when children are starting infant school and they are compared with others. Comparison is never healthy, because the normal rate of growth is extremely varied. In the majority of cases, small stature is due to genetic factors, malnutrition in the first two years of life, or a delay in development or growth (for which there is no specific therapy), but many parents are demanding from their paediatricians the same treatment given to Leo Messi.'

'These are the negative consequences of media divulgence regarding a therapy associated with a famous footballer, and the erroneous interpretation that parents and the population in general have made,' protests the doctor. 'None of this would have happened if everything had remained within the confines of doctor–patient–parent confidentiality. My duty is to insist that this particular course of medical action will do nothing for children who do not have the hormone deficiency, especially taking into account the costs against the lack of benefits. But it is imperative for those who do suffer from the deficiency, as Lionel does. That's why he started receiving the treatment in 1998, when he measured 1.27m; and after continuing with the treatment in Barcelona, he now measures 1.69m. Without this cure he would not have grown to his genetically intended height.'

Chapter 8

Across the pond

17 September 2000

English	Spanish (Spain)	Spanish (Argentina)
goalie	*portero*	*arquero*
bus	*autobús*	*colectivo*
Danish pastry	*bollo*	*factura*
biro	*bolígrafo*	*birome*
flip-flops	*chanclas de dedo*	*ojotas*
apartment	*piso*	*departamento*
skirt	*falda*	*pollera*
round (in shape)	*esférico*	*redonda*
t-shirt	*camiseta*	*remera*
coat	*abrigo*	*sobretodo*

… and in Spain, the word *coger* means 'to get' or 'to catch', while in Argentina it means something altogether more vulgar, which is best left unmentioned.

They say that the same language is spoken in Spain and Argentina and, in effect, the language of both countries is *castellano* – Castilian, denoting standardised Spanish – but the differences are numerous, and not just in terms of the meaning of particular words or expressions of slang (charming or otherwise). It is a question of different ways of life and, on occasion, different ways of understanding life. Almost all Argentine families have some Spanish or Italian ancestors, but more than a century after great-grandfather left the Iberian peninsula, or the Italian boot, becoming a *gallego* (slang for Spaniard) or a *tano* (slang for Italian), things have changed significantly. History has opened up a chasm, creating profoundly different cultures, such that today, if one abandons the current path and returns to the country of origin, adapting is no mean feat. It is always a difficult challenge: more so if the one who must face it is a boy of barely thirteen. It requires a lot of willpower to leave behind one's childhood, one's hometown, school, friends, the team that you love, the Malvinas and Bella Vista grounds, and part of your own family. And, above all, without any guarantees for the future.

Leo Messi and his father Jorge leave Rosario for Barcelona on 16 September 2000.

Let us take a step back and find out why father and son are embarking on an Aerolíneas Argentinas transatlantic flight, how they came to the decision to try their luck on Catalan soil, and what they are expecting from their journey.

At thirteen years of age Leo is already a well-known figure in youth football. The newspapers dedicate double-page spreads to him, he is talked about in the minor leagues, and even in Buenos Aires his game has been very positively evaluated by River Plate. Two years previously, Fabián Basualdo, former defender for both Newell's and River, represented Leo for a number of months, attempting to direct his career as well as possible, until the Messi family realised that it was unnecessary for someone so young to have an agent. But one fine day in 2000, Martín Montero and Fabián Soldini, of Marka – a company with Rosario headquarters dedicated to the buying and selling of players – introduce themselves at number 525, Estado de Israel. Lionel's father Jorge does not want to speak about these people, because as the story unfolds it is revealed that they did nothing to help his son

– in fact they did rather the opposite … such that there are lawsuits and appeals in various court cases even today. Legal disputes aside, let us continue with the story.

Montero and Soldini want to represent Lionel. They are convinced that the young lad could have a bright future with any great team, be it in Italy or Spain, from Inter to Milan, from Real Madrid to Barcelona. They make assurances that they have contacts and friends in high places. The Messis do not succumb easily to empty promises. Until the boy manages to land a trial in Europe, no one is going to take care of the bills.

It did not seem to be an impossibility, given the precedent set by Leandro Depetris, the boy who had gone to Europe to train with the Milan youth team. The only thing to do was to see if these friendships and contacts were not simply a ruse. They were not: in August 2000, Montero and Soldini call Horacio Gaggioli, one of their associates in Barcelona. Gaggioli, a Rosarino who has been buying up real estate in Barcelona since the 1970s, works with the football agent Josep Maria Minguella, Barça shareholder number 2292, transfer advisor to then president Joan Gaspart, and future candidate in the elections that resulted in Joan Laporta becoming club president.

'I saw a home video of the lad; Horacio, Martin and Fabían assured me that it was worth me taking a look. So I called Charly, who is a good friend of mine,' recalls Minguella.

'He told me about a really good kid … Something like Maradona. I thought he was talking about a boy of eighteen or nineteen – when they told me his age I was surprised,' adds Carles (also known as Charly) Rexach, who was the technical director of FC Barcelona at the time. 'He'd have to be absolutely phenomenal for us to take an interest. It wasn't club policy to sign kids from outside Catalonia, let alone a non-EU player. They assured me there was no one else like him. I travelled quite a lot in South America, but we decided to bring him to Barcelona to train with us over a few weeks so that the coaches at the club could have the chance to watch him at their leisure. That was the best solution; it was better for him to come to Spain with his family when it suited him than for us to plan a trip to Argentina. Anything could have happened – he could have been ill, or unable to play that week … For us to go over there would have been unhelpful.'

And so on Sunday 17 September 2000, Lionel arrives in the capital of Catalonia accompanied by his father and Fabián Soldini. Horacio Gaggioli is waiting for them at El Prat airport to take them to the Plaza Hotel, in the Plaza de España at the foot of Montjuïc, where years later Leo would debut with the first team in the Olympic stadium. The city can be seen from the windows of the hotel: if things go well, if there is a place for him at Barça, this will be his new home. There will be a house, money, a job for his father and maybe even a team for his older brother, Rodrigo.

It seems strange that an entire family should put all their faith in a thirteen-year-old boy. Before they got married, Celia and Jorge had already thought of emigrating to Australia – they wanted a new life in a new world. Things were not bad, but they knew they could not achieve much more. Their life in Argentina could not change for the better. They were looking for a new opportunity for their children, and Leo could receive his medical treatment in Barcelona and continue to improve his football at a great club, as his talent deserved. But it was not an easy decision. The Messis asked themselves time and again whether or not they were doing the right thing. Before leaving, they gathered the family around the table and asked each one of them what they wanted to do, making it clear that if even one of them did not want to go, they would all stay in Rosario.

The trial is arranged for the afternoon of Monday 18 September. Leo is stunned by all the sporting facilities. He makes them take a photo of him by one of the gates of the Miniestadi (the reserve and youth team stadium), just like the multitude of tourists who visit the Nou Camp every day. Then he goes into the dressing room to change and joins the youth teams on the second and third grounds. During the course of a week he trains and plays a short match with children his age. Jorge watches in silence from the stands, just as he always used to do at the Rosario grounds. Not wanting to disappoint his father, Leo scores five goals and another, which is disallowed, all in a single match. Dad had promised to take him to buy a tracksuit if he managed to score six. In the end he has to keep his promise.

All the coaches who see him comment that the Argentine kid plays very well, but it is Rexach who must make the decision regarding his future. Charly is on the other side of the world, in Sydney, Australia, where the Olympic Games are taking place. He has gone to observe the football tournament, which will conclude with a Spain-Cameroon final, eventually won on penalties by the Africans. And so, Leo's stay in Barcelona is extended until his return, scheduled for 2 October. The matter has been left up in the air and needs to be resolved as soon as possible, so a match is organised between cadets, aged fourteen–fifteen, and first-year students at the Miniestadi third ground on Tuesday 3 October at 5.00pm. Charly wants to see how Leo fares against older lads.

'I was coming straight from a meal and I arrived at the ground five minutes late. The two teams were already playing,' recounts Rexach. 'I had to run halfway round the pitch to get to the bench where the coaches were. It took me seven or eight minutes to get all the way round. By the time I sat down on the bench I had already made my decision. I said to Rifé and Migueli [the youth team coaches]: "We have to sign him. Now." What had I seen? A kid who was very small, but different, with incredible self-confidence, agile, fast, technically polished, who could run flat out with the ball, and who was capable of swerving round whoever stood in his way. It wasn't difficult to spot it; his talents, which are now known to everyone, were more noticeable at thirteen. There are footballers who need a team in order to shine – not him. To those who tell me that I was the one who discovered Messi, I always reply: if a Martian had seen him play they would have realised that he was very special.'

The boss has agreed; the deal is done. Two days later, Leo and his father are on a flight to Buenos Aires. They return home happy. Via a third party, Charly Rexach has assured them that they will soon be invited back to Barcelona so that the details of the contract can be formalised. To this day, Jorge does not know Charly personally, although he agrees that the fact that his son plays for Barcelona is thanks to the coach's stubbornness.

The adventure on the other side of the Atlantic has gone well. But in the final stages things do not turn out to be so easy. There are still many difficulties to overcome. Today, Rexach – who is known as the Pedralbes Kid, one of the most emblematic figures of Barcelona FC – recalls all the issues precisely, over a coffee in the bar of the Princesa Sofía Hotel, a stone's throw from the Nou Camp.

'First of all, he was foreign, and the law doesn't allow a foreign child to play in any national league. A considerable handicap. Second, he was a kid. He could end up not becoming a Barcelona player, whether due to his own choice, injury, or age. Third, what are his parents going to do? We'd have to find work for them if they moved to

Spain. And finally, the boy has a growth problem, he needs treatment.' Rexach explains that he weighed up the pros and the cons, and he was convinced that they had to take a risk no matter what 'and sign him, because he's so good'. Nonetheless, not everyone at the club is so convinced and when the moment comes to make a decision, questions arise. Some see Leo as being too small and scrawny and think that this is just about a nifty little player. Charly responds immediately to such objections: 'Bring me all the nifty little players, I want them all in my team.' Even the club president, Joan Gaspart, wants an explanation of the matter, asking if it is worth them taking on the responsibility of the family of a thirteen-year-old boy. And Charly says yes, it is a necessary risk. Meanwhile, time ticks on. October and November pass by without the anticipated decision having been reached. On 4 December Minguella calls Rexach. They meet in the restaurant of the Pompey Real Tennis Society, in Montjuïc. Horacio Gaggioli – who at that time represented the Messi family – is also present. He is the most insistent: 'Charly, we've got this far. Either you play him or the boy goes elsewhere ...' Gaggioli remembers adding: 'I wasn't bluffing. We had already begun talks with Real Madrid.'

'They didn't trust me, they didn't trust Barcelona. They wanted a written agreement or that was the end of the negotiations,' says Rexach. 'I knew for sure that I couldn't let that kid slip through our fingers, so I grabbed a paper napkin and wrote something to the effect that the club promised to sign Leo Messi if the agreed conditions were met. I signed it and I gave it to him.'

Both Minguella and Gaggioli also signed the paper napkin (a relic which has been conserved with care), an agreement of honour that is, nonetheless, insufficient. Before packing all their bags and leaving for Barcelona, the Messis want some guarantees. Starting with the cost of the journey and extending to the house and a job for Jorge, who will have to leave his job at Acindar in order to follow his son and the rest of the family. Charly Rexach works hard to resolve the problems, but it is not easy. 'At the beginning we couldn't discuss a contract. He was a kid who was going to play youth football, but it was a signing that had to be made, and we made it.'

On 8 January 2001 a final agreement is reached in Via Veneto, another Barcelona restaurant. Joan Lacueva, then director of professional football, meets with youth academy coordinator Joaquím Rifé, who is looking towards the future and wants the club to make an effort to woo Messi. And he asks for a report from the enthusiastic Rexach, who simply writes that Messi is incredible. Two letters are therefore written to Jorge Messi: one from Charly, who confirms the sporting agreement made with the family in Barcelona, and the other from Lacueva regarding the financial terms. In it he includes details of the house they are to rent, the school, and the 7 million pesetas (approximately equivalent to £40,000) the footballer's father would receive as remuneration for a position at the club, which is as good a way as any of remunerating the footballer himself, who would only have been entitled to a study grant.

The letter is enough to convince the Messis to pack their bags. On 15 February 2001, in the depths of the Barcelona winter, the entire family touches down at the Catalan airport.

Chapter 9

Provisional licence

6 March 2001

The photo on his first Barcelona ID badge shows him with a plump face and a quiff. And a smile – that was soon to disappear because during the first few months of his new life on Catalan soil, things do not go very well for Leo. On 6 March, a few weeks after his arrival, the Federación Catalana provides him with a provisional players' licence and the next day he is able to debut at the Amposta ground wearing the number 9 Blaugrana shirt (Catalan for 'blue and claret'). He even scores a goal. But he is a foreigner and cannot play in any national competitions, which means he cannot join the children's A team, which should be his team: instead he has to make do with the children's B team, which plays in the Catalan regional league. To make matters worse, by March the teams are already formed and competing, and although he is good, it would be difficult – and unfair – to sacrifice one of the kids who has been playing since the beginning of the season in order to give Leo a place.

Another thing: Newell's is not willing to make the necessary transfer arrangements so that Barcelona can enrol him in the Real Federación Española de Fútbol (Spanish Football Federation).

And that's not all – there is worse still to come. On 21 April a Tortosa defender tackles him hard: the result is a fractured left leg. It is the first injury in Leo's career. First he needs a splint, then a plaster cast and finally rehab – he won't be able to play again until 6 June.

A week later it happens again. Another injury, this time while walking down the stairs – torn left ankle ligaments. Luckily this injury is less serious – he is out for three weeks.

The only good news on the medical front comes from all the tests and x-rays he was subjected to by the endocrinologists and the club medics. After studying his medical history and growth problems thoroughly, they decide that it is possible to wean him off the growth hormone treatment very gradually. A personalised exercise programme and controlled diet should help the youngster achieve a normal growth rate. Although, ultimately, he will still have to put up with daily injections for a few more years.

As for the rest, his Barcelona experience has started off on decidedly the wrong foot. So much so that by the end of the season, between one thing and another, Leo has only played in two official fixtures and one friendly tournament (excluding training matches). Add to that all the other problems that Leo and his family have had to face and things couldn't really get much worse.

In brief: after staying at the Rallye Hotel, the Messi family move into an apartment on Carlos III avenue – so far so good. Adapting to the new school and new study programmes is more complicated. Leo is enrolled in the Joan XXII state school, in the Les Corts neighbourhood near the Nou Camp. He is still a child who has very little desire to study (he will not achieve level four of his obligatory secondary education, due to his increasingly numerous footballing obligations, among other reasons). Nonetheless, he does not create any problems for his teachers. He is serious, polite and always remains quietly in his corner.

If he manages at least to deal with the situation, by

contrast the youngest in the family, María Sol, does not manage to acclimatise to the new way of life.

During the Spanish summer vacation, when they reunite again in Rosario, the family weigh up their options and reach some decisions. Jorge and Celia (who has had to return early to be with her sister, who has undergone an operation) decide that María Sol and the boys should stay in Argentina. They ask Leo what he wants to do. Does he want to return to Barcelona or go back to his old life in Rosario? The boy has no doubt in his mind. He makes it clear that he wants to succeed in Barcelona, there is no need to worry about him. And so, only five months after their arrival, the family is forced to divide in two. On one side of the ocean, Celia, María Sol, Matías and Rodrigo; on the other, Jorge and Leo.

The situation becomes even more difficult than predicted for Leo, who returns to Barcelona on 20 August, now fourteen years old. Summer is over, school and training are starting again. The transfer from the Argentine Football Association is not forthcoming, meaning that he can only play in tournaments and friendlies. There is nothing he can do except put maximum effort into his training sessions and direct all his energy and hope into the friendlies that he plays. It is an attitude noticed by the coaches and his cadet B team colleagues.

Luckily, transfer season begins at the end of the year and continues into the beginning of 2002. In December, Leo's father signs his second contract, which supersedes the one signed in May and helps straighten a few things out – at least from a financial point of view, given that the family situation is not too wonderful due to late payments and bureaucratic problems. In the course of a few years, Leo will sign six contracts committing him to Barcelona FC, which, on the one hand, is testament to his incredible progression as a footballer; and on the other to changes in priorities and internal conflicts at the club. There are many such examples: from the director who gets annoyed because he has not been informed of the negotiations and throws the contract in the bin, to the one who would not stand for one kid costing the club so much money. Finally, in February, the FIFA documents arrive, allowing the Spanish FA to arrange Leo's signing. And on 17 February 2002, almost a year after his arrival in Barcelona, Leo is permitted to enter the championship. He plays against Esplugues de Llobregat at the Can Vidalet ground. Messi only comes on after half-time, but adds three gems to the final scoreline of 1-14. Little more than a month later, on 29 March, Leo wins his first Barça title. With much elation, they win the league thanks to a 6-0 victory over El Prat. The bad days are over and the successes keep coming: the Thaygen tournament in Switzerland, and most importantly, the Maestrelli Trophy in Pisa, Italy, from 27 April to 7 May. The B team defeats everyone from Inter to Chievo to Brescia, they draw with Juventus and they knock out Parma in the final. Leo is crowned player of the tournament and suddenly finds his voice …

'At first we thought he was mute,' says Arsenal captain Cesc Fàbregas, who was his team-mate at the time. 'Then, thanks to PlayStation and that trip to Italy, we discovered that he knew how to talk.'

'Until that moment,' recalls Víctor Vázquez, another of the B-team champions, 'he would always return to the dressing room, sit down in a corner, change, and leave without a word. In Italy he began to gain confidence.' Particularly with Víctor, who nicknamed him 'dwarf'. To get back at him, Leo would respond in *lunfardo,* Argentine slang. It was impossible to understand him. Coach Tito Vilanova agrees that the Maestrelli Trophy was an opportunity for Messi to spend time with his team-mates, get to know them and overcome his shyness. 'Because he wasn't timid at all on the pitch,' says Vilanova. 'When he played it was like watching Maradona when he was his age.'

He gained not only the praise of his coach, but also the respect and sympathy of his peers. The 2001–02 season, which had not begun all that well, ended magnificently at home and away. In the end, victories over Madrid and Espanyol in the Villarreal and San Gabriel tournaments were the icing on the season's cake.

By the 2002–03 season he was in the A team: 30 league games (he was the only player to play in every game), 36 goals (five more than Víctor, the striker), three hat-tricks, one four-goal match, and two titles (the Liga de División de Honor and the Copa Catalunya). And that was without counting trophies like the Ladislao Kubala Memorial Trophy, or the summer triangular tournaments.

Facts and figures help to summarise and evaluate the campaign begun by Leo at his mere fifteen years. He measures 1.62 metres, weighs 55 kilos and is the smallest on the team (the tallest, Gerard Piqué, measures 1.91m), although not quite the youngest (Ramón Massó Vallmajó does not turn fifteen until October). But he is a fundamental part of this talented team, led by Álex García. The only time he is unable to shine is during the Campeonato de España Cup. Neither he nor Frank Songo'o – son of Jacques, the ex-Cameroon goalkeeper from Metz and Deportivo de La Coruña – is able to play (although he still celebrates the victory with the others), because the rules state that only those born in Spain or with a Spanish ID card can play in this particular tournament. An issue which causes many problems and headaches in years to come.

Chapter 10

Puyol's mask

Conversation with Álex García

The appointment is at the Nou Camp ice rink. The young professionals are playing. On the other side of the glass separating the cafeteria and the sports facilities there are some difficult exercises and one or two rather inelegant collisions. Álex García knows one of those exercises very well, albeit on a very different type of surface. At 43, he has a career as a midfield goal-scorer under his belt (he debuted in blue and claret on 5 December 1990, in the most famous team of all, the Dream Team), as well as nine years as a coach for the Barça youth team (where he coached Messi for an entire season).

Let's go back to the 2002–03 championship.
'It was my second year as an A-team coach. I had a very talented group of kids. I had Cesc Fàbregas, Piqué, Víctor Vázquez and Leo …'

What was he like?
'Very receptive, always attentive to everything, quiet, shy, reserved, with great class. He was a different type of player, when he got the ball he was unstoppable, he had a devastating sidestep. He would get annoyed on the pitch if you didn't pass it to him, or if he didn't do as well as he wanted, but he never argued over a referee's decision or over a foul.'

And what was he like with the rest of the group?
'Well, they looked after him a lot, they defended him because he was like their little brother and because the opposition always pounded him, so Piqué or Víctor would always be by his side. Everyone knew he was important to the team, that at any moment Leo could seal a match.'

And has he ever had any problems with you?
'No, he really hasn't. I knew that he was far from home, from his family, that he lived here with his father. I could imagine his nostalgia; sometimes I asked him about it, but he acted like nothing bothered him. He held everything inside. At fifteen years, Leo already knew what he wanted, he was conscious of the fact that he had an opportunity at Barça, he knew what it meant to make a sacrifice – both his sacrifice and his family's, and he didn't want to waste the opportunity he had been given. In terms of football, the only thing that displeased him – he never said anything but you could see it in his face – was playing out of position. I moved him all over the pitch so that he could develop all his skills. It was almost a given in the youth teams. So I played him as a midfielder, sometimes as a centre forward, or on the right or left wing. But he didn't like it. Within a few minutes he would drift towards the centre behind the strikers. You couldn't stop him.'

What can you teach to a kid like that?
'I think he has introduced us to the street football style, "playground football", as they say in Argentina – the dodge, the feint. We in turn have tried to instil in him our attacking kind of football, the Barça kind – getting the ball a lot, playing as hard as we can, going forward in only two or three touches, driving the ball towards the centre of the pitch and

then pushing forward through the opposition's half. Every player should be able to show off his talent.'

The best memory of that year …

'There are many images of Leo going round in my head but the most incredible story is definitely the one about the mask.'

Let's hear it.

'It was the last game of the league: Barça-Espanyol at the Miniestadi. We only needed a draw to become champions. We were winning 1-0, when all of a sudden Leo clashed with a parakeet [Espanyol] defender. He lost consciousness momentarily and he was taken to hospital in an ambulance. They said he had a fractured cheekbone. Two weeks' recovery. He couldn't play in the Copa Catalunya, which was only two weeks later. The news saddened the whole team, who had just beaten Espanyol 3-1 and been crowned champions. Well … the first week passes and in the second the Barcelona medics tell us that Leo can train if he wears a protective mask. Two months earlier, first-team member Carles Puyol had suffered a similar injury and he had opted to wear facial protection rather than undergo surgery. We went to find the mask to see if Messi could use it. The medics agreed to it and allowed him to play in the final on 4 May wearing the mask.'

What happened in the final?

'The match begins and after two plays I can see that Leo is lifting up the mask a little bit. It doesn't fit him, he can't see. After two minutes he comes over to the bench and yells at me: "Here's the mask, boss," and he throws it at me. "Leo, if you take it off I have to take you off the pitch," I tell him. "I could get into a lot of trouble, and you …" "No, please coach, leave me on a little bit longer," he says. In five minutes he gets the ball twice and scores two goals. The first time he gets it in the middle of the pitch and dodges round the goalie; the second one is a cross from the touchline from Frank Songo'o, which he finishes beautifully. We were 3-0 up at the end of the first half and I said to him: "You've done what you had to do for your team, you can rest on the bench now."'

It's a lovely story. But tell me truthfully, did you ever imagine that Leo would make it this far?

'Not so quickly, no. I was convinced that Messi had a lot of talent and that he'd make it to the first team – but an explosion like that? No. Everything has happened very quickly. That's why I believe that if he doesn't suffer from any serious injuries, Leo will leave his mark on a whole era.'

Chapter 11

Debut

16 November 2003

The Dragão stadium is beautiful. Blue, contrasting with the green of the pitch; an open structure that allows a glimpse of Porto all lit up. The white cover closes in the space and provides a view of the pitch. Manuel Salgado's construction, which seats 52,000, was built in order to replace the old Das Antas ground, as well as to host Euro 2004. The inaugural match between Portugal and Greece was held here. It is the backdrop against which FC Porto usually play – a beautiful location and well floodlit for the debut with the first team. Particularly since the date in question is Sunday 16 November 2003, the day of the stadium's inauguration. The crowds have gathered, curious to see a new footballing moment for the city, to experience its magic directly, to wager whether or not the home colours will bring them luck, and to spend half an hour with their eyes trained on the sky admiring the golden blaze of fireworks.

For once, the match is perhaps of lesser importance. A bit of football, very few emotions, a decidedly boring fixture, which, in keeping with the script and to the delight of the home team, ends with a 2-0 victory to Porto.

Lionel Messi debuts in the 74th minute. He is the third substitution for Barcelona, invited to take his place as one of the protagonists of this Portuguese fiesta. This Barcelona team has been obliged to look to youth team players to fill the teamsheet. The internationals have been called up to their respective countries, occupied elsewhere in the Euro 2004 qualifying rounds or in friendlies. So there they are, the promising youngsters, called upon for a trip to Portugal: Jorquera, Oscar López, Oleguer, Márquez, Fernando Navarro, Xavi, Ros, Santamaría, Gabri, Luis García, Luis Enrique, Expósito, Thiago, Jordi, Oriol Riera and Messi, who had scored three goals for the youth A team at Granollers the previous day.

Leo replaces Navarro; he is wearing number 14. And he cannot wait to show what he is worth. So much so that he makes himself noticed in the fifteen minutes he is on the pitch by creating two scoring chances. At the final whistle, Frank Rijkaard comments that 'he is a boy with a lot of talent and a promising future'.

Leo is sixteen years, four months and 23 days old. In the club's history, only two players younger than that have worn the Barcelona first team shirt: Paulino Alcántara – who debuted against Català on 25 February 1912, aged fifteen years, four months and eighteen days – and the Nigerian Haruna Babangida – who was brought on by Louis Van Gaal to play for a few minutes against the AGOVV in 1998 during a pre-season match in Holland, aged fifteen years, nine months and eighteen days. This is undoubtedly a good sign for the young boy who arrived from Argentina two-and-a-half years ago.

In any event, the magical night in Porto is, for the time being, an isolated incident, an exception. Messi will have to wait until the July 2004 Asia tour in South Korea, Japan and China before wearing the first team shirt again.

In the meantime, Barcelona Football Club has seen many changes. On 15 June 2003, Joan Laporta wins the election and becomes the new club president. Frank Rijkaard arrives to preside over the dugout and, on 21 July, Ronaldinho is presented as the new Messiah to 30,000 people at the Nou Camp.

After the *annus horribilis* that was the 2002–03 season (knocked out of the Champions League by Juventus in the quarter-finals; brought down by the Novelda 2nd B team in the Copa del Rey; sixth in the league, 22 points below the champions, Real Madrid; two coaches, Van Gaal and Radomir Antic, and two presidents, Joan Gaspart, and Enric Reyna in the interim), the club's shareholders hope that things will improve and that they will recover the lost ground with regard to their historic Madrid rivals. They need a change of direction. And the changes come. Not only in the first team, but also in the youth teams. Joaquím Rifé is dismissed from his position as football director, and along comes Josep Colomer who, during his tenure, appoints Ángel Guillermo Hoyos as the youth B-team coach, class of 1987. He is an Argentine winger who has played for Talleres Córdoba, Gimnasia y Esgrima de Mar del Plata, Boca Juniors, Chacarita, Everton (in Chile), Deportivo Tachira (Venezuela) and Real Castilla. Hoyos and Messi immediately get on well. They talk about football and, of course, Leo's passion for Newell's. They very quickly understand each other. The new coach's first impression occurs on Japanese soil at the beginning of August 2003, where the youth B team is about to compete in the Toyota International Youth Under 17 Football Championship. 'When I arrived,' says Hoyos, 'we did some light training to loosen up. Nothing particularly hard or revealing. But after five minutes I could hardly believe it. Of course, they had told me about him. But I didn't realise the extent of it: Leo was fierce.'

A thought that is reinforced during the first match against Feyenoord in Aichi. Fifteen minutes after kick-off, Barça are already down by a goal. Leo calls for the ball, dodges past four defenders and the goalkeeper, and gifts Songo'o a goal. Hoyos cannot believe his eyes: on the one hand he is surprised by the boy's generosity, not at all selfish like so many others his age (or older); on the other hand he is dazzled by his class.

Leo goes on to be chosen as player of the tournament. It is a title he will receive again at the XXIII Torneig de Futbol Formatiu Memorial Jaume Serra in Sitges, at the third Memorial Salvador Rivas Miró in Sant Vicenç de Montalt, and at the Torneo dell'Amicizia, which is played at the end of August in San Giorgio della Richinvelda, in the Italian province of Pordenone. The youth B team defeats Parma, as well as host region Friuli-Venezia-Giulia, Hansa Rostok, Eintrach Frankfurt and Treviso, and in the final they beat Juventus 4-0. The team racks up 35 goals in total, but Leo cannot forgive himself for having missed a penalty. Although the wound is somewhat healed by converting one in the final, the error still haunts him. At first, Hoyos tries to console him by saying the goalkeeper will be able to tell his children and grandchildren that he once saved a penalty taken by the greatest player in the world; then he sets him to work training daily from the penalty spot, explaining that over the course of a season he will have to shoot five or six times from there and any one of those could be decisive. It could be in a championship game or in an important tournament. They are words that will come back to Leo when Argentina win the Under 20 World Cup thanks to two of his penalties.

Nonetheless, the Hoyos/Messi winning partnership (only a single defeat, at the hands of Real Madrid in the José Luis Ruiz Casado Sant memorial tournament) does not last long – only for the pre-season. The club's directors are in no doubt: Leo is outgrowing this particular league. They decide to move him up, along with Gerard Piqué, to the youth A team.

It is here that the youngster's incredible rise begins. In just one season he moves from the youth B to A team, then up through the Barcelona ranks from Barça C in the

Third League to Barça B in the Second B League, not forgetting his brief moment of glory with the first team as well as reappearances in the youth leagues to help out his ex-team-mates. Here is a more detailed account of Messi's performance and shining moments during his time with each of those three teams.

The youth A team – he arrives on the third match day of the league. He stays until Christmas, although for a few weeks he also plays for the Barça C team, returning at the end of May for the Copa del Rey. He plays in eleven championship matches and scores eighteen goals, one of which is truly incredible. It is against Real Betis during the final of the Nerja tournament. Messi finds himself in the centre of the pitch and, seeing that the goalkeeper has moved much too far forward off his line, shoots hard. The ball flies in a perfect arc: goal and victory.

Barça C team – at the end of November 2003, things are going badly for the team, who have only managed nine points in fourteen games. Enter the reinforcements: Messi and Alfi from the youth A team. They win their first match on 29 November against Europa. The two of them play extremely well. But the best moment comes on 4 January 2004. They are playing against Gramenet in Santa Coloma. The Blaugrana are losing 2-1. In the 87th minute it is Leo's turn to shine. A header and a left-footer – wham bam – two goals in the blink of an eye (in addition to the equaliser), and the Flea brings home the victory for his team. Five goals in ten games, a determining factor in helping to get out of the relegation zone, and Leo moves on to better things. He is too good for the Third League, it would be better to try him in a higher league, despite the fact that he is only sixteen years old.

Barça B team – on 16 March, he plays his first match at home against Mataró. Coach Pere Gratacós admits that they had to create a special training programme just for him, as he would have to face older boys who were taller, stronger and more experienced. The coach also confesses his astonishment at the way in which the youngster was able to switch teams, team-mates, coaches and formations, and yet still give it his all. He plays five matches and only the first is a victory – but Gratacós says that he was acclimatising and eventually showed what he could do. He adapted to the league and in the match against Girona he was the best on the field, which, like snakes and ladders, takes us back to square one: the youth B team. 'Others would have got annoyed, but not him,' says Juan Carlos Pérez Rojo, his youth team coach. 'When the youth B team needed him, he immediately said yes.'

It happens in the last three games of the 2003–04 Liga. Three teams are still in the running for the title: Espanyol, Barça and Premià de Mar. The decisive encounter with Espanyol is on 15 April. If the parakeets pull it off they will be one step away from the title. By contrast, Barça cannot afford to put a foot wrong if they want to keep their options open until the end. So Leo pulls a majestic game out of his hat, and when the opposition, losing 2-1, start looking dangerous while desperately chasing the draw, Messi responds in his own way – with a goal that seals the deal.

Two weeks later, the team is celebrating, having won the title. His 36 goals in official matches, and 50 counting friendlies, are worth a considerable amount, not to mention his first professional contract. The negotiations are not easy given the many differences between the club's directors and Jorge Messi, who deals with the matter personally. Eventually, however, a deal is reached. The Barça bosses know that should Leo decide to leave the city, he would have other options. Cesc Fàbregas has already been lost to Arsenal during the confusion that followed the dismissal of Joan Gaspart. They do not want history to repeat itself.

Chapter 12

Videotape

29 June 2004

Hugo Tocalli tells the following tale: 'They brought me a videotape of a boy who was playing in Barcelona. I really liked what he could do, but … in those sorts of cases I'm always worried that the tape is from some footballing agent. Besides, the kid was very young … So I said to myself, no … I'll wait a while. I go off to Finland with the Under 17s and when I get back I find out more about this player. Everyone has told me great things about him. I go and see Grondona (Julio Grondona, the president of the AFA – the Argentine Football Association), and I schedule an opportunity to see the kid, in two friendlies, against Paraguay and Uruguay.'

The kid was Leo Messi, an unknown from the other side of the Atlantic. And the famous tape that was sent to Tocalli (who was then responsible for the Federación Argentina youth division), came from Claudio Vivas, assistant to Marcelo 'el Loco' ('Crazy') Bielsa, who at the time was manager of the Argentine national team. Vivas, at that time an ex-Newell's player and coach, had been curious about this fellow Rosarino, an ex-leper like himself, whom he had met many years previously at the Escuela de Fútbol Malvinas, and who was now making waves in Europe. So curious, in fact, that he decided to submit a tape of some of his fellow countryman's best moments for the coach's judgement.

It works, and the two proposed friendlies are subsequently organised in order to see him in action. The first request sent to Barcelona at the beginning of May has his name spelt incorrectly, asking for them to spare 'Leonel Mecci' some time to come over to Argentina; the request is politely rejected. He has Copa del Rey commitments. The end of June is more suitable. The AFA are in a hurry to see him play. Leo has lived in Spain for three years, he plays in the Barça youth leagues, and there is a risk of losing him and seeing him in a *Furia Roja* (Red Fury – Spanish national) shirt. It is not such a remote possibility given that only a year earlier during the Copa de España in Albacete, Under 16 coach Ginés Menéndez had offered Leo the chance to play for Spain. 'No thank you' was the reply he received. Despite living on the Iberian peninsula, Leo feels deeply Argentine. But who knows, perhaps after some insistence, the kid might change his mind? Either way, it is better to pre-empt the Spanish Football Federation.

'He arrived one Monday to train with the Under 20s,' recalls Tocalli. 'He was a very shy kid, he didn't know anyone and no one knew him.' While his team-mates – the likes of Pablo Zabaleta, Oscar Ustari, Ezequiel Garay – had already made names for themselves in the local championship, he has not. He stays in a corner of the dressing room at the Argentino Juniors stadium, hardly uttering a word. When the moment arrives to train and play ball, his attitude changes. Suddenly he is not as timid as perhaps he first seemed. The boss likes him – he values his ability and speed, but he does not come across too strong.

The match against Paraguay is on 29 June. Leo is not starting, partly because of his age, partly out of respect to the team, and also because they do not want to put too much pressure on him. In the second half, in the 50th minute, when the Argentines are already winning 3-0, Tocalli approaches him. He puts a hand on his shoulder and says to him: 'Go with the trainer, who is heading down to the pitch.' Surprised and excited, the Flea bursts onto the pitch wearing the sky-blue-and-white shirt for the first time. And he shows what he can do: he picks off his opponents and scores a goal.

'You could see it in the way he played,' says Tocalli. 'If he was good in training, on the pitch he was something else.' The friendly ends 8-0 and the youngster has seriously impressed the coaches. So much so that, that very night, Tocalli receives a call from his friend and youth coach predecessor, José Pekerman. 'He asked me where I had found the boy. He thought he was fantastic. "You're going to start him in the next match against Uruguay, right?" he asked me.' But no. In the match against Uruguay, in Colonia, he is not in the starting line-up. When he comes on, however, he surprises everyone again. The next day, Sunday 4 July, the Buenos Aires sports magazine *Olé* writes: 'Young Messi is the real deal. He scored two goals, four assists, and was the one to watch in the 4-1 victory over Uruguay.'

Leo's double trial has been a definitive success. He has really impressed them. And now Tocalli has no doubts about including him in the squad for the FIFA Under 20 World Cup qualifiers in South America the following January.

A bit of trivia: aside from Mauro Andrés Zanotti who plays in Ternana, Italy, Messi is the only 'foreigner'; he is also the youngest in the group. While he has just turned seventeen, the others are aged between eighteen and 20 and have extensive experience at all levels of the Argentine championship.

Time for the South American qualifiers. They are played in Colombia – in Armenia, Manizales and Pereira, cities along the central southern Andes, in the so-called 'coffee-growing region', far from Bogotá, the capital. They are played at high altitude – from 1,650 metres in Armenia, to 2,500 in Manizales – and the Argentines do not find it particularly easy to acclimatise.

Messi debuts against Venezuela on 12 January 2005 at the Centenario de Armenia stadium. As usual, he is not in the starting line-up, but is on the bench. He comes on fifteen minutes after half-time to replace Ezequiel Lavezzi, who today is a tattoo-sporting Napoli centre forward. At that moment the Albiceleste are winning 1-0. Thanks to Leo, eight minutes later the scoreboard reads 2-0. The match finishes 3-0. The Venezuelan defeat is incontestable and Messi's contribution is significant. The scenario is repeated at the Palogrande stadium in Manizales, this time against Bolivia. At the beginning of the second half, the boss sends the number 18 on in place of Barrientos in order to form a more attacking line-up. 'And after five minutes, Messi showed everyone that he is first-class material,' writes the Argentine newspaper *Época*. 'He latched onto the ball halfway up the pitch, made an unstoppable run and crossed it into the back of the net. An excellent shot that must surely be in the running for the title of best goal of the entire Under 20 South American championship. And in the twelfth minute, Messi made it 3-0.'

Two days later comes the clash with Peru, and for the first time Messi is in the starting line-up. He will only start in three matches; for all the others Hugo Tocalli will put him on in the second half. Why? 'That was my decision,' says Tocalli, justifying himself. 'The boy still hadn't got into the rhythm of the entire team, he was used to playing in the Barça youth leagues, he didn't have the same intensity that's needed to play in South America … they were very demanding matches. And to add to that his opponents were from the '85 leagues and two years make a big difference at that age. So I decided to use him with caution so as not to tire him out or give him too much responsibility.'

It is a choice that yields good results which are obvious by the last match, against Brazil in Manizales on 6 February. Messi comes on for Neri Cardoso in the 65th minute. Ten minutes later he makes the most of a pass from Barrientos and seals a 2-1 victory with a smooth shot into the back of the net, his first goal against the eternal rivals. At the end of the run, Argentina qualifies in third place for the FIFA Under 20 World Cup in Holland, behind Colombia and Brazil. Messi has scored five goals – the second highest goal-scorer after the Colombian Hugo Rodallega, who netted eleven. Rodallega is a nineteen-year-old who makes no concessions, be it on the pitch or in stirring up rivalries: 'I'm undoubtedly better than Messi,' he declares, 'but the big difference is that he plays for Barcelona and I play for Quindío.' Leo responds with humility: 'I have nothing to say, I play for the team.' And FIFA rightfully counts him among the eleven best players in South America – an accolade that helps to win over the selector.

'I loved him,' confesses Tocalli. 'I loved his change of pace from zero to a hundred in no time at all, his trick of dodging past his opponent, his ability to move extremely fast with the ball still glued to his foot. He demonstrated that, despite his stature, he was able to score many goals; he had a very good left foot and he would strike the ball well.'

For Hugo Tocalli, however, the match against Brazil was his last as the Under 20s coach. Pekerman, who has just been named manager of the Argentine national team, wants him by his side as a full-time assistant in the run-up to the Germany World Cup. Francisco 'Pancho' Ferraro takes over the reins of the Under 20 team due to play in Holland in June. During the final four months in the lead-up to the trip to Europe, Pancho alters his team. In come Agüero

– today a much sought-after striker for Manchester City (who played back then for Independiente, an Argentine team) – and Gago (who was then at Boca Juniors and today plays for Roma); out go Boselli and Zanotti. At the last minute he has to replace José Sousa, from Estudiantes de La Plata, who has fractured his left hand. Likewise, he ends up having to replace many other players, just as his predecessors have had to do, as those who are committed to starting with their various Argentine teams are unable to play. Messi becomes a key figure on the team: he has just won the league with Barcelona and everyone is expecting him to reach his full potential in Holland. One thing for sure is that the Argentine team is one of the favourites to win the tournament. They are going for their fifth title in this competition. They won three out of four times (in Qatar in 1995, in Malaysia in 1997 and in Argentina in 2001), all under Pekerman's reign, and let's not forget the 1979 victory in Japan, where Diego Maradona was the protagonist.

It is Saturday 11 June: they are playing the United States at the FC Twente stadium in Enschede. Surprise! Messi is not in the starting line-up, he is on the bench and the Albiceleste lose 1-0.

It's a bad start to the tournament but Leo keeps everybody calm: 'I'm in a very good state of mind and I think I'm up for playing for 90 minutes, but I have to respect the coach's decisions.' He adds: 'The team will pick up the pace because we have some good players. We have everything we need to qualify.' He is spot on and he proves it on 14 June against Egypt. This time he is in the starting line-up. He scores the first goal, weakening the African defence, leaving Zabaleta to seal the scoreline definitively. The third match against Germany is a tricky one: it decides who goes into the last sixteen. The Germans have one point more than the Argentines, so a draw will suffice for them to go through.

But Messi makes his mark. He gets the ball in the middle of the pitch, slaloms past the defenders and makes a precise pass – Oberman lets the ball go past him and Neri Cardoso scores to make it 1-0.

The path to the final is full of obstacles: the first is Colombia, the winning team in the South American playoffs. Messi is suffering from an absence of players able to pass to him; nonetheless, in the twelfth minute of the second half he manages to level the score, making up for the first goal scored by the 'coffee-growers'. The introduction of Gago, Pablo Vitti and Emiliano Arementeros brings fresh legs to the team and, in the 93rd minute, Julio Barroso manages to avoid extra time. Spain awaits them in the quarter-finals. It has been widely written about as a greatly anticipated match, because the Spaniards are the current European Champions and they reached the final of the last Under 20 World Cup, although Brazil clinched the title in the end. Speaking of duels, there are great expectations about seeing Messi and Cesc go head to head, two eighteen-year-olds (Leo's birthday was the day before the match), friends from Barcelona and rivals on the pitch.

'I've got on well with Messi ever since the first day we met in the youth academy. I've spent three amazing years with him, scoring goals and doing one-twos. I've had a great time with him, it was amazing to play alongside him,' says the 'Wonderkid' – as the Arsenal fans call Fàbregas.

'Cesc is a good friend of mine – we met back in the Barça youth leagues. He's an impressive, well-rounded player, with many attacking and defensive skills,' replies Messi. And he assures everyone that he and his team have great respect for Cesc and Llorente's Red Fury team. The game is actually very balanced at 1-1 until the 70th minute. Then Spain loses concentration and Leo ups the pace: first he serves up the advantage goal on a silver platter to Gustavo Oberman, then two minutes later, after chipping the ball over the head of one of his opponents, he scores the 3-1 winner.

'The Argentine team is the rightful winner, they played better than we have,' admits Iñaki Sáenz. Regarding Lionel, he comments: 'He is talented, he makes good decisions, he looks for the goalkeeper and he knows what to do.'

The semi-final is the scene of the classic Argentina-Brazil clash, both four-times champions in this tournament and the memories of all the previous duels weigh on their minds – like in Qatar in 1995, when the goals of Leonardo Biagini and Francisco Guerrero claimed victory for the Albiceleste. The Argentines are playing with black armbands as a symbol of mourning – after two weeks in a coma due to a road accident, Independiente goalkeeper and national Under 17 player Emiliano Molina has just died. Within eight minutes the Albiceleste are already dominating, thanks to a torpedo-like shot from Messi from outside the area, which just edges in at the goalpost, rendering the Brazilian goalie's spectacular dive completely futile. Renato equalises in the second half, but at the last minute, after Leo gets past his opponent for the umpteenth time, Zabaleta picks up a rebound off a Brazilian defender and manages to score. And then comes the final, at 8.00pm on 2 July at the Galgenwaard Stadium in Utrecht. The opposition are Nigeria, who have beaten Morocco in the semi-finals. The previous day, a Dutch TV channel had presented Messi with a golden clog, the trophy that declares him player of the tournament. 'I'm very happy and I thank you for this prize,' he says. 'The truth is that I'm very surprised at everything that has happened to me here.' And the surprises continue into the final. In the 38th minute, Messi controls the ball down the left-hand touchline; he begins a 45-yard zigzagging run and gets into the box. Dele Adeleye realises that he cannot snatch the ball from him and instead knocks him down. There is no doubt in referee Terje Hauge's mind: it's a penalty. Leo takes it without a run up, softly, with his left foot, to the right of Vanzekin – who throws himself in exactly the opposite direction: 1-0. In the 52nd minute Chinedu Ogbuke levels the scoreboard for Nigeria. In the 73rd minute Agüero is fouled by Monday James in front of goal. Leo steps up to the spot once more and shoots with precision into the left-hand side of the goal. Goooaaaal: 2-1. The Argentines win their fifth Under 20 title. Leo Messi is the star player.

'What can we say about him? The final images of last night sum it up,' writes *Clarín* the next day, 'with the trophies for best player and highest goal-scorer of the tournament, the champion's medal around his neck and the sky-blue-and-white flag over his shoulders.'

Chapter 13

The football is his toy

Conversation with Francisco 'Pancho' Ferraro

With an air of intelligence in the dugout and a soothing, calming voice, Pancho – as he is known to everyone in the footballing world – has an enviable CV, between national youth teams, and clubs in both South America and Europe. But some of his best memories are still of those days in June and July 2005, when he led the Under 20s to their fifth world title.

'It's true, I am proud of that victory on both a personal level and as part of the team, I'm proud of what the boys did, and of players like Messi, Agüero and Gago, who made a name for themselves at international level.'

Do you remember the first time you saw Messi?
'Yes, it was in the South American qualifiers in January 2005, I was lucky enough to spend almost 40 days with the team. José Pekerman had asked me to take over the Under 20s and Hugo (Tocalli, the coach) wanted me to be there alongside him in Colombia to see how things were run.'

What was your first impression?
'That of a nice, polite, shy boy. He was the youngest of the group. He came from Europe and he still wasn't fully integrated, and he didn't have the physical stamina to play 90 minutes. That's why, after discussing it with Hugo, we

always brought him on in the second half, where he could make a difference.'

You didn't bring him on in the first game in Holland against the United States either ...
'He had a slight injury, which is why he was on the bench, but from the second match against Egypt he was in the starting line-up, and indisputably so. He had come better armed both physically and mentally from Barcelona. He had debuted with the first team, he was stronger and he knew how to handle a higher-level match. He played in midfield, not as a playmaker; from three-quarters of the way up the pitch he could create risky situations at any moment. His presence on the team made all the difference.'

And how did he get on with the group?
'He was happy, and even happier when he was on the pitch with the ball. He shared a room with Agüero and he never bothered us. On the contrary, we could all see that they were happy and they got on very well. They were very considerate to their peers and to the staff. Very respectful. They brought sobriety to the group and kept low profiles – they were very humble. In fact, within a team full of honest people, they were two extremely respectful and professional boys.'

You say that Messi was always happy when he was on the pitch with the ball ...
'Yes, it bears repeating that Leo loves to play, and the football is his favourite toy; he has so much fun with it and he can control it like nobody else. It's incredible to see him on the pitch with the ball glued to his left foot; he drives it forward at a dizzying speed and he's aware of everything that is going on around him; he reads and anticipates the play. That's very difficult – only the greats can do that.'

Like Maradona?
'Diego was one of a kind. It's true that for some time now everyone has been comparing the two of them, especially after Leo's goal against Getafe. All I can say is that both have truly been bewitched by a magic wand. But Messi doesn't need to be compared to anyone, he is a brilliant and unique footballer, a great one, one who can create surprises in every game and that is what people love about him.'

What did that Under 20 World Cup mean to Messi?
'It was his explosive moment as a footballer. It was his chance to make himself known across half the world. Before he went to Holland, very few people in Argentina knew of his talents; when he returned he was an idol. Best player, highest scorer of the tournament, those two goals of his in the final … He was already a star, the footballer that an entire nation had been waiting for.'

And an entire nation was hoping that he would play in the 2006 World Cup against Germany. But Messi stayed on the bench. You were at the World Cup with the kids who were sparring with the team; you've known José Pekerman for years – what happened in that final match?
'We were down one substitution due to Pato's [Abbondanzieri's] injury and at that moment José will have decided to go for some other play, a different footballer, a different tactical move. But I have no doubt that Pekerman has been one of the best youth coaches. Who else could have brought the best out of an eighteen-year-old boy like Messi?'

Let's leave polemics to one side and talk about his development after that World Cup.
'I think Messi keeps on progressing and for the moment he has no limits. He progresses while keeping the same

low profile as always. He doesn't like being evaluated, he doesn't do things just for the sake of doing them, he just wants to play in peace. He surrounds himself with his loved ones, his parents and his siblings, and they support and protect him, just as they did in Holland during the World Cup.'

Chapter 14

A friend

Conversation with Pablo Zabaleta

'He's a very good person,' says Leo's mother Celia, of Pablo Zabaleta. And she is happy that her son is close to the Under 20s captain who won the World Cup, was later a winger with RCD Espanyol, and is now at Manchester City. He grew up in Arrecifes, and before making the move to Europe he cut his teeth at San Lorenzo (Argentina). And although he is only 27, everyone already considers him a veteran, or in other words, someone you can trust.

When did you meet Leo?
'In the Under 20 team when we won the Holland World Cup, which was an amazing experience and a joyful moment for all of us. That's where the beautiful friendship was born. We also became close with Kun (Agüero) and Oscar (Ustari). That was a great team …'

What was so special about it?
'There was a good atmosphere, great camaraderie, and everyone really wanted to win …'

But Leo didn't find it easy to integrate …
'No, I don't think he did … The problem was that no one knew him. He had come here very young, to Spain, and he had taken a different path. In Argentina, the players move

up to the first teams very young and that makes them grow up faster, it makes them find the right rhythm. Leo came from Barcelona, but it didn't take him that long to adapt and by Holland he really took off. The world went crazy for the way he played.'

And after that World Cup there were many more important moments.
'In Budapest I shared a room with him on the day of his debut with the national first team, although it wasn't a great game for Leo. A happy moment that we shared was winning the Olympic gold in Beijing.'

And what is your relationship like, now that you live in Manchester?
'We speak a lot on the phone and we see each other when the national team meets. Before, when I lived in Barcelona, we used to go out to an Argentine restaurant. Our favourite dish? A good rump steak. On other occasions we'd meet up in the afternoon to drink *mate* and talk football – the Argentine league, the national team, and whatever was happening in Spain.'

What is Messi like from a friend's point of view?
'He's a pretty normal guy. He's someone who likes to be at home and who loves his family very much. I think he's an even better person than he is a footballer.'

And what is he like as a footballer?
'As a player he's a gem. He has the heavenly gift of handling the ball really well. He impresses me with his ability to move the ball at such speed. It's incredible, what he's capable of doing, the way he gets round the other players, the way the ball is always glued to his foot. As he has shown

us many times, he's capable of taking a team to greater heights, of deciding a match. And he doesn't feel the pressure. Unbelievable. Leo is similar to Maradona, although Diego is unique and to compare them is crazy. As a friend I'm happy that he is doing so well.'

So, what did you mean when you said that 'he's an even better person than he is a footballer'?

'I said that out of humility towards Leo. He hasn't changed since I've known him. Fame hasn't made him lose himself, the praise hasn't gone to his head. He is still a great friend.'

Chapter 15

Soap opera

3 October 2005

The 2005–06 Liga begins on 26 August. The 75th Liga season has a new protagonist in the form of Robinho, the jewel in Real Madrid's crown, who it is hoped will sparkle alongside the other Brazilians in the league, Ronaldinho and Ronaldo. It is a league marked out as always by an eternal Real Madrid-Barcelona duel. The reigning champions play the first match away, against Alavés at the Mendizorroza stadium. Messi is neither on the pitch nor on the bench. Strange, given that only two days previously the young Argentine was the indisputable star of the Gamper Trophy. The explanation is given via an official announcement:

'FC Barcelona has decided not to play Leo Messi in the match against Alavés as a matter of caution, in light of the outstanding legal issue that will shortly be resolved within the confines of federal regulation relating to non-EU players.'

What has happened? On 8 July the Spanish Football Federation modified its general regulations regarding 'naturalised' players: in other words, non-EU players between the ages of seventeen and nineteen who have moved up through the youth teams of a Spanish club. The modification should allow the young player in question to play in the league, even if by doing so their club exceeds the three-foreigners-per-club limit in their line-up. Messi meets all of the required criteria to fulfil this regulation, which means that despite the club's three non-EU positions already being filled by Ronaldinho, Eto'o and Márquez, he should be able to play. But the new ruling – criticised by certain clubs, who see it as an ad hoc measure for Barcelona and Leo – must first be accepted by the Professional Football League (PFL) and ratified by the Consejo Superior de Deportes – the High Sports Council. In other words, 'due to the temporary situation, the FC Barcelona legal department have advised against allowing him to play'.

It is a difficult scenario to comprehend, given that in the 2004–05 season Leo played in a Champions League game with the first team against Shakhtar Donetsk, as well as in seven league games – with no professional licence and no EU documents, only his contracts for the youth team and the Barcelona Second Division B team. He had debuted in the Catalan derby against RCD Espanyol on Saturday 16 October 2004 in the Olympic stadium in Montjuïc. He comes onto the pitch to replace Deco and gets his first touch ten minutes later, after a pass from Belletti: some interesting action, but nothing exceptional that merits recording. Nonetheless, it is an unforgettable night for Leo – the realisation of a childhood dream, just as he was quoted in *La Capital* as saying that his goal was to 'make it into the first team'. Although, at that time, he thought he would do it at Newell's, his favourite team.

And he not only gets his premiere, he also scores his first league goal. It is 1 May 2005, the Nou Camp scoreboard indicates that there are three minutes remaining, and Barça are 1-0 up against Albacete. Frank Rijkaard brings off Samuel Eto'o, substituting Messi into the unusual position of centre forward. The youngster, only seventeen years and ten months old, takes advantage of a ball from Ronaldinho and beats the keeper, Valbuena, with a smoothly-timed shot.

It is a moment of pure elation: Leo does not know what to do with himself, and ends up being hoisted onto his friend Ronnie's (Ronaldinho's) shoulders, screaming joyfully. He is the youngest player in the club's history to score in a league game (a record later broken on 20 October 2007, when Bojan Krkić scored against Villarreal).

Things have gone well for him in the first team, but after that 1 May match, the Argentine will not play another official match that season – not even after Barça have done enough to ensure their seventeenth league title.

At the start of the 2005–06 season, he does not even play in the Spanish Super Cup against Betis. In the first leg he is on the bench, in the return leg he is not even on the teamsheet. In fact, even before the official communication from the club, something is not right and the board knows it. Messi is an unresolved case. Complaints begin pouring in to the club. Why wasn't this dealt with before? Why hasn't he been naturalised, given that Argentines can opt to take on dual nationality (Spanish-Argentine) after two years of residence in Spain?

With news of the possibility that Leo might not be able to play in the league come other suggestions, such as forfeiting him to another club who have a non-EU spot open. A suggestion that is immediately dismissed. The rumours about possible interest from other European clubs, like Inter, become more and more persistent. The Italian club's president, Massimo Moratti, has never tried to hide his interest in the player and has even made a financially attractive offer to Jorge Messi – who tries to use this bargaining chip to put pressure on Barcelona to resolve the issue.

Meanwhile, on 31 August (the closing date for new team signings), FC Barcelona renew Messi's licence as a youth player naturalised in the team that plays in the Second Division B. And on 16 September, the news that the player has signed a professional contract goes public. It will last for nine years, until 2014. According to various sources, his fees will increase to 3 million euros per season and the buyout clause to 150 million euros.

In reality, the announcement about the contract had already been made in June. 'A week after his eighteenth birthday, Leo Messi has received his greatest present. Team secretary Txiki Begiristain has travelled to Utrecht, Holland, with the player's father, in order to draw up his new contract, which guarantees him a place at the club until 2010,' reads the Barça website on 30 June, while the youngster is playing in the FIFA Under 20 World Cup.

There are various theories about this discrepancy over dates: some maintain that Messi, now legally an adult, simply accepted the new deal; others reckon that the contract was ultimately modified in September, because the player's father was not satisfied with some of the clauses about incentives; there are those who think that the length of the contract was increased, from the usual five years to the final nine; still others believe that the September agreement was nothing more than a declaration of intent, implying that a professional contact would be signed in accordance with all regulations the following year. The fact remains that the issue of the contract adds new material to the ongoing soap opera, which takes a new twist on 20 September. An overwhelming majority of the PFL committee votes against: the rule proposed by the Spanish Football Federation and the Association of Spanish Footballers concerning naturalised players will not come into effect. Those who are firmly in agreement with the Blaugrana president talk of a conspiracy against Barça, hatched by the powers that be in Spanish football. One thing for sure is that Messi cannot play in the league. He *can* play in the Champions League, however, without any problem. After examining the documents sent over by Barcelona, UEFA has agreed that he can play. They recognise his naturalised status. There is nothing extraordinary about it – Leo has already played many games in the European competition the previous season. And in the first Champions League match, against Werder Bremen, the most dangerous Group C opponent, the Argentine shines. He comes on in the second half. He wins a penalty, which is converted by Ronaldinho, and which puts paid to the hopes of the Germans. It is an important moment, which can only point towards him being placed in the starting line-up for the next match, against Udinese at the Nou Camp. But on the following day, 26 September, news arrives that puts an end to previous issues. At 1.00pm, Lionel Andrés Messi Cuccittini appears before Fernando Alberti Vecino, the judge presiding over the civil register, and proclaims 'that he does not renounce his Argentine nationality; that he swears allegiance to the King and obedience to the Constitution and Spanish laws; that he chooses Catalan civil residency; and that he petitions for the right to be inscribed into the Spanish civil register'.

In short, Leo has secured Spanish nationality: he is now a citizen of the EU. Barça presents the documentation to the Spanish Federation. The response is immediate and positive: 'In accordance with the rule in force [the Federation] recognises the aforementioned footballer's right to play with his club, taking into account his Spanish status, which is valid for any purpose.'

On 1 October, the sixth match day of the league, Leo will be able to join his team on the pitch against Zaragoza, with a weight lifted from his mind. That Saturday the Nou Camp crowd treat him as if he is a national hero. Barça is losing 2-0. Leo comes on in the second half but does not produce any miracles, although in the final moments Rijkaard's team manages to pull off an extraordinary draw. All should be well that ends well – but not this time.

Two days later, on Monday 3 October, Deportivo de La Coruña – Barça's next opponents – send a letter to the PFL, copied to the Spanish Football Federation Competition Committee, in which they petition for an injunction, requesting an investigation into the Barcelona player's naturalisation case. 'The player's national licence,' write Deportivo, 'has been obtained (and therefore given) outside the usual period for obtaining licences, which ended on 31 August and will not open again until December.' The crux of the demand 'is the reestablishment of equality in the competition, which it is believed has been violated, although of course once the inquiry has been carried out, this matter of undue infraction of the rules will come to an end'. The Alavés bosses, who had already threatened to kick up a fuss, go even further: they petition the Professional League to ban Messi from playing. From their point of view, his licence to play is null and void 'in the eyes of the law, given that processing it implies an evasion of the law'. Why? Because 'Barcelona could not arrange Messi's professional licence before 31 August, the date when the window for such licences closes, since at that point he was still a foreigner,' explains Javier Tebas, who is not only the legal advisor for Alavés, but also vice president of the PFL. 'Now they have given him Spanish nationality and have obtained a youth licence for him, with the intention of backdating it to 31 August and with the hope of playing him, despite the fact that the window for new signings is closed.'

In other words, Leo cannot rely on his EU residency until January. Moreover, 'given the contract that has been signed, how can Messi play with his youth team licence for the first team?' asks Tebas.

Joan Laporta loses his patience, declaring: 'We have sufficient legal basis for playing him. I don't know what else they want from us. We tried to do everything by the book and now that he has a Spanish passport they keep creating problems. I don't know why everyone is taking such an interest in damaging the player's career. They are stirring up trouble to prevent Messi from playing with Barça.'

The Blaugrana president goes on the counter-attack, making historical references: 'I don't want to imagine the possibility that nowadays, in an era when democratic rights and liberties exist, we are going to drag up the past, like the Di Stéfano case.'

A few details to refresh the memory: Alfredo Di Stéfano, known as the Blond Arrow, arrived in Spain from Argentina in 1953 to play for Barcelona. But the intervention of people in high places ended up turning the matter into a national issue and invalidating the signing. Even the advisory board got involved in the matter, stating that, given the player's importance, he shouldn't be given an exclusively Catalan residency, and putting forward the 'fair' proposal that the footballer play alternating seasons for Barça and Real Madrid. Luckily for the Whites, it was a solution the Catalan club rejected.

But the past does not come back to haunt Barça. Laporta's concerns are only phantoms that do not reappear. One thing for sure is that the Messi case ends up all over the sports pages across the country and provokes a scandal in Argentina. The first ruling from the Spanish Football Federation's Competition Committee appears on 18 October, stating that 'due to his naturalisation, Messi can continue to play as a Spaniard'. This last is followed by outrage from Alavés and Deportivo, appeals and counter-appeals, rulings and fierce debates, but in the meantime, Leo keeps playing. With the exception of the match against

Deportivo, when Rijkaard decides to rest him because he has just returned from a match with the Argentine national team, and because the Galician team had threatened to contest the fixture if the Argentine was playing, the Blue and Claret number 19 continues his hard work in the league. The issue continues in dispatches until the following year, but does not really make itself felt on the pitch. And so the Flea debuts at the Santiago Bernabéu on 19 November. It is his first time playing in this classic derby. Less than a month later, on 14 December, he receives the Golden Boy award at the Nou Camp, the annual prize awarded by the Turin sports publication *Tuttosport* to the best Under 21 player. Thanks to his achievements in the Under 20 World Cup, Messi steamrollers his opponents: Wayne Rooney only scores 127 points against the Argentine's 225. It is another source of recognition, which comes at just the right time: the Germany World Cup is only six months away and all these honours transform the Flea into a more desirable entity in the eyes of both small and large sponsors.

From McDonald's to Pepsi, Spanish oil and gas company Repsol YPF to La Serenísima yoghurts, Lays crisps to Storkman shoes, Garbarino electrical appliances to MasterCard, dozens of them are bidding for Messi, who has just shared a set with Maradona. They are pictured together signing a television: 'Look at what they're signing, they're the best.'

Lionel plays with everyone and everything. 'Football: 30 pesos. Tennis ball: twelve pesos. A kilo of oranges – three pesos,' runs the MasterCard advert while showing clips of the youngster having fun with a football, a tennis ball and an orange, concluding: 'Discovering there's hope after Diego – priceless.'

He plays with sad children for Bubbaloo, he dances with the ball to a tango rhythm for Pepsi. And that's nothing compared to the latest campaigns, like the one with the Messiah who ascends to the heavens for A-Style, an Italian caps and sportswear brand, or the one where Messi appears disguised as a footballing grandma for an Air Europa advert at the end of 2007.

But there is no point wasting time describing images, it would be easier just to go to YouTube to see how advertisers have made use of the image and abilities of Messi the juggler to sell anything and everything.

By the end of 2005 and beginning of 2006, it is undeniable that in the public sphere Leo is considered a coveted trophy – as proven by the war sparked between American sports giant Nike and German triple-stripers Adidas.

Chapter 16

A breath of fresh air

Conversation with Fernando Solanas, Head of Sports Marketing at Adidas Iberia

Is it true that Nike and Adidas, the giants of the sports store world, ended up in court over Messi?

'It's true, but let me tell you the story from the beginning. It was in 2003 that I first made contact with Jorge, Lionel's father and agent. At that time Messi had a contract with Nike, just for sportswear: in exchange for his image, they supplied him with trainers, clothes, etc. Jorge told me that they were happy with the American firm, who had made the bid for him two years earlier when he was only fourteen and played in the FC Barcelona youth team. It had not occurred to him to change sponsor. But I did not want to lose the contact and the following year (when Nike's sportswear contract was ending) I spoke to him again, making him see that there was good profit to be made if he negotiated with us.'

Let me see if I've got this right. In 2003 Messi was only sixteen years old and already a multinational company like Adidas was trying to 'steal' him from the competition ...

'It's our job to be on the lookout for the stars of the future. That's why we go to the experts in every sector. I played football. I love the sport and I might have a fairly good eye for players, but when it comes to deciding where to invest, I trust only the opinions of the coaches, the scouts, the "talent-hunters": in short, those who work alongside the youngsters. And five years ago all of them were saying that Messi was the gem in the Barça youth squad. They predicted his explosion ... I couldn't waste any time.'

OK, let's continue with the story ...
'Once the Nike contract has ended, Jorge decides not to sign with anyone else. He keeps receiving sports products from Nike because they sponsor Barcelona, but he wants to wait before making a deal for his son. I see him play in the Under 20 World Cup in 2005, wearing Nike gear. Messi is already a first-team player at Barça and things go very well for him in Holland. At that moment I think some very interesting offers start to land on Messi's doorstep from other European clubs, like Juventus.'

And what happens in terms of sponsorship?
'Two days before leaving for Holland, Jorge signs a letter of intention with Nike. Then things get complicated: they negotiate for many months without reaching an agreement ... until we intervene. We make an interesting offer, both in terms of money and in terms of representing the Germany World Cup. And in January 2006 we sign a contract until June 2010.'

They say that in terms of money ... Adidas offered five times the annual income offered by Nike ... and we're talking more than a million dollars – true or false?
'The figures are always confidential, we can't reveal the conditions of the contract.'

Alright, let's continue with the story because this is where the war between Adidas and Nike begins. Why, when Messi first wore his Adidas Predator outfit and scored a goal against Zaragoza in the Copa del Rey did Nike scream at the top of their voices: 'Messi has a deal with us and we're going to do whatever it takes for him to honour it'?
'Yes. Nike took the case to the courts and the judge cautiously ruled that Leo had to play in Nike equipment, so as not to hurt the supposed rights of the American firm.'

But in the end you won the battle, correct?
'I wouldn't call it a battle, but yes, the latest ruling was the one that determined Messi had no obligations towards Nike. Since then we have gradually started working with Leo.'

What does Leo represent to the football world and to sports marketing?
'Leo is something new, a breath of fresh air, the new Maradona. On the pitch it is like he is animated. In short, a very attractive personality.'

No one disputes his appeal on a footballing level, but as a personality … isn't he a very shy and modest kid?
'That's exactly what people like about him, that he's normal, he's a kid who loves being with his family and friends, who plays PlayStation and doesn't notice the buzz he generates. His simple nature is his greatest advantage. Too often sports stars seem to inhabit their own universe, very far from us. Leo, with his shyness, is close to all the fans.'

Let's talk about your campaign, 'Impossible is Nothing', in which Messi is one of the key figures.
'They are real stories that our icons tell. The idea is to convey to the consumer that nothing is impossible. And in this

case Leo tells his life story: an eleven-year-old boy who had the physical stature of an eight-year-old, but who didn't let that stand in the way of succeeding. Through hard work, perseverance, willpower, nothing is impossible. Leo is a perfect example. It is worth remembering that at thirteen he crossed an ocean, arrived at Barcelona, and after starting in the youth teams he has made it as a global football star.'

What does Leo sell?
'Authenticity.'

Where does he sell?
'He is strongest in Latin America, Spain and Asia, especially in Japan.'

Why Japan?
'Because Leo is small. It sounds silly, but it isn't. The Japanese identify with a little player who is skilled with the ball.'

Chapter 17

Boy of the match

22 February 2006

It is cold in London – intensely cold. The first leg of the Champions League quarter-final is being played at Stamford Bridge. The ground is muddy, which has provoked no end of controversy in the press. The atmosphere is heated – very heated, and very English. On one side is Chelsea – with a rational game, defensive, vigorous and impetuous, the most convincing team in Europe. On the other, Barça – talented, imaginative, with a taste for the spectacular. A lovely footballing model, but one that is often considered fragile, a machine easily broken. Both sides lead their respective leagues and, by the end of 2005, they have done incredible things. The new year has not started too well, however: in the Premier League, Chelsea let in three goals at Middlesbrough and they suffered the unspeakable in the FA Cup against modest Colchester. Barça are without Eto'o, who is playing in the African Nations Cup. With Xavi injured they have been knocked out of the Copa del Rey at the hands of Zaragoza, and without Ronaldinho they have lost two league games. The defeat against Valencia is tough, since they are closing in on Barça in the table, reducing the gap to six points.

Leaving circumstances to one side, the match offers myriad points of interest. Like the duels: between Ballon d'Or winner Ronaldinho and the runner-up Frank

Lampard; between Eto'o and Drogba, voted best and second best African players. And let's not forget the duel between the coaches: on the one hand emotional, hysterical José Mourinho and on the other, cool, calm Rijkaard: two completely opposing characters.

Moreover there is the eternal theme of revenge, or vengeance, which is always present in football. Few have forgotten the defeat and the three goals in nineteen minutes that the Blues had inflicted on the Blaugrana on 8 March 2005 in the return leg of the Champions League last sixteen. Barça led with a relative advantage after their 2-1 victory at the Nou Camp, but were left helplessly chasing the comeback after a series of defensive errors, which, according to Rijkaard, were due to a lack of maturity and concentration. Despite Ronaldinho's exploits and a string of missed chances, this Barça team, who already thought of itself as the new Dream Team, had to deal with the sight of Mourinho running onto the pitch and blowing kisses to the fans, as well as the insults, the shoving and the violent brawl between the players and the security guards, which even implicated the Dutch coach. The journey home was bitter, as the errors were rehashed over and over and referee Pierluigi Collina was accused (by the Spanish press) of not having given various penalties, nor having seen Carvalho's foul on Valdés in what was eventually a 4-2 victory led by Terry. Accused, in other words, of having favoured Chelsea.

It is well known that in cases such as these, history matters. It triggers headlines on every sports page and almost creates the impression of a television drama entitled 'Revenge'; there is more and more tension felt among the players, who go onto the pitch now at 8.45pm. The teamsheets are announced: Chelsea are missing Drogba, who is replaced in the attack by Hernán Crespo, while Asier del Horno and Claude Makelele are confirmed at the back.

Meanwhile Thiago Motta joins Edmílson in the centre for Barça. Andrés Iniesta, who has been in the starting line-up for some time, is on the bench. Leo Messi is sporting the number 30 fluorescent yellow shirt. To many, he seems no bigger than a kid when he comes onto the pitch. How will he be able to deal with this kind of tension, which is difficult enough even for the big boys? It seems that he doesn't feel the pressure. Is it down to a youthful lack of inhibition? Or is he simply fearless? The answer comes in the third minute, when the first shot on target comes from the Argentine and Petr Cech saves it comfortably. Leo is definitely fearless. And he demonstrates it continuously in the coming minutes as he scurries into every available space like a little mouse. He runs up and down, stealing balls, passing accurately, working well with his team-mates, creating the first real chance and sowing the seeds of panic among the Chelsea defence. A nightmare for Del Horno, who leaves a stud-mark impression through his right sock in the 31st minute. No caution, and no protest whatsoever from the Flea. Play continues. But a scuffle leads to the Basque defender being sent off six minutes later, leaving Chelsea a man short. What happens? Messi controls the ball three-quarters of the way up the pitch, resists an extremely tough tackle, and battles shoulder to shoulder with Robben, who manages to steal his position and snatch the ball, but the little guy will not back down. He chases him to the edge of the pitch, trying to overpower him from one side or another. Finally, with an unexpected burst of energy, he seizes the ball near the corner flag. Robben is now in front of him – he succeeds in nutmegging him but no sooner has he done so than he is flattened by a blue locomotive.

'I saw the defender coming at me fast and deliberately, and I tried to jump out of the way … But I didn't make it,' the Argentine later explains. The yellow shirt is knocked to the ground, along with Del Horno's blue one. Players gather around them, causing a commotion. Robben and Gudjohnsen start arguing with the linesman. Deco and Ronaldinho throw themselves at Del Horno. Puyol almost comes to blows with Robben. Motta and Edmílson try to calm the situation. Terry argues with Terje Hauge, the Norwegian referee, while Ronnie mutters something in his ear. Then comes the red card: Del Horno protests, Motta applauds, Makelele complains. The game recommences and Mourinho readjusts his team. He substitutes Joe Cole, sending on right back Geremi, and moving Ferreira into position to mark Messi. But nothing changes, neither the foul nor the recent beating has fazed the youngster, who continues to take centre stage; he doesn't let up, he pays no attention to the Blues' exasperation, and soldiers on with his fearless solo performance. He continually empowers the right flank of the pitch, creating juicy chances for Ronaldinho and Deco, although they fail to take advantage of them. Leo is too isolated – without the team behind him, he fails to make an impact. In the meantime, ten-man Chelsea are adhering strictly to their coach's instructions: 'Just get the 0-0 draw.' Now they have the perfect excuse to hang back and wait for an opportune moment to strike. The Blues are in complete control and it's not long before they make it count: spurred on by Drogba's entrance at the beginning of the second half, the English team takes the lead in the 58th minute. It is Motta who ends up sliding the ball into his own net while trying to clear a free kick by Lampard. Now they need to turn the game around. Once again it is Messi who is trying everything possible, motivating the rest of the team and ignoring the chants and whistles from the Stamford Bridge crowd at every turn. Fast, direct, he skips away, destroying the defence, shooting, making incredible passes – but nobody is there to receive them. He puts in a gentle shot from the edge of the area which grazes the goalpost to the left of the Chelsea goalkeeper. And he stands there as if stunned, with an ironic expression, wondering how he could have done better. He is the most determined, and finally the team gets behind him. In the 70th minute Terry turns the tables for Barça: Ronaldinho takes a free kick that beats Cech to level the score and Barcelona start to play some good football and create chances. And it's Messi again: he sends a golden opportunity to Larsson, who has come on for Motta. Three minutes later, Terry launches himself onto the Argentine in the area to prevent him from controlling the ball. Penalty? The referee ignores the incident. In the 79th minute Eto'o heads a great pass from Márquez into the net. They have done it.

Unbeaten until that moment at Stamford Bridge, after 49 matches (38 wins, eleven draws), José Mourinho must face up to the blow of his first defeat. And he doesn't digest it very well. He blames it on the referee and Leo: 'Am I disappointed with Del Horno's sending off? Did you see the match? Either way I'm cross with the authorities: write that if you want ... But what can we do? Ask for them to retract Del Horno's red card? Suspend Messi for his theatricals? Nothing will change the result ... Because let's be serious, Messi put on an act. Catalonia is a country of culture, you know it is. And I've been to the theatre many times and it's very high quality over there. And Messi has learnt from the best ...'

'Whoever says that Messi put on an act obviously didn't see what really happened,' says Eto'o. 'They were pounding on him from all directions,' insists Rijkaard. Leo simply says: 'I have a cut on my knee, one on my thigh and another on my foot. My whole body is bruised, but I'm not in pain because we won.' He adds: 'It has been an incredible game.'

Everyone else is in agreement, starting with his team-mates, who hug him as he leaves the field, while the fans who came to the match chant his name. The following day the descriptions are flowing – people are talking of 'dedication', 'genius', 'a footballing virtuoso', 'Barça's treasure', 'the birth of a great star', 'the best', 'the bravest', 'the best in the match'. In the context of his age and his nerve, his performance is compared to the likes of Pelé in the 1958 World Cup in Sweden, of Maradona in the Under 20 World Cup in 1979, of Cruyff against Benfica in 1969, of George Best. He is showered with praise, it is as if the boy has passed the test of maturity with flying colours and, with him, the entire team.

The return leg at the Nou Camp is on 7 March. In the 23rd minute Leo Messi is off, stealing the ball from Robben – but suddenly he puts his hand to his left knee and falls to the ground. 'In the play when I collided with Gallas, I had already felt the first stabs of pain, but I decided to keep going,' he would say later, 'and in the next play I realised that I couldn't go on.'

There has been no rough play, no knock, but Leo is lying on the ground. He grimaces with pain, his hands holding back his hair and covering his face to try to hide his fear. The crowd falls silent. His team-mates look at each other, downcast. He leaves the pitch, distraught. Rijkaard hugs him, emotional. It is a difficult moment for a player who was applauded by 90,000 Nou Camp spectators – not as a drama queen, but as the puppet master who had pulled the strings of the Stamford Bridge victory.

Muscular tear in the upper part of one of the right hamstrings – a four-centimetre tear. The Barcelona medics say that recovery will take four to six weeks. But luck is not on Leo's side. When the time comes for him to play again, more problems arise in the same area: he can still feel the scar. He was supposed to play against Villarreal but does not, he should be playing in the Champions League semi-final against Milan but is not. In the end he goes 79 days without football. And he watches the Champions League final from the stands.

There had been talk of the possibility of him playing for a short stint on this great occasion – Barça-Arsenal at the Stade de France, Paris – perhaps for a few minutes at the very least, but despite the seemingly healed injury, Rijkaard decides not to risk it. His team-mates go on to lift the cup for the second time in Barça's history. Sad and alone, Leo does not go down to the pitch to collect his medal.

Chapter 18

Difficult, very difficult

Conversation with Asier del Horno

Defender, born 19 January 1981 in Barakaldo (Vizcaya). Height: 1.81m. Weight: 72 kilos. Debut: 9 September 2000, Deportivo-Athletic Bilbao 2-0. Sporting career: 1999–2005 at Athletic, 2005–06 at Chelsea, 2006–07 at Valencia, 2007–08 at Athletic, 2008–2010 at Valencia, 2010 at Real Valladolid, 2010–12 at Levante UD. Ten caps with the Spanish national team. Titles: one Premier League (2005–06), and FA Community Shield (2005). That's how his CV reads, but the ex-Chelsea left back has many more things to say.

What happened at the 2005–06 Champions League final sixteen Chelsea-Barcelona match at Stamford Bridge?
'It was a special match, given what had happened the previous year. The atmosphere was tense. Everyone could feel it. We were quietly confident. Mourinho had prepared us for every detail of the encounter, trying to block every possible Barça manoeuvre. In the midfield we had people like Makelele, Lampard and Essien, who protected the defence but Messi kept on getting through. I came face to face with him two or three times and I tried to stop him with all my skills and experience.'

Did Messi surprise you? Perhaps you weren't expecting to come face to face with a kid like that?
'In every match there's always one player, the one you least expect, who makes you suffer.'

In the 31st minute, you gave him a kick that merited a yellow card. What had the Argentine done to you?
'Nothing, it was an incident during the game and I don't remember the details.'

Is Messi one of those forwards who provokes the defence?
'No, he doesn't provoke. He doesn't say anything. There are many provocations in football between defenders and forwards, but that's not his style.'

Moving on to the 36th minute of the first half …
'Messi had nutmegged Robben just by the corner flag. I tried to stop him and he went past me. He started to roll around on the ground and they sent me off. Messi was sharp, he was smart, it looked like it was an incredible tackle and in reality it was nothing …'

So José Mourinho was right when he declared after the match that 'Leo Messi put on an act, and a good one'?
'Lionel exaggerated, without a doubt.'

Leaving the past aside, let's talk about Messi's characteristics as seen from the point of view of a left back.
'The key thing about Messi is that he drives the ball forward very well, quickly and with the ball always glued to his boot. His speed gives him time to change direction, surprising whoever is marking him at that particular moment.'

How can Messi be stopped?
'It's complicated. It's difficult, very difficult. Depending on the situation you're in, given his divine inspiration ... Playing on the opposite touchline, when he dodges into the centre, it's difficult to stop him. He has speed, he has skills ... argh, he's a real problem for any defender.'

Any advice for your colleagues?
'I wouldn't know ... I can only say that defenders need to keep tightly in line, be aggressive, be speedy and hold the position well.'

Chapter 19

Not even a single minute

30 June 2006

There are others who are considered the big stars. Ronaldinho, more than anyone else; according to commentators and fans, he will be the one who will shine the most. Many predict he will be crowned best World Cup player and highest goal scorer. Because – among other reasons – according to the majority of the world's coaches, players, newspapers and TV channels, Brazil is favourite to take home the title. Betting on Barça's number 10 is easy and logical. He has just had a spectacular season: Ballon d'Or, Liga and Champions League winner. The only thing that remains in order to crown him king is his second world title. Here is the list of potential candidates: fellow Brazilian Ronaldo, from whom everyone expects the umpteenth resurrection; David Beckham, the pop star of football; Zidane – facing the final challenge of his career. They are closely followed by the likes of Figo, Ballack, Torres, Van Nistelrooy and Del Piero.

In terms of Argentina, the name on everyone's lips is Juan Román Riquelme. Twenty-eight years old, born in Buenos Aires, an attacking midfielder, he plays for Villarreal and as yet has no World Cup on his CV, but selector José Pekerman has put his trust in him.

The Albiceleste have been built around him and their game largely depends on Riquelme having a good day.

He is a silent footballer, charged with the responsibility of leading the team. He needs to be solid, he needs to play imaginatively and make magic, he needs to move between the lines and get the crucial passes to the strikers. And Messi? Well … Messi is in the running in the category of medium-level stars, or rather, promising youngsters. He has been dubbed the new Maradona and the World Cup should be his chance to surprise the whole world at just eighteen years of age, after establishing himself on the international scene at Stamford Bridge.

Along with the Portuguese Cristiano Ronaldo and the Ecuadorian Luis Valencia, fans have included him in the list of six candidates from whom the best young World Cup player will be chosen (the other three, nominated by FIFA, are Cesc Fàbregas, the Swiss player Tranquillo Barnetta and the German Thomas Podolski). The title was inaugurated on 1 January 1985. The player in question will have to distinguish himself on pitches throughout Germany in terms of style, charisma, clean play and a passion for football. The Argentines want to see Messi in the starting line-up and they have pinned all their hopes on him; they want to see confirmation of all the amazing stories that are told across Europe about the heir to Maradona – and they want that confirmation in the shape of a national shirt. Since the days of the Pibe de Oro (Maradona's nickname, golden boy) they have dreamt of a different player, a spectacular, magical player, whom they could love and worship the way they did – and still do – Diego. When it came down to it, it was Maradona himself who, a few months previously, asked that the number 10 shirt be given to Messi – a shirt number which the Argentine Federation had retired in his honour.

Leo may have grown up far from his native country, but in the last few months he has returned home in order to recover from the injury he received against Chelsea. He has had time to get some exposure, give interviews and shoot some ad hoc adverts for the World Cup. Both multinational and Argentine companies have bet on him in order to benefit from the effects of a global stage. Not least, German sporting brand Adidas, who have plastered entire buildings from Rome to Buenos Aires via Berlin with enormous posters of his face. On the eve of the World Cup, at least in terms of publicity, he is definitely beating his team-mates by miles. He undoubtedly has the highest level of media coverage of any Albiceleste player. But such publicity can generate jealousy – yet another obstacle in the youngster's path to being accepted in Pekerman's team.

He has recently been invited into the group, thanks to his success in the Under 20 World Cup. His debut with the main national team is on 17 August 2005. It is during a friendly against Hungary in Budapest, at the stadium dedicated to Ferenc Puskás. He comes on for Maxi López in the 65th minute. And he is on the pitch for little more than 40 seconds. On his second touch, he dribbles the ball past Vanczák. The Hungarian grabs him by his brand-new number 18 shirt; Messi lifts his arm and pushes him back. Bam! He catches the defender full in the face. German referee Markus Merk is in no doubt. He elbowed him. And he pulls out the red card in front of the disbelieving Argentines. Sent off in his first match. Not the scenario that Leo had imagined. He is to spend the rest of the match crying. His coach and team-mates think the referee's decision is excessive, but their words of consolation are in vain.

After an unfortunate debut, there are other matches that offer an opportunity to move on and get into sync with the squad. But it is not easy. As is already obvious, Messi is shy. He hardly speaks to his team-mates, or the staff. There is no shortage of anecdotes illustrating this, like the time during training in Madrid when the boss invites the whole squad to a barbecue – an Argentine social ritual *par excellence* – in order to encourage group bonding. Leo does not open his mouth, not even to ask for some meat. It is a silence that is apparent and worrying to the others. And Messi does not even emerge from his silence in order to conform to expected formalities. At Christmas, for example, when all the Argentine players go over to visit the manager after spending time with their families, Messi does not show up. And the AFA are often unable to locate him.

The lad adheres neither to the team hierarchy, nor to the unwritten rules that are essential to Argentine football. He is not a rebel, he does not behave badly, and he does not do it intentionally, it's just the way he is. In the training sessions before his debut with the main national team, for example, he finds himself face to face with Gabriel Heinze. He faces up to him one, two, three, four times, repeatedly giving him the cold shoulder. Heinze, now a Newell's Old Boys defender, is reaching boiling point and is about to avenge his wounded pride. Pekerman has to intervene to save the little guy's skin, and the honour of one of his players. It is a scene that will be repeated with others in Nüremberg, the Argentine team's base over in Germany. The least one could say about the young Barcelona footballer is that he is shameless. And without ignoring the issue of unwritten rules, which are steeped in history, it has to be said that Messi is young – too young. To draw parallels yet again, at eighteen years of age, despite being an emerging figure, Maradona was not even selected by César Bilardo for the 1978 World Cup. Messi is in Germany, but it should be remembered that no Argentine player since the 1930s has played in the final stages of the competition at only eighteen years old. The lesson that has had to be learned by men who have sat 'willingly' on the bench is that it is necessary to protect newly emerging talents at all costs – the weight of defeat must not be allowed to rest on their shoulders. There is actually a risk of harming them. And in these cases, history carries a lot of weight.

So too does the injury of 7 March. Messi is seemingly completely recovered; he has already played various friendlies before the World Cup; but there are those in the dressing room who say his muscles are still bothering him. In terms of his state of mind, he is happy in the lead-up to his first World Cup. In his pre-tournament statements he reaffirms what everyone has been saying: the Brazilians, with his friend Ronaldinho up ahead, are the favourites, but 'we also have a good team. And the national team is made up of many great players. Of course we are going to take it one step at a time, one game at a time. And there will be excellent opponents and every match will be very complicated. But I believe that Argentina can win the World Cup.'

The Albiceleste is in Group C, known from the beginning as the group of death: Ivory Coast, Serbia and Montenegro and Holland. It will not be an easy ride, especially with the disaster of the Korean and Japanese World Cup weighing on their minds.

Saturday 10 June at 9.00pm in Hamburg sees the first match against the Ivory Coast. During a training session five days earlier, Messi suffered a contusion, making it difficult for him to play. The manager's idea is to pace him, allowing him to go on later in the competition, apart from anything because they are not convinced he is 100 per cent fit. In fact, they state: 'We cannot promise anything that could create expectations. In each successive training session we have seen improvement and a return to form. And he is getting better bit by bit. We are grateful for the effort he has made to be here with us.' On the bench he goes. From his 'privileged' vantage point Lionel watches as Crespo scores his 30th Albiceleste goal with his usual opportunism. He watches as

Riquelme, in a moment of divine inspiration, looks into the stands and sends the ball exactly where it needed to go. And he sees the unmarked 'Conejo' Saviola punish Tizie with his first touch. He watches as the 'Elephants' (Ivory Coast) fight back and try to create chances without getting a goal – they only manage it towards the end, thanks to Drogba as usual – penetrating the Argentine defence, led by the impeccable Ayala. The result: 2-1. The Albiceleste look promising, even without Leo. Commenting on the game, Pekerman remarks: 'To me, football is always the same. I have expectations of this squad from an analytical point of view, not based solely on desire. We put up a great performance in terms of defence in our first match, holding off dangerous Ivory Coast players. True, we lacked presence. But the good thing is that we never lost our nerve.' It does not take much reading between the lines to realise that he is satisfied with how things have gone, which is obvious given that, in the second match against Serbia and Montenegro – which concerns him, despite the fact that they have lost to Holland – he has no intention of changing his teamsheet, except to put Lucho González in place of Esteban Cambiasso. In short, at the Gelsenkirchen stadium on 16 June, Messi is on the bench again. He has Carlos Tévez to keep him company, and 65 minutes to witness three goals and wonder how many he could score. Then he is on his feet, in his fluorescent outfit, warming up along the touchline. The warm-up is a promising sign. He returns to the dugout, following gestures and instructions, and finally assistant coach Hugo Tocalli lets him put on the blue number 19 shirt. His World Cup debut comes in the 74th minute. He comes on for Maxi Rodríguez, joining the game at the same time as Carlos Tévez, the other youngster on the team.

In the stands, Maradona lifts his arms in the air, screaming and cheering along with the thousands of Argentine fans. They sing: 'Olé, olé olé olé, Me-ssiiiii, Me-ssiiiii!' Someone holds up a poster with the Flea's face next to the World Cup trophy. Underneath it says: 'This is my dream.' Others wave a placard that reads: 'He's Argentine and he's the Messiah.' The demand of one little girl brandishing a placard – 'José, let Messi play (please)' – is finally answered.

Up until now the Albiceleste have been playing well, no complaints, but when the Flea comes on things change: the number 19 forces a team who were starting to rest on their laurels to wake up, he gets them moving again, he makes them start accelerating more and more. They pass him the ball and he's off like a shot, with the sole objective of making it to the opponents' goal. He creates quite a spectacle as he skips along. A free kick is taken quickly and Leo is onto it, zooming along on the left-hand side of the penalty area. He reaches the line, lifts his head and slides the ball in front of the goalposts in a perfect position for Crespo who, anticipating the Serbian defence, stretches out his foot and takes the total number of goals to four. In the 87th minute Tévez passes to Crespo, who passes back to Tévez who, after having scored the fifth goal, shows his generosity by sending the ball down to Messi, who is motoring up the right wing. He gets past the defender and scores the sixth goal, sliding the ball between the post and the goalkeeper's hand. Then he pauses to point to the player who gifted him the goal. Crespo rushes over to hug him, the crowd goes wild.

This time it is a fantastic World Cup debut, although as usual the man in question plays it down: 'I wasn't thinking about my debut. I was thinking about winning a match that I really wanted to play in. In all honesty I still haven't thought about the fact that I'm now a World Cup player and that I fulfilled a dream today.' And now? Now Pekerman has a decision to make, a dilemma to resolve. 'His country wants him to play Messi from the start. And not to wait until the 74th minute. And the press, who see what sells, want it too. And, my dear friends, what press and what country wouldn't want it?' writes Pep Guardiola in *El País*. 'Only he (Pekerman) knows what he is going to do with this genius. No one doubts that Messi will give him the same over 90 minutes that he gives in fifteen. Yesterday was like that sweetie that a mother keeps hidden in her bag, well hidden, ready to give to her child when he won't stop crying. And it always works, even if only for fifteen minutes.'

At the end of the day the decision is not so difficult, the hot potato burns less because the last match in Group C against Holland is insignificant. Both teams have already qualified for the last sixteen, now they are just playing for first position in the group. Pekerman can kill two birds with one stone: Tévez and Messi in the starting line-up, Saviola and Crespo rested to avoid any yellow cards that could mean missing the next match. In the end, everyone is happy – especially those who want to see the little genius from Rosario play again.

On 21 June at the Waldstadion in Frankfurt, Lionel is awaited by Johan Cruyff, Michel Platini, Franz Beckenbauer and, of course, Diego Armando Maradona, dressed inevitably in his Albiceleste shirt. In other words, the crème de la crème of World Cup football.

Leo is the last to disembark from the team bus, iPod headphones in his ears, the last to change, after having a look at the pitch and chatting with fellow Barcelona players from the orange-clad team (Van Bronckhorst and Van Bommel) and the last to start his warm-up. When the time comes to go on the pitch, he waits respectfully in line. On his feet, he is wearing a pair of Adidas boots designed especially for his World Cup appearance. On them is his name, the sun from the Argentine flag, the phrase 'The Hand of God' and a date: 22 June 1986. The following day it will be twenty years since Diego scored two goals against England in the 1986 World Cup, one with the hand and one with the foot.

Expectation is mounting in the stands. What wonders will Lionel have for them this time? If he wreaked havoc in fifteen minutes, who knows what he will do in 90. And even if this isn't his night, the effect of his presence on the pitch is almost palpable. In the first half he plays along the right wing, marked by Tim de Cler. He has eleven touches, losing the ball once and making seven good passes. In the second half he switches to the left wing, where he is marked by Kew Jaliens. In 23 minutes he only gets three touches, only one of which is played the way it should be. In the 69th minute Pekerman substitutes him for Julio Cruz. There is very little of note: an inoffensive left-footed kick and one or two brilliant passes – one deep to Cambiasso, intercepted with difficulty by Van Der Saar, an incredible ball to Maxi Rodríguez and a beautiful 'one-two' with Riquelme with a final shot that ends up going just wide.

It was the most highly anticipated match of the first stage of the World Cup, a clash between two powerful teams with many great precedents (the 1978 final being among those that stand out), which, nonetheless, was disappointing. Some journalists maliciously imply that the number 19's rather ordinary performance will give Pekerman the perfect excuse to put him back on the bench. And back he goes.

On 24 June, his nineteenth birthday, he is back to being a spectator for 84 long minutes. And this time Argentina are not doing well: Mexico, coached by the Argentine Ricardo La Volpe, have pushed them against the ropes. When Messi comes on for Saviola, the score is 1-1. The game is heading into extra time. And it is then that the boy from Barça changes the team's rhythm, he gives it the necessary depth and sends the ball from foot to foot, building up to an amazing Maxi Rodríguez goal. Albeit with more difficulties than anticipated, Argentina have made it into the quarter-finals.

In Berlin, on 30 June, they face host team Germany. There are 120 minutes of play, of which Leo Messi plays not even a single minute. It is a mystery, the polemic of a match that ends with Argentina losing on penalties (4-2, after a 1-1 scoreline at the end of extra time).

Let us rewind the film of that decisive match, in order to understand how it is that the player who could have played a crucial role in winning the World Cup ended up on the bench.

Pekerman replaces Saviola with Tévez in the starting line-up, and Lucho González also starts. Two players who work well with the team – no complaints there. Pekerman is forced to make his first substitution in the 71st minute, when Pato Abbondanzieri is injured in a skirmish with the giant Germans. Leo Franco comes on in his place. The next to come off is Riquelme – 'he was tired', says the boss. Cambiasso replaces him. The manager is trying to achieve a balance, or rather, he is trying to bolt the door and defend the scoreline. Argentina are winning 1-0 thanks to a header from Ayala, but the players are continually trapped in their own half and they blame the Germans for the hard blows they receive. In the 79th minute the final substitution is made with Cruz coming on for Crespo, just moments before Klose heads in the equaliser. To rectify the situation would have required speed, skill and creativity, which Cruz does not possess and which Tévez can no longer muster due to tiredness after playing for the length of the match. Essentially, they needed Messi. Popular consensus seems to be that if he had come on, Argentina would have sealed the match before it got to the penalty shoot-out stage. He would have taken charge of transforming the situation.

Why didn't Pekerman send him on? Why did he choose Cruz over him? 'In that moment we needed a striker in the box and that's not Messi,' he explains in the press room after the tears, after the fight between Oliver Bierhoff, Frings and Cruz, and before announcing his resignation. 'We were always considering him [Messi] as a good option, I knew we could count on him,' says the manager. A statement reinforced by his comment that 'Argentina may have had alternatives, but we could not instigate them'. Hugo Tocalli today confirms that version. 'In order to counteract Germany's play in the air it was important to send on Cruz. We were winning 1-0 in a match we were controlling well, in which we had dominated, and then Abbondanzieri's unfortunate injury ruined all our plans.' But his explanations do not convince anyone, and one by one various theories emerge on the topic:

1. Mistake: Pekerman simply got it wrong. He misinterpreted the game, he made a hurried decision and he made the change when he should not have done so.

2. Mystery: Only the manager will ever know the truth and it will go down in Argentine footballing history as one of its many secrets, like Rattín's sending off in England in '66, Maradona's drug-taking in the United States in '94, or the red card against Ortega in France in '98.

3. Bad advice: Pekerman let himself be influenced by the heavyweights in the dressing room, who were annoyed by Messi dominating the media spotlight. In other words, Messi says he wants to play and this irritates team leaders like Juan Román Riquelme and the captain, Fabián Ayala, who ensure their feelings do not go unnoticed and call him to order at a press conference. They are the ones who convince the coach to leave Messi out of the starting eleven.

4. Etiquette and values: Pekerman could not erase or ignore etiquette, values and players who had earned their right to be on the pitch over many years.

Whatever happens, no one will ever know which of these theories is correct. José Pekerman remains silent and does not revisit the subject. A year later, in an interview with sports magazine *Marca*, when they ask: 'What happened with Messi? Wasn't there some sort of dispute over him?' he replies: 'I am proud of him and I was the one who included him in the Under 20 team when no one knew who he was. In Argentina the problem is that we have so much faith that just a little bit of Messi gets us very excitable. And people were expecting Messi to be the great Maradona of this World Cup. And he was just taking his first steps with Argentina, a great team. I hope this experience will serve him well in the future.'

And Leo Messi? He also stays silent on the topic. That night in Berlin he is one of the few who does not appear before the cameras and microphones. It is not only due to his disappointment over being knocked out of the tournament, but also because he is angry at what some of the press are saying about his behaviour during the penalty shoot-out. 'They said things like that I didn't care if we went out – which could not be further from the truth. If anyone had been inside the dressing room,' he confesses in an interview with *Mundo Deportivo* five days later, 'they would have realised what I was feeling at that moment.' He will not be drawn on the issue of Pekerman giving him so little in the way of opportunities. 'He decided that was the way it was going to be … He did it that way because it had been working. Players like Saviola and Crespo had been doing really well, and that's that.'

That's that. Time to turn the page.

Chapter 20

Positive discrimination

Conversation with Jorge Valdano

When he is asked how he wants to be introduced, he replies, 'ex-footballer'. This despite the fact that he was the Real Madrid general director; and aside from winning one world championship in an Argentine shirt, he has been many other things in his lifetime: coach, sporting director, writer, commentator. Words are without a doubt among his best weaponry; metaphor is his indispensable tool; he considers analysis a pleasure.

Let's talk about Messi, a footballer who started out at Newell's, like you. Let's begin at the 2006 World Cup. An entire nation had pinned their hopes on him and instead he didn't even set foot on the pitch in the decisive match. Why?

'Pekerman is a man who knows talent when he sees it and he has never kept it hidden away. We can try to imagine that there was some problem we don't know about, probably a physical issue. Maybe he wasn't at his peak. That said, I'm with those who thought it was a shame that Argentina collapsed without Messi. In the last match many things happened: Abbondanzieri was injured, Riquelme got tired, Argentina were 1-0 up – all factors that penalised Messi. The match seemed under control. Germany were not getting anywhere, but the truth is that in their desperation to equalise Messi could have taken advantage of the opposition's disorder to score another goal. But these are all speculations, I prefer to deduce that Pekerman's thoughts are worth more than mine because he was dealing with the facts on the ground.'

And while we're on the topic, there has been much talk about Messi's youth, his maturity, the etiquette of Argentine football and the dressing room …

'Maradona played in his first World Cup when he was 21 and it was not a happy experience. He was not entirely mature enough yet. With Messi there was positive discrimination: we were thinking that if he had played he would have turned the match around …'

Now that we have dealt with that topic, let's talk about Messi and Maradona.

'Maradona's game was more nuanced. Diego could finish but he could also be the strategist. Messi is more intense than that. With his assets, his physical, mental and technical speed, he is always tempted to go for the goal. Diego sometimes used to put his foot on the accelerator, whereas Messi lives with the pedal to the floor. It's a youthful sin. As Menotti used to say, he needs to learn to be Joe Bloggs, a "Jack of all trades". He can't always be Messi, because if you're continually explosive then the opposition will have their guard up constantly and it's more difficult to surprise them. Their similarities? The same thing happens with Leo that used to happen with Maradona, he's an individual who carries such weight that he can manage without the team. He's not like Zidane or Platini, who need the team around them in order to display their collective intelligence. Messi needs his team-mates to pass him the ball, after that he does the rest on his own. Their differences? Physicality. Diego came to Napoli eight kilos heavier and he was still a decisive influence. Messi's game requires him to be explosive, so it is imperative he stays in perfect shape. Look at the injuries he has sustained: it seems like his muscles break him because of the amount they require of him.'

What do you think of Messi today?
'He has matured. He has a natural ability to deal with the competition. He gives the impression of being happy whenever he has the ball at his feet – he is not conditioned by context, nor by the expectation he has generated. And that is the mark of a great player, not getting stage fright. At the crossroads of his career, where you can really measure the limits of his personality, he has given us some astounding performances. We're dealing with someone who plays incredibly attractive football, and who, even with three men marking him, with his back to the goal and hemmed in at the corner flag, can be dangerous.'

What will his future hold?
'I would have liked to have had his future ... he has every reason to become the first great player of the twenty-first century. The twentieth century was carved out by Pelé, Maradona, Cruyff, Di Stéfano. He could dominate this decade, along with Cristiano Ronaldo. He's in the best possible position. Mother Nature has given him all the tools he needs. Now, he must take charge of that talent. He has an advantage: he looks at himself with a certain sense of distance. In addition, the off-pitch Leo doesn't make the headlines – that only happens when the ball is at his feet. That's another difference between him and Maradona. Diego was doubly attractive: on the one hand as a footballer and on the other as the rebel, the provocateur. He was always a volcano on the edge of erupting.'

Chapter 21

The devil

10 March 2007

Barcelona – This time, Don Fabio's nightmare is about a nineteen-year-old boy, Leo Messi. An Argentine flea who ruins his party. Capello had never won on Barça territory (not with Juve, nor with Roma, nor with Madrid), he was getting there, against all predictions. And then along came the little guy, once, twice, bringing the scores level each time and, just when it looked like it was going their way, in the 90th minute he pulls the most beautiful sequence out of his hat, the speediest dribbling, a cross into the centre: 3-3. Capello and his men are like children who have had their lollipop snatched from their mouths.

What is indisputable is that the Spanish derby has been strange, exciting, volatile, full of goals. It begins with the two captains, Puyol and Raúl, who take to the pitch and make the sign of the cross. They need it: Barça must wipe the expulsion from the Eden of Europe from the memories of the Nou Camp's 98,000 spectators, while Real Madrid is playing a game of survival – their last chance to stay in the running for the league title. The standard prediction is that the ball will be controlled by the Blaugrana, the favourites, spread across the pitch in a daring 3-4-3 formation, so that Madrid are even less marked than usual. Very few are prepared to wager a bet because Capello's men like to get their own way against their eternal rivals. And, against predictions, within five minutes they are already dominating the scoreboard. The blond Guti passes to Higuaín along the left wing. The young Argentine plays an apparently innocuous ball: it is Thuram who turns it into a lethal one, with an incredible clearance that lands at Van Nistelrooy's feet. The Dutchman takes a shot from outside the box. Pathetic diving from Puyol and Valdés. It's in – 1-0. Now it's Rijkaard's turn to be nervous. Leo Messi comes on after just five minutes. Xavi sends him a deep pass, leaving only Casillas between the Argentine and the goal. The Whites are left rooted to the spot. Equaliser.

The defenders on both sides are foundering. One of the most nervous on the Barça team is Oleguer: he is to end up being sent off in the 45th minute after receiving his second booking (for a foul on Gago). The first comes in the twelfth minute, when he grabs Guti inside the box. Penalty and yellow card. Van Nistelrooy makes no mistake. Fabio Capello cannot believe his eyes. The president told him not to come away with a defeat, but to be in the lead gives him a proper chance to breathe.

It doesn't last long. Leo Messi is proving a nightmare again, as he latches onto a rebound from Casillas. It's not easy, but he scores anyway. In under the crossbar. Credit for the equaliser must go to Ronaldinho, however, who has finally awoken from his daze. He does what he does best, unbalancing two or three opponents, doing a one-two with Eto'o and shooting at Casillas, who manages to get a hand to it at first, but can do nothing about Messi's sudden rebound. Four goals in 27 minutes: this is the type of spectacle that the Spanish crowds

> love. Relieved of their fears, Barça seem to take charge of the situation. The Whites' defence is wavering, then comes the sending off, followed by a second half with only ten men. Rijkaard takes off Eto'o and sends on Sylvinho. The Blaugrana maintain control of the ball, but the Whites are dangerous. The advantage hangs by a thread. Guti takes a free kick: Sergio, Ramos and Puyol go up to meet the ball. The White defender gets a touch on the nape of his neck, the ball flies under the bar and into the back of the net. Victory? No, along comes Messi to save Barça and keep Madrid at arm's length. And Capello is back to the same old problem.
>
> Luca Caioli, *Corriere della Sera*, 11 March 2007

Yes, Capello … at best he had forgotten what Messi was capable of doing. And yet in the final of the Joan Gamper Trophy on 24 August 2005, it was precisely he who had asked about that devil (as he described him) who had driven the Juventus defence crazy, provoked three yellow cards, created one goal, and looked dangerous throughout the 90 minutes. At the end of the match, decided on penalties, Juventus had gone home with the cup thanks to six shots on target from the penalty spot. But Leo had been chosen as player of the match and was the genuine surprise of the game. Fabio Capello, who had instantly recognised the youngster's talent, joked with Frank Rijkaard, saying: 'Well … if you don't have room for him in your starting line-up, give him to me, we're ready to sign him.'

Perhaps Fabio Capello thought everything would turn out well for him on the evening of 10 March 2007, just as it had on 22 October 2006 at the Bernabéu. 2-0 to the Whites and everyone at home happy, with a Messi who had put in a good effort for at least 70 minutes, with a repertoire of left-footers, assists that were wasted by his team-mates, and breakthroughs into the box. And all while receiving a series of forceful tackles from Emerson that pushed the regulations' boundaries. To the extent that, by the end of the match, he would be diagnosed with a sprained right ankle in the external lateral ligament, which would keep him out for a week.

But he hadn't managed to score.

This time the tables are turned. Has Messi got something against Don Fabio, who is currently the England manager? Absolutely not. Is it that playing against Capello brings him luck? Not that either. It's a different issue altogether. 'Playing against Real Madrid,' says Messi, 'is always particularly motivating for any player.' That is a fact and he has demonstrated it since the first time he set foot on the Bernabéu ground on 19 November 2005.

Everyone remembers that match because of the show put on by Ronaldinho (two incredibly stunning goals, not to mention everything else he did) but also because of the 'standing ovation' given by two Real Madrid supporters to the Barcelona number 10. That was undoubtedly the photo opportunity of the match. Unforgettable. It was shown on all the TV channels. Editors and journalists even went as far as tracking down the two men, one with a black moustache, the other with a beard, who were on their feet applauding. The media people wanted to know why they paid such tribute to him. Their response? How could they not applaud a superstar and his magic, even if only as a sporting gesture? But as well as the Gaucho (Ronaldinho), the people in the stands were also very impressed with Leo's performance.

Let's take a quick look at the highlights from that day. In the third minute, Sergio Ramos feels obliged to knock down the Flea on the edge of the area, in front of goal. In the fifteenth minute, Leo is the one who, after a fantastic piece of footwork, provides Eto'o with the chance to score the first goal. In the 26th minute, Messi's spectacular change of pace traps Roberto Carlos. In the 30th minute Messi penetrates the defence, but Iker Casillas blocks the shot. Barça are within reach of the second goal. In the 40th minute, Ronaldinho slaloms and crosses to Messi, but the header is wide of the goalpost. In the 47th minute Messi tries again. It's wide. A defender clears the ball. In the 55th minute Casillas denies Messi's third shot. In the 69th minute, Messi is replaced by Iniesta. These minutes and notes record that he played a fantastic game in his *Clásico* derby debut, all that was missing was the goal to take his display of speed, angles and lethal assists to the level of perfection. But the strongest memory from that match is an abundance of courage on the part of a debutant, who showed respect for nothing and nobody, who did not suffer an ounce of the 'stage fright' so beloved of his compatriot Jorge Valdano, who proved it from every part of the pitch, who took initiative and assumed responsibility, despite there being superstars on the pitch like an inspired Ronaldinho and an Eto'o on best form. These are feelings that will be widely confirmed, disputed and reaffirmed. It is a shame that he misses the return leg due to the injury he suffered at Chelsea. It is the same injury (only on the other leg) that he will sustain on 15 December 2007 against Valencia in Mestalla, five days before the classic derby. Sharp pain in the left leg, head bowed, biting on his shirt, and he's off. Goodbye classic derby. Against Real Madrid, Barça have to lose the player who made all the difference at the start of the season. The ultrasound confirms it: tear in the upper part of the femoral biceps in the left thigh. Out for four to five weeks (he will play again 36 days later, on 20 January, against Racing Santander). And he will get injured again on 4 March 2008 in the Champions League quarter-final match against Celtic in Glasgow. Another femoral biceps tear in his left thigh. Another five weeks out before returning to the field.

Pause for a question: Why does Messi endure so many tears and breaks, to the point where people are already calling him 'the porcelain star'? Accumulated muscle fatigue, an old injury that has not properly healed, an insufficient warm-up, psychological stress, an imbalance of pressure on muscular areas, bad posture throughout one's career, direct impact, a supposed difference in length between one leg and the other … there are many possible causes of injury. Furthermore, the complexity of the hamstring structure makes it difficult to pinpoint the causes and that in turn makes a player's recovery more difficult. In Messi's case, some people also factor in his physical particulars, his muscular and bone structure and his growth problems, stimulated by hormones. In any event, it is difficult to establish the precise cause, even for the Barcelona medics, who have often been slated by the press over prognostic errors with regard to recovery times. 'They told me,' explains Jorge Messi, 'that his muscular mass is made up of explosive fibres, like those of a sprinter. That's what gives him his trademark speed, but the risk of a break is considerable. In any event, Leo is perfectly aware that he really needs to take care of himself.' Let's close the chapter on the issue of injuries and resume the story of the classic derby on 10 March 2007, although, admittedly, there is also an injury involved in this story. Leo has been out for nine weeks, but this time it is not because of his muscles but because of an incident during a match. On 12 November 2006, in a game against Real Zaragoza, opposition defender Alberto Zapater stamps on his foot. The fifth metatarsal of his left foot is broken. He has to go into surgery, where a pin is fitted to stabilise the fracture and he is given a skin graft to speed up the recuperation. Prior to the match in question he played some good games, 'but,' he says, 'I still hadn't scored. That was my unfinished business.' He manages to score a hat-trick, his first at the top level (he had previously scored more goals in a match, but only on a small ground of little importance) and although it doesn't seal a victory for the team it is at least enough to save Barça's skin *in extremis.* 'Because losing to Real,' he says, 'is always bloody awful.' And that's not all – a goal allows Leo to display a message (printed underneath his shirt) that reads: 'Have strength, uncle', to his godfather, who has just lost his father. It is his way of showing his full support at a difficult time. And there is another dedication made on that magical night. It comes in the form of kisses blown to Barça's emblem. After the third goal Messi runs along and repeats the gesture, because 'I owe a lot to Barça for what they did for me when they had the chance, and also to the fans for all the affection they have shown towards me, especially in these difficult few months.' Those three goals change the course of a negative season. From 10 March onwards Leo plays frequently, he doesn't waste any chances and he doesn't just score goals – he creates works of art.

Chapter 22

Jaw-dropping

Conversation with Gianluca Zambrotta

Two seasons together. Two very weak and sad seasons for Barça. And for the defender who arrived in Barcelona after having won the Germany World Cup with the *Azzurri* (the Blues – the Italian national team). But in the Nou Camp dressing room and on the pitch the current Milan player Gianluca Zambrotta had time to get a close-up of Messi and evaluate him.

What do you think of Leo Messi?
'I think he's one of the greatest talents to come out of the last ten or twenty years. It's undisputable that he's one of the best players in the world today, especially if we take into account that he's only 26 years old and still has a lot of time to grow.'

Do you remember the Barça-Real Madrid match on 10 March 2007?
'I wasn't at the ground but Messi's performance had a big impact on me. As it did on everyone, I imagine. He had already shown us great things back in 2005 at the Bernabéu, but in that classic derby he outdid himself. The most surprising thing of all is that a nineteen-year-old kid could be capable of taking the weight of a team like Barça on his shoulders, which is something very rare, and ensuring

they equalised again and again. And all this in an incredibly difficult fixture, agonising, tense, hugely competitive; all derbies are like that of course, but the truth is that the one in 2007 was particularly tough. What can I say? He has exceptional abilities and, above all, a certain maturity and sense of responsibility rare in such a young player.'

And what about that goal against Getafe?
'That I did see. For me it was jaw-dropping. "How did he manage that?" I wondered. The same question that my team-mates, the coach and the Nou Camp spectators were asking. It was an incredible goal, the goal of a star. The most beautiful goal I have ever seen anyone score. It was very similar to the one Maradona scored in '86. Although, from the ground, Leo's goal seemed to be even better than Diego's.'

From the point of view of a team-mate, what is Leo's secret?
'For him there is no difference between the Nou Camp and the football ground in his hometown. They are one and the same. He doesn't feel the pressure, or at least that's how it seems. The main thing is that there is a ball involved. He's like all the great, extraordinary players I've met: when they see a ball they become kids again, excited by their favourite toy. They won't let go of it and they would never stop playing. Try to take a ball away from Messi. You can't.'

Why?
'Because he has incredible ball control, it's always glued to his left foot, he's extremely fast, he moves well in small spaces with or without the ball, like Maradona. And he'll run rings around you to show you up. You never know where he'll go next. He could go to your right, to your left, or nutmeg you. In some matches the opposition have had up to three players marking him, but in the end he has

always managed to make an impact on the game. He's in a class of footballers where, if he's on form, he'll win you the match. He's already proven it many times. Although, in all honesty, I wasn't expecting such consistency, such high-level performance game after game. We were lucky to have him on the team.'

Is he an individualist?

'Driving the ball forward, dribbling, those are trademark elements of his game – he always wants the ball because that's how he has fun and how he entertains everyone else. It's like, when you play football with your friends and you're good, you always want the ball because you want to be the best and leave everyone astounded. No, he's not an individualist. He has grown and he knows what it means to play in a team.'

And what was he like in training and in the dressing room?

'He's a modest kid, very willing to work hard, he feels that he still hasn't reached his full potential. He's a fun guy, he jokes and fools around. He's one of those players who help to create a good atmosphere in the dressing room, one of camaraderie and friendship. He and I are not especially close, because there's a ten-year age gap, but we chat often. He seems like a mature kid who has his head firmly screwed on. With a great personality.'

Chapter 23

Leo and Diego

18 April 2007

'Barcelona Football Club are regaining ground.

Xavi ...

Messi swerves round Paredes.

He's hanging onto the ball, he's gone past Nacho as well.

Messi makes it all the way to Alexis, still with the ball.

Inside the box ... he swerves again.

The ball looks like it's going wide ...

Messi scores!

What a goal!

He has left four Getafe players and the goalie in the dust.

A right-footed shot. Nothing like the usual Messi!

Just look at that goal!

It's the 28th minute, midway through the first half.

Without a doubt, that could be the goal of the season ...

Amazing. The whole world is smiling and does not know what to make of that display of drive, speed, ability, dodging and finish. It really was truly impressive ...

I don't want to compare, but it reminds me of Diego Armando Maradona's goal against England in the 1986 World Cup. They are two different goals. They are two different players. I don't mean to say that Messi is Maradona, but it reminds me of that goal.'

That was the TV commentary of the Barcelona-Getafe game, on 18 April 2007, on Digital +.

And this is the voice of Víctor Hugo Morales on Radio Argentina on 22 June 1986 at the Argentina-England game, Azteca stadium, Mexico City.

> 'Diego's turn.
>
> Maradona has the ball.
>
> There are two men on him, Maradona's on the ball, the world footballing genius heads to the right, he gets past the third and there's only Burruchaga left to face him ...
>
> It's all Maradona!
>
> Genius! Genius! Genius! C'mon c'mon c'mon c'mon and
>
> Goaaaal! ... Goaaaal!
>
> Spectacular!
>
> Viva!
>
> What a goal!
>
> Diegoal! Maradona!
>
> Please excuse me, I'm quite emotional ...
>
> Maradona makes a memorable run, the best play of all time ... cosmic kite ... What planet did you come from? To leave all the England players by the wayside, so that the country would be a clenched fist screaming for Argentina ... Argentina 2, England 0.
>
> Diego! Diego! Diego Armando Maradona ...
>
> Thank God for football, for Maradona, for these tears ...
>
> For this score, Argentina, 2; England, 0.'

The shirts are different. So is the importance of the two games: one is a Copa del Rey semi-final, the other was a World Cup quarter-final against an opponent like England, whom Argentina were facing for the first time since the 1982 Falklands War. Although everyone denies it, non-footballing factors are making themselves felt, quite substantially … at least in the hearts of the fans.

The protagonists are different: Maradona, the cosmic kite, is 25, he is God, he is the world superstar. When the Golden Boy scored that goal, Messi the Flea still had not been born yet. He is a nineteen-year-old kid who debuted in the Spanish league and with the Albiceleste less than two years previously.

The excitement of the commentators is incomparable: the tears, the epic feelings and the South American rhetoric versus the rigour, at least on this occasion, of the Spanish commentators, and yet … the two goals are really quite similar, very similar, one seems to have been learned from the other. The first impression is correct.

The next day, the whole world sees history repeating itself. On global video archive YouTube, the goal unsettles Internet users. It is viewed thousands of times, as well as alongside Maradona's goal. It opens up an online debate as to which of the goals is better. Everyone has their own opinion, from expert ones to impassioned ones, while the media compares the two clips from every possible perspective, praising Leo's performance.

Headlines, commentaries and linguistic inventions of all shapes and sizes are to be heard and read: from 'Messidona', to 'The Foot of God', or even, 'Messi shocks the world'. There is no bias to speak of: the evidence is enough for even the Madrid sports papers, who are generally reticent about dedicating the front cover to their eternal rivals Barcelona. This time, however, they do not hesitate. The *Marca* front page headline reads: 'Twenty years, ten months and 26 days later, Messi repeats Maradona's goal.' And inside are quoted Víctor Hugo Morales' words: 'What planet did you come from?' It has not escaped anyone's notice that this is one of those events rarely seen on a football pitch.

Take the 53,599 Nou Camp spectators, for example: they are on their feet, grabbing hold of anything that can be waved, from the newspaper to the programme, a handkerchief or a scarf, waving *en masse*. And those who do not have anything of the appropriate colour still partake of the collective ritual, applauding until their hands hurt. A full-blown tribute.

Or take those who are on the pitch, like Eto'o, Deco, Gudjohnsen. The three of them hold their hands up to their faces. 'Oh my God, what did he just do?!' is the best translation of their disbelieving expressions. And it doesn't end there – in the live interviews at the end of the match, team-mates and opposition alike are brimming with praise.

'It was the best goal I have ever seen in my life' – Deco.

'He has eclipsed us all' – Jorquera.

'I only hope I don't see myself on TV in 30 years' time' – Paredes.

'Words do not exist to describe that goal. From over there on the bench I was awestruck' – Güiza.

Bernd Schuster, Getafe coach at the time, does not agree, but everyone knows what the German is like. 'We should have fouled him in order to stop him, even if it would have earned us a booking. You can only be so noble.'

The debate has begun and within a day it has spread all over the world. Although football is aesthetic and fantastical, some people insist on analysing it with numbers, figures and statistics.

So here they are: Leo's goal took twelve seconds compared to Diego's 10.8; he ran 60 metres, while in the Azteca stadium it was 62; he made thirteen touches against Maradona's twelve; he slalomed round five of the opposition, while Maradona left six England players in his wake.

The pictures of the action are superimposed, they are analysed side by side in order to compare and understand. People look for the similarities as if it were a children's game. Buenos Aires newspaper *La Nación* does it best, pointing out ten coincidences, from the spot where the play begins right up to the celebration (both run towards the corner flag on the right hand side of the pitch). Websites, TV stations and newspapers launch their polls. The questions are more or less the same: which goal was more spectacular, that of the Flea or that of Diego? Which did you prefer? Which did you think was better? *Marca*'s poll attracts 55,000 respondents: 60.62 per cent prefer Messi's goal, while 39.38 per cent opt for Maradona's goal. The result is the same on the Cadena Ser radio station, although the margins are closer: Messi wins with 52 per cent to Diego's 48 per cent. *Mundo Deportivo*'s poll records an overwhelming majority in favour of the Barcelona striker: more than three-quarters of the voters. Argentina's *Olé* website users award Maradona 74.3 per cent of the vote. It was predictable, because that goal is engraved in the country's collective memory – there isn't a single household in which that goal hasn't been watched on video or DVD at least once. In Argentina they have even made a 'flickbook' with the goal of the century. It's a 'handheld movie', you flick the pages and it is as if you are watching the film in action (in addition, the Icons of Argentina collection also includes the 'Hand of God' goal, Maradona's tricks with the ball in Villa Fiorito and Maxi Rodríguez's goal against Mexico; Leo Messi and his moment of glory are not yet part of this exclusive selection). And it should also be noted that in Argentina, Maradona is not just a footballer, but a people's hero, a living legend, a faith (the Maradonian Church parodies religion and worships Diego as a supreme god), and a national historic icon, like José de San Martín (the general who fought for independence from Spain), Carlos Gardel (the famous tango singer), Evita, Jorge Luis Borges (the famous author) or Ernesto 'Che' Guevara. It's natural that the Argentines should feel reticent about trading him in as if he were a mere football sticker.

What is certain is that these polls perfectly illustrate the extent of the passion felt on both sides of the pond. As well as the debate over which goal is better, another question arises: that of Messi's intentions, or in other words, to quote *La Nación*, 'Was Messi trying to imitate Maradona? Was it or wasn't it a big coincidence?'

The man himself will erase all doubts. 'Perhaps the play was similar, I have only seen it once on television,' declares Messi, 'but I never thought it could be the same as Diego's goal. They told me afterwards, but at that moment I wasn't thinking about anything, only of the joy of having scored a goal.'

And there's more, when they ask him to describe his achievement, Leo describes it thus: 'I saw a gap and I went forward, as always, to get forward and try to score. The two defenders were closing in on me and I wasn't getting anywhere, so I looked for someone to play a one-two and when I saw the gap I got past. Luckily it worked.'

That air of simplicity, as if it was something normal (and deep down it is, it is part of his job), is reminiscent of Maradona in '86, or at least it is if we go by the memories of Jorge Valdano. 'Diego insists that he tried to pass me the ball various times, but he kept finding obstacles that prevented him,' he says, although he is convinced that in reality Diego 'was never willing to let go of that ball'. Valdano offered Maradona the chance to pass; in Messi's case it was Eto'o. The parallels and similarities between the two goals are infinite, including the issue of the kick suggested by Schuster and supported by another Getafe defender. Listen to what 'el Negro' Enrique, who was present at the famous Azteca game, has to say. 'They say that the England players didn't try to foul Maradona. That's because they couldn't! Whenever they got there, he had already passed them.'

The same holds true in Messi's case. Let's stick with the anecdotes. In the Mexico World Cup it was Héctor Enrique who laid claim to his contribution to the goal and the previous pass; here, Xavi does the same. 'He told me,' reveals Messi, 'that with all the great goals everyone talks a lot about the goal, but he passed it to me and yet no one mentions it.' By contrast, there is no parallel whatsoever between what happened afterwards, among other things, because naturally the two situations were different. Perhaps there is not even any link between the words of the two protagonists. After the match, Leo says that it 'wasn't a big deal' and quietly goes out to dinner with his father and his friend Pablo Zabaleta. Unfortunately, the media attention forces him to move restaurant. There are too many people waiting for him at the usual one. At a jam-packed press conference at the Nou Camp the following day, a wet-haired, recently showered Leo says into the microphones that he has slept soundly and that 'he really has not stopped to think about the goal and what it means'. He is immune to the persistence of journalists, adding that the goal doesn't change a thing. 'I don't feel any kind of pressure, I am going to keep playing and enjoying myself as I have always done.' There is one thing, however, which he does not forget: the dedication, which he had already made at the time and now repeats. 'I dedicate it to Diego. I want to send him all my support and best wishes and hope that he gets out of there as soon as possible and recovers, because that is what the whole of Argentina and all football fans everywhere want.'

Diego Armando Maradona is in hospital. He was admitted as a matter of urgency during the night of 1 April.

An alcohol relapse has caused acute alcoholic hepatitis. According to his personal physician, Alfredo Cahe, he was on the brink of death. In Argentina they even announce his death. Luckily it is not the case, and during the beginning of May Maradona is discharged from the Avril neuropsychiatric clinic where he had voluntarily submitted to therapy to help overcome his alcohol dependence. The first thing he does upon leaving is to appear on the TV programme *ShowMatch* to recount his version of events and attack those who tried to bury him before his time. And during the interview with his friend Marcelo Tinelli, he also finds time to talk about Messi's goal. Let's hear from Maradona: 'Those who made that comparison were exaggerating. They really over exaggerated. To start with, my goal was more beautiful than Messi's. And what's more, I scored it against eleven internationals from England, a world champion team, and in a World Cup. Leo scored his against Getafe, in the Copa del Rey in Spain. It's not the same.' Maradona restores his goal's reputation and accuses everyone who has dared to make comparisons as having exaggerated. Months later, in an interview with *El Gráfico*, a weekly Buenos Aires sports paper, he is even harsher. 'What was the first thing you felt after seeing Messi's goal against Getafe?' they ask him. Annoyed, he replies: 'It has nothing to do with mine.' 'The circumstances no, but the action itself was similar, Diego …' they insist. 'No, no, leave it, they are nothing alike. I scored millions of those kinds of goals in training, they're just not on tape. If we're going to talk seriously about this, don't make me say something I don't mean …'

Unfortunately the debate doesn't end there.

It is 9 June: Barcelona-Espanyol, in the 43rd minute of the first half.

Here is the commentary that was broadcast on one Argentine TV station:

'Now it's Messi.

It's Messi who faces up to the opposition,

Messi to Eto'o in the area.

Eto'o has his back to goal and is surrounded by four defenders.

Eto'o takes the ball out wide to the touchline.

Zambrotta …

Messi couldn't get there …

With his hand, with his hand, like Diego.

I'll yell it anyway:

Goaaaaal!

It's Diego! Tell me it isn't! To me it's Diego. It's the same guy …

He's reincarnated, I don't believe in that but … he's reincarnated. There can't be so many coincidences. Explain to me how two things can happen again in such, but I mean *such* a similar way, to two different men … Messi, or Maradona dressed as Lionel Messi, goes down, puts on a Barcelona shirt, and levels the game with his left hand.'

And for those who are still in any doubt, here's Michael Robinson's commentary from Digital +: 'He has scored two Maradona-style goals in the same season. The two against England – one against Getafe, one against Espanyol. He has repeated them both.'

The Hand of God strikes again, with all its similarities and debates. On 22 June 1986, Maradona anticipated Peter Shilton, 15cm taller than he was, coming off his line. With his jump, Messi overpowers Carlos Kameni, who is 19cm taller than he is. Despite the protests of the England players, Tunisian referee Alí Bennaceur allows the goal when his assistant points to the centre spot. Despite the technology available in 2007 and to the Espanyol players' despair, Rodríguez Santiago also allows the goal. Maradona is reluctant to admit what everyone already knows, 'that the Hand of God was the hand of Diego! And the same hand that also stole from England.' Just after the match, Messi is only sorry that the goal 'didn't gain anything; it only won us one point' and not the league. He celebrated 'in a normal, joyful way for having drawn the match'. There is certainly no reason to be ashamed at having done something sneaky.

Diego and Lionel, Messi and Maradona, the disciple and the master. Ariel 'the Tiger' Zárate, a 29-year-old from Entre Ríos, who performs in a group of four Argentine musicians, has dedicated a song to the subject, called 'El Pie de Oro llegó' ('The Golden Foot has arrived' – a play on Maradona's nickname 'El Pibe de Oro', meaning Golden Boy). It goes like this:

On 24 June in '87
A year after Argentina became champions
A star was born, a new dream
The Golden Foot was born in Rosario.

With a magical dodge, a great, little player
At seven in the juniors for Newell's Old Boys
Over here they turned their back on his problem
And he had to emigrate and go to Spain,
He made his second home in Barcelona
And he made it, thanks to sacrifices and love.

In 2004 he debuted with Barça
And his dream was realised with the Under 20s
(The Golden Foot has arrived!)

(Chorus)
Go for it Lionel

The world is waiting to see you run again.
We want to see the magic in your feet.
(repeat)

He has a heart as big as a lion
When he comes on there's hope
The fans want to cheer his goal
In a match with the sky-blue and whites,
We cheer you on from every corner,
The national team are hopeful,
We want to see you with Argentina, as champion!

(Chorus)

Passion is awaking throughout the world
We want to see you with Argentina, as champion!

Now Messi has his own songwriter, just as Maradona had El Potro Rodrigo. Apart from songs, the similarities between the two have been talked about and written about numerous times, too many to count, even before that April 2007 goal. Lionel has always been compared to Maradona in one form or another. The first to draw parallels were his Newell's coaches, from Enrique Domínguez to Ernesto Vecchio, via Adrían Coria. 'I have seen him do stunning things with the ball, which not even Maradona could do at that age,' insists Vecchio. Guillermo Hoyos, his coach in the Barcelona youth B team, makes the same point. 'Messi is the closest I have seen to Diego. In drive, in determination. Leo single-handedly altered the outcome of dozens of games! He is like Diego, they attack him, they attack him again and he keeps going practically from the ground. You'd have to kill him to stop him. He has no problem handling himself. The ball gets carried along by the arch of his foot and the only thing he has to worry about is speed. He already has a good feel for the ball and he does it in a different way to everyone else.'

Since then there have been many who have talked about it, in every stage of the Barça number 19's career. River Plate ex-number 10 Norberto Alonso says, for example: 'There are things about him which remind me of Maradona. Like the way he bursts forward explosively. And the speed with which he plays. But Diego had that game-altering vision which Messi lacks.'

Arsenal coach Arsène Wenger has no doubts. 'Messi is like Maradona but with a turbo attached to his feet.' Nor do footballers past and present, like Eto'o: 'Messi is the Diego Armando Maradona of the future', or Deco: 'He reminds me a lot of Maradona. Sometimes I hear people say that he should beware of the fame so that what happened to Diego doesn't happen to him. But Leo's situation is different, because he is in a healthy environment in which he is loved and protected.' And Franz Beckenbauer: 'When we see him run with the ball we are reminded of Diego Maradona at his best, with good reason.' Some do not deny the parallels, but they have words of warning for Messi. 'Between Messi and Maradona,' maintains Héctor 'El Negro' Enrique, '86 World Champion with Argentina, 'there are two things they have in common: their running style and their speed. Diego has that run and that short sprint, which makes mincemeat of you, and it's difficult to take the ball off Leo. On top of that, he doesn't just shoot for the sake of shooting, rather, he looks for the far post and dodges from right to left like Diego. The bad thing is not that he's compared to Maradona, but that Leo believes he is Maradona.' Something that also concerns Gabriel Batistuta. The ex-Fiorentina striker and highest-ever goal scorer for Argentina says: 'Leo shouldn't try to imitate Maradona, he only has to be himself and do the best he can. Because otherwise, even if he reaches Diego's level, he will only be seen as the second Maradona.' The discordant voices are few in number, one of them being Pelé, although it is fairly natural bearing in mind the issue relates to Maradona. *O Rei* ('The King' – Pelé's nickname) is convinced that 'Messi is a different guy. Maradona used to come from behind. Messi is a bit quicker. On the other hand Diego was a better armed footballer.' Another discordant voice is that of César Luis Menotti, 'el Flaco', selector of the Argentine World Cup 1978 team. 'He is not the new Maradona. In Argentina, and in other countries as well, every time a kid comes along who has good technical skills and abilities and who is decisive, the whole world declares him as the next Diego. Messi is a very good player, left-footed, skilled, powerful, he plays for Barcelona and he's Argentine. But he is not Maradona, he is Messi.' Writer, journalist and psychologist Walter Vargas is categorical, maintaining in his book, *Football Delivery*: 'Messi is not and never will be Maradona. I say he will not reach those heights, and I even think that it will be difficult for him to come close.' There are many contrasting opinions. But there's more: the Argentine Olympic Committee even carries out a study, overseen by Miguel Toderi, in order to scientifically compare the two players. The result? A truism. They show that Messi and Maradona share a series of physical traits: low centre of gravity, muscle mass, height, weight, development and, of course, they are both left-footed.

In these cases it is better to leave science to one side and stroll through La Boca, Buenos Aires, around the Bombonera (the Boca Juniors ground), to chat to fans great and small. Rodrigo, in his blue and yellow Boca Juniors shirt, does not want to hear or speak of the matter. He has seen Maradona play and he won't hear of any comparisons. He lists Messi's weaknesses, from his taking of free kicks to his vision of the game, and he glorifies Maradona's gifts, asking his inquirer if he remembers the number 10's first goals with the Argentinos Juniors. Let's move on to Luis, who has a photo of Maradona in action in his completely *bostero* (Boca fan) shop, with the inscription, 'Your children and your children's children will ask about him.' But then, while walking through the streets, you see some little kids playing with a ball. Two of them are wearing Barcelona shirts with Messi's name across their backs. Julián, aged ten, the most chatty of them all, says emphatically: 'I'm a Boca fan, but I like Messi, I like the way he plays.'

Perhaps preference has to do with age? 'In one of his most beautiful verses, *El Poeta murió al amanecer* [*The poet died at dawn*], Raúl González Tuñón writes: "Some people, the oldest ones, denied him from the start. Others, the youngest ones, denied him later on." That is what happens in the footballing world generation after generation. And the same thing happens to Messi,' explains Horacio Del Prado, commentator for Radio Nacional in Argentina. 'The old folks who maintain that Messi will never reach the level of Maradona forget what everyone always says when a new superstar appears: he'll never make it. They said that Maradona was chubby, too small and that he would never become a champion at the level of the greats. The great goalie Hugo Gatti was one of the ones who talked incessantly about how round Maradona was, and Diego scored four goals against him.'

Let's leave opinions aside and examine other reasons for the perpetuation of the comparison. It's simple: ever since Maradona retired in 1997, the Argentines – and others too – are always in search of a successor. It's not unusual, it always happens when a great player goes. First, time is needed in order to accept the dissolution of the legend, then time is needed in order to find someone who is reminiscent of them, who makes us relive the lost magic. And who makes us think back to old times – because memory is a fundamental aspect of football; because in order for a young player to sell, it is easier to hang a tag around his neck saying 'New Pelé' or 'New Maradona'. That way everyone knows what we're talking about. Often they get it wrong, the name designation doesn't work, or the candidate for successor does not fulfil all the promises. As was the case, just in terms of 'New Maradonas', with Ariel Ortega, Pablo Aimar, Juan Román Riquelme, or the 'Apache' Tévez. It is a difficult crown to bear. Even more so when there are so many coincidences, as there are in Messi's case: little; left-footed; grew up at Newell's, where Maradona spent a brief stint; matured at Barcelona, the first European club to experience 'Maramondo'; Under 20 world champion, like Maradona in 1979. And debuted with the national team against Hungary, exactly like Diego. And it is even more difficult when Maradona himself invites you onto his TV programme, *La Noche del 10* (*Number 10 Night*) and singles you out as his heir. 'Leo has been chosen to be one of the greats. Many think that he already is, but in my opinion,' says Maradona, 'he has hardly begun playing. He can give even more than he has already given and, when he does, it will be his moment.' When they ask him about it in *El Gráfico*, he responds that of course Leo is the best current Argentine player, but in response to the next question – 'Will Leo be able to overtake you?' – he offers: 'If it is for the good of Argentine football, let him overtake me.' Despite all his proclamations and blessings, the old king is reticent to concede his sceptre. It is up to the pretender to show that he will grasp it with honour.

Chapter 24

A long career ahead of him

Conversation with Frank Rijkaard

An ashtray, a packet of tobacco, a can of Pepsi and he begins to talk. The former Barcelona coach is relaxed, he has no urgent appointments and he willingly speaks at length, discussing the little boy who debuted with the first team on 16 October 2003.

You played impassioned games with Milan against the Napoli of Maradona, and you were Messi's coach for five years. In short, you are the best placed to resolve the issue: 'Is Leo the new Diego?'
'I have many memories of Maradona – those clashes with Napoli, in the Italian championship, they were historic; but when Diego played in Italy at 26, 27 years of age, he was already made. Messi is still very young, he has his whole career ahead of him. I understand why many people compare Leo to Diego. They are both Argentine, they're both little and they both have great qualities, but comparisons are always complicated. Back then, Maradona represented football. It's clear that he was, and is, football. Leo is a unique footballer, but in order to compare him to Maradona we will have to wait until the end of his career.'

And what about that goal against Getafe?
'I have seen a lot of football, many great players and many more goals ... I have to say that Leo's goal against Getafe

was one of the most spectacular that I have seen. It was a genuine work of art. I remember that after it happened I felt immensely happy for him, for the team, for the crowd; but, in all honesty, I wasn't that surprised.'

Why?

'Because you see it every day in training, when he's playing, you know that he can do incredible things and he's capable of doing things like that.'

Were you therefore not surprised by the discussion about the similarities to Maradona's goal in the 1986 Mexico World Cup?

'I thought it might happen. Because it's true that they are quite alike, although I think Leo accelerates even more than Maradona. Thousands of clips of the two goals were posted on the Internet, and I've seen at least another twenty similar ones.'

Let's return to Leo's debut with the first team.

'Leo was already talented when he was at the youth academy, but you have to reserve judgement. You have to wait and see because the transition into the first team is fundamental. It's the real test. Well, Leo surprised all of us because instead of encountering difficulties, his skills improved by playing with great footballers. In the Gamper [trophy], against Juve, everyone realised what the boy was worth.'

What are his characteristics, his qualities?

'It doesn't matter if he is playing in front of ten spectators or 100,000. Leo is the same as always, he always feels secure and has the same desire to win. He is the boy who says: "Give me the ball, I want to play, I want to be creative, I want to show my talents." And when he gets it, it's a difficult task to stop him without fouling him. He is extremely fast, he has great ball control, an exquisite touch and he can dribble in a way rarely seen throughout the footballing world. And let's not forget, he's explosive, and although he's not very tall, he is very strong. You can see it when he clashes with the opposition – it's not easy to knock him down.'

How has he changed over the years?
'When he debuted he was a very well balanced person, calm, respectful and very shy. Over time, he has changed a lot, but without losing these attributes. Now he is more sure of himself, he is conscious of being an important player in the team. Everyone values him and he is perfectly aware of it. His attitude has not changed, but he is not the silent boy he was all those years ago. He is funnier, he likes to joke around when he is with his team-mates or surrounded by people he knows ... I have to say that from day one the team has behaved very well towards him, the group has accepted him. Sylvinho, Deco, Ronaldinho, they've helped and advised him. Great players always recognise a special player.'

What kind of relationship did you have with Leo?
'I care about him a lot. At the beginning, I felt he needed my sympathy and support, because of his age. Later on I saw that he needed it less: he knows what his options are, he knows how the footballing world works. He has assumed many responsibilities and he will assume many more, for his team-mates, his club, and the shareholders. He is already mature enough to do so because he has developed as a person and as a footballer, he has experienced some wonderful moments, and some very difficult ones.'

Like when he was injured against Chelsea and you hugged him as if you were his father?
'To me it was a natural thing to do. I felt his suffering, I knew

how important it was to him to play in that match. Getting injured is unbearable. The only thing I could do was console him, and say: "Don't worry, you'll be better soon." It was a very emotional moment, very beautiful, although it wasn't nice at all. But you have to deal with these things in your career. They are the things that make you grow, that motivate you to keep playing, to make it to the top.'

Tell us some advice, or the most important advice, you gave Leo.
'Finish the action: shoot, or cross it, don't keep dribbling. Because there is more of a risk of losing the ball or getting injured. You can't dribble for 90 minutes, nor can you dribble past ten men and the goalkeeper in every match. You can do it once a year, not every Sunday. That's the advice I gave him years ago and it seems that he took it on board. He demonstrated as much this season: in many games he has scored one or two goals, or given a team-mate an assist. In short, he has improved his football and he is showing his maturity. He needed to, because Leo sees a lot more than others do on the pitch. He can achieve more than others. What he can't do is wear himself out pointlessly, not pace himself and not make a difference.'

Rijkaard lights another cigarette and then, continuing his train of thought, adds:

'There is a sense that Maradona used to transmit, and now Messi also transmits, the joy of playing. They are two people who have fun with a football. It seems that they are always asking for the ball … and they're saying "Let's play".'

Chapter 25

You have to prove it

Conversation with Carlos Salvador Bilardo

Call him the oracle, the professor, the grey matter, the father of a new school of footballing thought (Bilardism, of course), or simply, the *Narigón* (nosy one). All of them are titles that Bilardo has garnered over the length of his successful career as a footballer and coach, as much in his own country as abroad. His philosophy is well known: 'Winning is all that matters,' and 'No one remembers the runner-up,' and of course 'A final is a question of life and death.' Now, after a stint in politics as sports secretary for the province of Buenos Aires, the medical doctor who dedicated himself to football has returned to his true love: he is now the general manager of the Argentine national team. And, as always, he enjoys reflecting on football in his usual frank and ironic way.

It's possible that you were the coach who has had the greatest rapport with Maradona. You had it in the national team that won the World Cup in Mexico in '86; in Italy in '90 when the Albiceleste reached the final; and in Sevilla; and you were by his side in the 2010 World Cup. In short, you know Diego very well, and you follow Messi's development, which leads us to ask: 'Is Leo the new Diego?'

'In Argentina, and not only in Argentina, when a new player breaks onto the scene there is always a comparison to be made with Maradona. Many people have gained the title of new Maradona … the problem is that they have to keep proving that they're on his level. In his day, Diego proved he was the best in the world. Messi is doing very well, he's on the right track, but if he doesn't win a World Cup, as team leader, he will never get to Maradona's level. Just as has happened with other great footballers who haven't been crowned world champions. I'm thinking of Gullit, Cruyff, or Platini.'

Leaving the future aside, let's talk about Messi's goal against Getafe and Maradona's goal against England, which you saw from the dugout …
'They are two similar goals, in different situations: one at a national level in the quarter-finals of a world championship, the other at a club level in the semi-finals of the Copa del Rey.'

OK … but did it surprise you?
'It surprised me the way that Spain went crazy for Messi. They couldn't talk about anything else. And here as well: they didn't stop showing it on TV over and over again.'

And from a technical point of view?
'It surprised me that from the moment he got the ball until the execution, Messi maintains the same level of power. Maradona changed rhythm and Messi always moves in the same way. He does the same as all left-footers who play on the other touchline. When they get the ball on the right hand side and move inwards they have the whole width of the goal in which to score.'

Which of the two do you prefer?
'I'll stick with Maradona's goal. Maradona had people coming at him continuously, and the central defenders staggered

their attack: first Butcher and then Fenwick. Messi ran 30 metres without anyone trying to tackle him. That's why he gets more touches with his right foot, his weaker foot. He leads with it, and then he always sidesteps with his left foot. It's very difficult for the defenders to get at him because he comes bounding along and he goes very fast. In the end, the central defenders wait for him in a line, and it's easier for him.'

Messi and Maradona … let's consider their qualities.
'From three-quarters of the way up the pitch, up to the goal, they are two players who can decide a match, they have quick, short steps, it's difficult to take the ball from them and they also kick well.'

Can you compare them in other respects?
'Comparisons are an eternal feature of football. How many times has Maradona been compared to Pelé, Platini or Cruyff in order to ascertain who was better? But times are changing, just like with medicine. The knowledge of a doctor today is not the same as it was twenty years ago.'

Anything else?
'I still don't know Messi very well. With regard to Diego I can say that he is a man who knows his football, tactically and technically.'

Chapter 26

Disappointment

15 July 2007

Sadness and anger. These feelings and many more occupy Messi's thoughts and words in the middle of June. The reason is simple: Barcelona haven't won the titles they were hoping to take home. From eight possible titles, they have had to make do with the Spanish Super Cup – nothing more. A particularly poor outcome. And for someone like the Flea, who thinks only of winning, he cannot but feel bad about it. And think about how 'we started well. Then we were knocked out of the Champions League too early. Then, when we thought we had got past the most difficult part, we went out of the Copa del Rey. If you add it all up, it's painful,' he explains in an interview with *France Football*. He doesn't speak of the league, the hardest blow to deal with. In February, it seemed as if the Blaugrana had it in the bag and that the persecution of Capello's Real Madrid was nothing more than a dream to keep the championship alive and to have something to say to the media. However, it wasn't to be: points lost in the final moments, particularly against Betis and Espanyol, end up gifting the title to the Whites. Why not give a financial incentive to Mallorca, Madrid's rivals in the last fixture on 17 June at the Bernabéu? (It is common practice in Spain to reward teams who beat your local rivals.) Messi sees nothing wrong with it if it helps them win, but despite the Argentine's good intentions and expectations, the miracle, which seemed possible in the 65th minute, is not forthcoming in the end. And so, the last chance to save the season disappears, leaving only disappointment. In short, nothing has turned out as expected and 'the hero is left without a prize', as the *El País* headline reads. Because in fact, on an individual level, it has been a positive season for Messi. The Argentine has played an indisputable starring role in many magical nights: it was he who momentarily thwarted Real Madrid's inconsistencies with his famous hat-trick. Then came the Foot of Maradona and the Hand of God II, wonders and tricks that did not amount to anything. The goals scored and the award for best foreign Liga player are nothing more than a meagre consolation prize.

Luckily, football doesn't stop. Awaiting him are the national team and the Copa América and, with them, the chance to recover from the blow he has suffered. And the possibility of being in the starting line-up in an important tournament, not simply part of the squad, as happened to him in the Germany World Cup.

Alfio 'el Coco' Basile, the selector who has assumed José Pekerman's post, is counting on him. He knows that the Flea has a huge amount to contribute to the national team and that he has a fundamental role to play in his plans for the team. He does not want to repeat his predecessor's errors. He calls him up for the European mini-tour, in Berne and Barcelona, where they will face Switzerland and Algeria, with a view to playing him in the continental championship which will take place in Venezuela, where the whole world is convinced that Messi will play the leading role. In a poll on the tournament's official website, Leo is winning by a considerable margin (33 per cent of the votes), beating the Chilean Matías Fernández and the Venezuelan Juan Arango. Brazilian Real Madrid player Robinho, who will eventually be chosen as best player and will be awarded the title of highest goal scorer, with six goals, is bottom of the list with only eight per cent of the votes.

On 24 June in Maracaibo, four days before Argentina's opening match against the United States, Messi celebrates his twentieth birthday and the media wheedle out of him an obvious wish: 'To win the Copa América and be the highest goal scorer.' Argentina has not won it since 1993, making the pressure and expectations enormous. The expectations placed on Messi are so high that, in contrast to what happened in Germany, both the squad and the coach fuss over him. Coco even provides him with a mentor: 'La Brujita' Juan Sebastián Verón. The 32-year-old ex-Boca, Sampdoria, Parma, Inter, Lazio, Manchester United and Chelsea player, who has had newfound success with his first love, Estudiantes de la Plata (an Argentine team), offers advice to the twenty-year-old Messi both on and off the pitch, and defends him against accusations that he is an arrogant soloist. 'Messi is reserved. He doesn't hang out in a group drinking *mate.* He prefers to play PlayStation. To me it's like he's my little brother, who I have to take care of. I have to keep him safe!' he explains in *El País.* And in fact, Messi does need taking care of because Messimania has been unleashed in Venezuela. It's madness, the kid can't take a step without being surrounded by hordes of fans, shirts with his name on are selling like hotcakes to adults and children alike, and on the pitch he barely has to touch the ball to get a standing ovation, even when he misses. If he is not in the starting line-up, as happens in the game against Paraguay, within ten minutes the annoyed crowd are calling his name.

It is a blind love, which reaches its peak at the Lara de Barquisimeto stadium. Messi is walking towards the dressing room tunnel, tired and distracted, when out of the blue he sees a girl. Leo has seen that she is about to throw herself off the stands – worried, he waves his arms and shouts: 'Stop, what are you doing …?' The love-struck twenty-something doesn't listen to reason and jumps. Luckily she falls on her feet. Soldiers and security guards pounce on her, but before they can take her away she manages to embrace her idol and plant two kisses on him. Leo looks decidedly perplexed, as does Simon, the referee, who grabs him by the arm demanding an explanation, convinced that it was some kind of attack.

'It was unbelievable. I was signalling to her not to jump and she ended up jumping anyway. I swear I didn't know what to do,' he will later confess to *Clarín*. 'It was at least a four-metre drop. She could have killed herself, and on top of that they got her out of there pretty quickly without even seeing if the poor girl was okay or not.'

The incident happens on 8 July, in the quarter-finals. Argentina have just beaten Peru 4-0, and in the 61st minute Messi has scored that longed-for goal. He did not score in the previous matches, against the United States, Colombia and Paraguay, although he has been decisive in mobilising and transforming the Albiceleste machine. Like in the debut against the Americans, when he serves the ball up on a plate for Crespo to score his second goal, or during the 25 minutes in which he plays in the second half of Paraguay-Argentina (Basile wants to rest him for the quarters), when he brings a bit of spice to an otherwise boring game. But he was still missing the goal, and scoring it against the Peruvians is a weight off his shoulders. And in the semi-final against Mexico in Puerto Ordaz, he re-establishes his position, creating another masterpiece. According to the commentators, 'They should pack up and go home'. 'That's what geniuses do,' says Basile. 'Shall we pack up and leave? What more do we need? Why should we continue after having seen that goal?' The commentators of Tyc Sports, an Argentine TV channel, agree with Coco. And that's not all.

Here's little Carlos Tévez: 'What Messi did was brilliant. He didn't have many clear opportunities to score, but the first ball he got was an incredible goal.' Mascherano: 'It was one of those moments of genius that we've come to expect from him. Nothing he does surprises me any more. He's extraordinary.' Cambiasso: 'It was a stunning goal.' Heinze: 'There are no words to describe Messi's goal.' In essence, a goal that ended up taking its place among all the clips of the Flea's best goals posted on the Internet.

But what has he managed to pull out of his hat this time? Let's see the replay. In the 60th minute Heinze, who scored the goal that put them ahead, passes to Cambiasso. The Inter player, with two defenders closing in on him, returns it to Heinze who looks for the shot from his own half; Tévez receives it outside the box with his back to the goalkeeper. He controls it on his chest, plays it down, turns and passes to Messi who is off, quick as a flash. He gets into the box, lifts his head, sees the goalie and sends the ball through the air with incredible grace. A perfect arc, a chip which beats Sánchez, the desperate goalie, who jumps backwards and stretches out a gloved hand, but doesn't even manage to get a finger to the ball, which curls in under the crossbar. Leo watches the ball until the net billows, then he runs towards the corner flag to celebrate with the Argentine fans. Verón, his mentor, is the first to reach him, the boy jumps on his neck while from the dugout Coco throws up his arms, applauds and laughs delightedly.

'Did you feel they should have packed up and gone home after your masterpiece?' 'No, stop it, stop it. It was a beautiful goal, nothing more. The important thing is that it helped Argentina get to the final.' That is Messi's response to the question from *La Nación* the following day. But they push him. 'Do you think it was the most amazing goal of your career?' 'Maybe, I don't know, I have scored a few good ones, like the one against Getafe. The truth is I haven't really seen it on TV. Everyone says it was really good: I saw the goalie come off his line and I took the chance. It turned out well, didn't it?'

Same old Messi, unshakable in his modesty. Although he claims the rights to his dream: that of beating Brazil in the final. Leo had said since the beginning that he wanted to play against Brazil, and his wish has been granted. He wants to put that 3-0 from a friendly at Wembley the previous September behind him.

His friend Ronaldinho will not be there, which Leo says is just as well; neither will Kaká. In any case, although they have lost the opening match against Mexico and only managed to win the semi-final against Uruguay on penalties, the Green and Golds are still tough rivals to beat. Moreover, finals are a different story – you can never be certain what will happen. Something that does become painfully certain is that Argentine dreams are buried with a resounding 3-0 thanks to the beast Júlio Baptista, Albiceleste captain Ayala's own goal, and Daniel Alves. They corner the elegant team and they do it well. At the José Romero stadium in Maracaibo, Argentina make no impact, it's as if they don't exist. And Messi? 'He did little to change history,' says *Clarín*. 'With neither frenzy nor football, Leo ended up being fenced in by his Brazilian marker and remained trapped in his labyrinth.' The images are more revealing than commentaries or critiques. Messi sitting on the pitch with a lost look in his eyes; Dady, the physio, shaking his head at him in a consolatory gesture; FIFA president Joseph Blatter presenting him with his medal, and Messi coming down from the stands only to take it off and hold it in his fist. He has been chosen as the best young player of the Copa América. But what good is that … in the wake of this new disappointment, there is nothing but anger and sadness.

Chapter 27

An electric kid

Conversation with Alfio 'El Coco' Basile

Seated at his usual table in the back corner of the La Raya restaurant in Buenos Aires, Coco is chatting with a group of friends. Among them are players, journalists, old acquaintances – a regular get-together. Every so often, the unmistakable deep, rough voice of the Argentine coach is heard above the background hum and the noise of glasses clinking and cutlery scraping. Claudio Codina, the owner of the restaurant who is like a son to Basile, gently interrupts the gathering and joins him in talking about Messi. With a cigarette between his fingers and a glass in his hand, the words flow thick and fast from the mouth of the Bella Vista ex-defender.

'I love Leo very much, because he's a great lad. He's humble, he doesn't think highly of himself, he doesn't think of himself as a star and the fame hasn't gone to his head. He's a good person. He's the son every parent would like to have, or the one you'd want to date or marry your daughter. People everywhere love him and not just because he's an incredible footballer, but because of his personality. Incidentally, let me tell you a story.'

Tell it, tell it … please.

'We were in Oslo, in a little field surrounded by huge buildings. It was an evening training session, almost nightfall, and there was no one around. But something happened that you don't expect in a country like Norway, where you'd think even the football fans are cold … All of a sudden the lights went on and the windows opened in houses around and we started to hear people yelling from all directions: "Messi! Messi! Messi!"'

And what did he say?
'Nothing … it embarrasses him, in the best sense of the word, when people call out to him or praise him. You can see him practically suffering when the spectators shout his name. And the girls … they go crazy, as we saw in Venezuela … Such affection for that little face, for that shyness, for the humanity he exudes … Those are attributes that he gets from his parents. He has an incredible family, who really protect him. When I saw his mother, she said to me: "Look after him for me Coco, please look after him for me."'

And did you look after him?
'Of course. I tried to help him, I tried to relieve as much of the pressure as possible, the way they do at Barcelona. They also protect him because they know what he means to their team. But Leo doesn't get overwhelmed by the pressure. When he gets onto the pitch he doesn't think about what's going on around him, he only thinks about playing with the football. He loves the football.'

While we're on the subject, let's talk about Messi in terms of football.
'I met him when he was only fifteen years old and I thought he was very good; now he's an outstanding footballer. He has speed, acceleration; he can dodge, he's always capable of creating something new; he is in great shape and has enormous talent. He's an electric kid. As I always say, I find it exciting to watch Messi play.'

As you did in the Copa América when Leo scored that goal against Mexico, and you said: 'They should pack up and go home. That's what geniuses do.'
'Was I wrong?'

We don't even need to answer that ... Let's move onto another genius, Maradona, whom you know well and with whom you have shared ups and downs. Can Messi be compared to the number 10, the way everyone is doing?
'We have to wait and see. Leo is not yet Maradona. He has only just begun. He hasn't forged a career path yet. He plays a similar game, but there's no need to compare them because people will want him to play like Maradona now. He has all the right criteria to be one of the greats, but we have to wait, for now he just has to keep doing what he's doing and enjoy playing.'

When he talks about you, Messi says again and again that you put up with him from the beginning, that you always let him play and gave him a lot of freedom ...
'From three-quarters of the way up the pitch Messi has the freedom to go anywhere, freedom to be inventive, to play the way he knows best, to make challenges, to dribble up the pitch, to soar. The best players need to soar.'

Chapter 28

Bronze and silver

17 December 2007

Let's try and get our heads around the numbers: one goal in eight matches in his first season with the first team; seven goals in 23 fixtures in the 2005–06 season; fifteen goals in 31 matches between the league and the Champions League in the 2006–07 season; eight goals in the first slew of fixtures at the beginning of the 2007–08 season; 21 goals in 22 matches since he scored the hat-trick against Real Madrid in March 2007. But the figures do not do justice to Leo's progression. Instead let's take a look at the headlines:

'Messi is worth the whole team' – *El País*, 20/09/07
'Messi plays Messiah' – *Marca*, 23/09/07
'Messi dominates' – *El Mundo*, 23/09/07
'Messi's got guts' – *El Periódico*, 27/09/07
'Messi was worth the entrance fee' – *La Vanguardia*, 30/09/07
'Messi is king of La Liga' – *Marca*, 08/10/07
'Messi's irresistible rise' – *Sport*, 09/10/07
'Messi does the mambo' – *Mundo Deportivo*, 09/10/07
'Messi starts to do what Maradona did before him' – *As*, 18/10/07

And it's not just the headlines on every page which celebrate the moment of glory, the divinely inspired play, 'the brilliance and inspiration' of the Argentine 'who turns everything he touches to gold'. The comments of the coaches, the rival teams, the football experts, both Spanish and Argentine, and the studies also document his explosion. There is talk of a 'footballer without limits', and it is stated that, given his mindset, Messi is capable of 'taking risks and directing the game'. There is talk of his extreme running speed: 4.5 strides per second, which beats the 4.4 of Asafa Powell, the speedy Jamaican who set a 100-metre world record of 9.74 seconds in Rieti (Italy) on 9 September 2007. There are discussions regarding his low centre of gravity, which allow him to control and drive the ball forward with characteristic ease. Comparisons with the number 10 are made continually.

In an exclusive interview in *Marca*, Diego does not argue with any of this; he simply explains that 'if Rijkaard puts Messi on the bench, Laporta will throw him out'. And after his team's harsh defeat at the Nou Camp, Zaragoza coach Víctor Fernández says what everyone is thinking: 'Messi could be the best in the world.'

As though besieged by an avalanche, the compliments swirl around Messi from September to November. And since it's not long before the nominations for *France Football*'s Ballon d'Or and the FIFA World Player, the hopes and the voting predictions become more and more outspoken. 'Messi is close behind Kaká,' writes *La Vanguardia*. 'Messi is a candidate for the Ballon d'Or. His performance and goals for Barça and Argentina make him a favourite,' announces *Marca*. It is a full-blown campaign in favour of the Flea, although everyone is conscious of the fact that Kaká is the favourite and probably already has the prestigious award in the bag. But either way, it is better to campaign, and give some impetus to the Argentine's cause. In the meantime, while awaiting the verdict, Messi is awarded the Bravo, the prize given by Italian sports magazine *Guerin Sportivo* to the best Under 21 in the European championships. Leo is the first Argentine and third Barcelona player to win it, after Guardiola and Ronaldo. It is 25 November. Just one week later, Ricardo Izecson Dos Santos Leite, 'Kaká' (a nickname given to him by his brother), lifts the Ballon d'Or. Messi is in third place. Bronze, with 255 votes. Cristiano Ronaldo is just ahead of him with 22 more votes, while Kaká has received no fewer than 444 votes.

The Brazilian, who is a member of the Reborn in Christ Church and a fervent evangelist, gives thanks to God 'for being lucky enough to be able to dedicate myself to this profession'. He believes that Milan's Champions League victory and his position as highest goal scorer are what helped him triumph over his opponents. Of Leo, he says: 'He represents ability and control of the ball. He is young and full of talent, I think he is very good.' The difference between them? It's simple, explains Kaká, 'Messi hasn't won any important titles this season, not La Liga, nor the Champions League, and I think that has counted against him.'

It is the same story fifteen days later at the FIFA World Player Gala 2007. With just one difference, which makes one of the top players extremely nervous. Kaká takes gold again with 1,047 votes, best player of 2007 according to his colleagues; but Leo moves up to silver (504 votes), overtaking Cristiano Ronaldo who, with 426 votes, has to make do with the bronze.

It is amusing seeing what happens in the room. The presenter announces Messi in second place and Ronaldo in third. The two of them stand up at the same time in the front row of the stalls in order to go up on stage. Messi buttons his jacket. It is the first time he has ever worn a suit and he looks decidedly unaccustomed to such attire. FIFA president Joseph Blatter and Pelé do the honours on the Zurich Opera House stage. Cristiano Ronaldo is the first to shake hands all round. He nods to O Rei and, without hesitation, picks up the second place silver trophy. Blatter has to motion to him and insist: 'Messi, it's for Messi.' The presenter repeats the result of the votes and asks them to switch trophies. An uncomfortable moment smoothed over by the presenter with a 'you did very well but you just missed it', to Cristiano Ronaldo.

The two of them change places for the photo and the ceremony continues without any problem.

'Blatter said that that one was for me; then, when I went to pick it up, it turned out that the other one was for Cristiano and this one was for me,' Leo comments at a press conference later. When asked how he feels, he replies: 'The truth is that I feel happy, all those people who voted, they gave me this prize ... Before it all happened I said that it was already wonderful just to be in the top three, so I'm very happy. It was all new to me, so I was just taking it in and enjoying it.'

Leo Messi shouldn't even have been there. The injury he picked up the previous Saturday at Mestalla had threatened his attendance at the gala. Then, at the last minute, the doctors give him a good report, so the Blaugrana expedition leaves for Zurich, headed up by Joan Laporta, who receives the FIFA Fair Play Award on behalf of FC Barcelona. Jorge and Rodrigo go along to keep Leo company.

Two days later in Barcelona, the father and brother find time to talk about their trip to Switzerland, the prizes, and various other things related to the champion they know so well. Is there disappointment that he missed out on the gold? 'Just the fact that he is second and third in the world at twenty years of age, means Leo is already a footballing icon. He still has time to make it to number one if he continues like this,' says Jorge, sipping a cup of tea. 'In all honesty, did you ever imagine that your son would get to this level?' 'No, I never imagined he would go so far. I was betting on Rodrigo, who was a good striker. He grew up at Newell's, he played with Central Córdoba, he played as a reserve in the first division, he had a motorbike accident that kept him out for a year, he trialled in Chile, and then I brought him here to see if he could find a Spanish or another European team.'

'The difference,' comments his older brother Rodrigo, 'is that Leo has an attribute that I didn't have: he has a lot of willpower, he has made a huge number of sacrifices to get to where he is. I didn't have as much willpower. I'm a lot more lazy.' But who instilled Leo with such a passion for football? 'I was never one of those frustrated footballers who wants their kids to be champions at all costs. I never aspired to that. It was my mother-in-law who used to take Rodrigo and Leo to play, not me,' declares Jorge. 'Yes, it's true that I coached him for a year at Grandoli, but I wasn't his teacher. I enjoyed watching him play.'

So then where does his passion come from? 'Back when I used to play, I loved football,' says Jorge. 'I woke up in the morning and went to bed at night thinking about football, maybe that has been passed down to Leo.'

'When my brother was five or six years old,' explains Rodrigo, 'there was no other present that could make him as happy as a football could. He was crazy about football like all the kids. But he knew how to be faithful to his childhood passion and he's pursued his dream. Because his happiness was, and still is, tied up with football.' And what does the job involve for a factory-worker-turned-football-agent father? 'For his own benefit I have to protect him from the expectations of interested parties who could harm him. There are people who seem trustworthy but actually they're criminals.

The world is full of them. It's not easy, I have had to learn, I have made mistakes, and bit by bit I have straightened out any issues along the way.' How is the father-son relationship? 'Good, apart from the generational difference, which creates a barrier. I try not to smother him too much, that's what he needs. I prefer him to be surrounded by youngsters his own age, his brothers, his friends. I don't want my son to think: he's always around. If he needs advice I give it to him, if not … I try not to get involved in anything. I tell him things and I can see that he often takes it on board. Money? Contracts? We almost never talk about those things, we chat more about football, the football here and the Argentine teams, like a get-together between friends.'

And how are things going with the older brother? 'I was by Leo's side during the first few years here, in Barcelona. They weren't easy years, we used to get very bored,' explains Rodrigo. 'They were sad times, we would spend them watching films or playing PlayStation. Then, bit by bit, his life changed, and so did mine. Every so often he likes to get off the pitch and go out to eat. In terms of nightlife? He doesn't like going out that much. I used to like going out, he would rather get a drink and have a chat. He spends a lot of time with us. He looks after Agustín a lot, my oldest child, who is turning five, and he loves my little girl, who was born in 2006. He also likes the meals that my wife Florencia makes – her roast chicken and *empanadas* could rival my mother's.'

A question for the head of the family: does all that money change a player and his family? 'We don't have luxuries, we still haven't finished the house in Rosario. Leo has a chalet here in Castelldefels: two floors, four bedrooms, a garden and a small pool. We live just as we did before, but people look at us and think we've changed; on the contrary, they are the ones who have changed. They look at us differently … they envy a boy who has done well. The money that Leo earns is put away safely so that he and his family shouldn't have any problems in the future.'

The last question, that has to be asked, is about his son's future. 'I think it will be good. He'll keep developing, he'll be even better.' Better than Maradona? 'Diego was one of a kind. Leo is different, these are different times; I hope he comes close to the number 10's level, in terms of the technical qualities he displayed and the results he achieved.'

(above) Messi, front row, second from left, with his first team, Grandoli. The man in green is his father, Jorge Messi. (Courtesy of the Messi family)

(below) Celebrating with the trophy after Argentina beat Nigeria 2-1 during the 2005 World Championships Under 20 final. The banner in the background says: 'Argentina I love you'. (AP Photo/Bas Czerwinski)

(above) Tussling with Brazil and Manchester United's Anderson in the semi-final of the men's football competition at the Beijing Workers' Stadium during the 2008 Olympics. (PA Wire)

(below) Edwin van der Sar and Rio Ferdinand can only watch as Messi scores Barcelona's second goal in their 2-0 win over Manchester United in the 2009 UEFA Champions League final in Rome. (AP Photo/Gregorio Borgia, File)

(above) From left, Barcelona's Xavi Hernandez, Carles Puyol, Lionel Messi, Thierry Henry and Andrés Iniesta celebrate next to the trophy at the end of the 2009 UEFA Champions League final against Manchester United. (AP Photo/Luca Bruno)

(below) Fighting for the ball against Real Madrid's Xabi Alonso, right, during a Spanish La Liga soccer match at the Nou Camp stadium in late 2009. (AP Photo/Manu Fernandez)

(above) Kissing his 2009 Ballon d'Or, or Golden Ball trophy, awarded to the Europe-based footballer of the year. (AP Photo/Francois Mori, File)

(below) Scoring the second and winning goal during the 2009 Club World Cup final against Estudiantes of Argentina in Abu Dhabi, United Arab Emirates. (AP Photo/Bernat Armangue)

Chapter 29

Physical thinking

Conversation with Roberto Perfumo, 'El Mariscal'

The La Biela waiters and clientele know him well. Some of them stop and greet him and ask for his perspective on the issues of the day. Once he has dished out his opinions to all and sundry, the Mariscal – ex-defender for River, Racing and Cruzeiro, one of Argentine football's best defenders, who is also a commentator and a social psychologist – finally sits down to have a cup of coffee. The walls are covered with photos of motor racing champions like Juan Manuel Fangio, Friolán González and Manuel Gálvez, who in the 50s and 60s used to frequent this café-bar, situated opposite the famous Recoleta cemetery in Buenos Aires. Those were different times. Today, the talk is about football.

What do you think of Lionel Messi?
'Technically speaking he's one of the few players in the world who can drive the ball forward without looking at it, and that allows him to watch the opposition and his teammates, and make an unprecedented pass. He can do it because he sees the whole pitch. He has a lot of precision while at the highest possible speed. He plays imaginatively, he's creative and every time he gets the ball, every time he challenges the opposition, it's an experience … everyone is

waiting for something to happen. And it does. In addition, for me Messi has physical thinking.'

What does that mean?
'He is mind and body. All at the same time. He has the same gift that Pelé, Maradona and Di Stéfano had. It's the speed with which his brain tells his legs what to do. Messi gets an idea and, bam! it's already happened. Do you know what I mean? Seeing the position of the goalie and shooting between the posts is done through intuition, not through thinking.'

Since you've mentioned Maradona, the obvious thing is to ask you about the comparisons that have been made and are still made continually …
'After Pelé retired, it took Brazil another 24 years to become world champions again. We are still in mourning for Maradona. We're all hoping a Saviour will appear, the new Messiah, who will take us to the top once again. Messi could reach that position, but he still needs time, he needs to develop his gifts and prepare himself for the opposition, he needs to reach his footballing maturity.'

What are his weaknesses?
'He still has a youthful sin: he doesn't always know how to make the best choices. Sometimes you have to make a run, sometimes you have to pass, it's useless to persist when a play is not going your way, it's better to choose the most simple and effective solution. He himself will realise that it's the ball that has to keep on running … these are things you learn with experience and with age.'

Is Messi already an icon?
'He is a simple guy, very humble, and kids admire him enormously.'

Why is that?
'Because of his look, because of his face. He reminds me of the *cuis* (a type of squirrel, one of the most common Argentine mammals). Add to that his natural magnetism when the ball is between his feet. I hope he never loses his passion for playing ball. That's the only way he will be the best in the world.'

Since you are so sure of your prediction … let's move on to talking about the future and, in particular, the risks.
'I hope that the money doesn't soften him. With millions of euros in the bank he still needs to run, train, play in the cold, the rain, the snow. I hope he doesn't become an advertising icon like Beckham; the risk is that you lose the passion for the game. I hope he never loses that "amateurism", that love of being on the pitch that guys like Pelé and Maradona preserved. Being Messi won't be easy, it will definitely be a headache. In any case, he is still climbing uphill to reach the top. The most difficult part will be once he is up there and has to maintain that level. Look at Ronaldinho.'

Meaning?
'Juan Manuel Fangio used to say, "When the bad times come, no one can endure them." That is what's happening to Ronaldinho. When things start to go wrong … you say to yourself, it's fine, I'll get back to form. But you don't look after yourself, you don't concentrate, they start to question you every blessed day, the environment doesn't help because friends of a champion are the worst kind, family is a disaster, and you keep careering downhill without being able to apply the brakes. You don't realise it and time passes. It's a lesson Messi needs to remember when he's at the top.'

Chapter 30

The long journey towards gold

22 May 2008

'I'm excited because it's the Argentine national team. And I always said that I want to play for my country. It's the Olympics ... it's an opportunity a player gets once in his career, if he gets it, right? It's possible that I might get the chance to be there and I would love to go. What if there's a conflict with the club? I don't think there will be. I think the club understands how I feel and ... there won't be any problems.'

It is just after 1.30pm on a grey Thursday. There is quite a buzz in the Hesperia Tower hotel in Barcelona, close to El Prat airport. Today sees the first gathering of the Argentine Under 23 squad. It is the beginning of an Olympic adventure for Sergio 'el Checho' Batista's boys. There is an atmosphere of reunion and re-acquaintance, between players, between players and coaches, between footballers and journalists – who have been positioned in the foyer for a while now in order to get an interview.

An exhausting initial training session is followed by a procession of white shirts towards the dining room; after the meal there is a press conference in the enormous auditorium. In theory it is only an introduction to the Catalunya-Argentina friendly, which will be played two days later at the Nou Camp, on Saturday 24 May. The adverts are promoting it as a challenge between two extremely young Barça stars

– Lionel Messi on the one hand, and Bojan Krkić on the other. But the sixteen-year-old from Linyola will not be on the pitch. Catalan selector Pere Gratacós would prefer not to play him to avoid a headache, since Bojan turned down Luis Aragonés' call for him to play for the Spanish national team in the European championship, claiming tiredness. Leo is there, however, and becomes the main protagonist before a crammed audience of Catalan and Argentine journalists. Checho is sitting beside him and observes the reporters pestering him with questions about all the issues currently facing Barcelona: the new coach, the possible departures of Ronaldinho and Deco – two team-mates with whom he is very close – before finally arriving at the topic of the Olympics. Messi speaks openly. He wants to go to Beijing. He doesn't think that missing Barça's Champions League qualifier will be too much of a strain on the team (the first leg is on 12 or 13 August, the return leg is on the 26th or 27th, against an unknown team). On the contrary he maintains that 'Barcelona do not depend solely on me to win matches. They want to form a team that aspires to win all the titles, if a player is absent on one particular day I don't think anything will come of it.' He is convinced that the club as much as the Barça fans will understand his decision.

He is wrong. Very wrong. It is immediately apparent upon hearing the comments from those in the room. While the journalists who have come from Buenos Aires might be satisfied with the position Leo has taken, happy that he has announced his Olympic dream and reaffirmed his desire to go for gold with the Albiceleste, the Catalan reporters are annoyed. They are coming off the back of two bad seasons for the club. The titles have vanished into oblivion one by one; the team that once dazzled the world has disappeared among dressing-room disputes and diatribes; its stars have

been extinguished, and others, like Ronaldinho, have not made the headlines for months; Frank Rijkaard, the coach who directed the show for five years, has been dismissed; they have announced the departure of the superstars who led the Blaugrana to victory in the Champions League and La Liga; in summary, Barça – as a club and as a team – is going through a critical stage of much instability. At a time like this, it is difficult to digest Leo's decision. 'But how … can Barcelona play the Champions League qualifiers with him not there? Who is paying him, Barça or Argentina?' And they dredge up the topic of the possible 8-million-euros-a-season 'megacontract', which Messi is to sign. And there's more: 'Messi is the player around whom the Blaugrana want to reconstruct a winning team, and he says "ciao" and he goes off to China. And if he gets injured, as has happened to him twice in this championship, who will pay?'

All this, and more, can be heard in the hallways of the Hesperia hotel. Few can stand the idea that the future Barça number 10 (everyone reckons he will inherit Ronaldinho's shirt number), the player who was so needed during long weeks of misfortune, can abandon them in this way.

The following day, in the Catalan sports papers, the headlines about Leo's declarations are mounting up. But they seem to understand the Flea's position. In keeping with their journalistic duty, many of them recall the regulations. 'In Messi's case, it is not possible for Barça to refuse because he is under 23 years old,' writes *Sport*.

In the offices of the Nou Camp they do not get the message. They have no intention of losing Leo during the Champions League qualifiers. They immediately consult the guidelines to see if there is any possibility of not conceding to the Argentine team. Leo's father Jorge Messi, who meets with Barça technical secretary Txiki Begiristain a few days later, announces: 'Leo will do whatever he is obliged

to do, to avoid being penalised by either party.' In other words, the decision to go to the Games does not depend solely on his son. If the Catalan club finds a way to prevent him, Lionel will have to resign himself to the fact and kiss his Olympic dream goodbye.

This is just the beginning of a tug-of-war between the AFA and Barcelona, which will go on for more than two months. In the meantime, having played the friendly against Catalunya (a match won by Pocho Lavezzi with one of his usual goals), Leo leaves for Argentina in a hurry. Coco Basile and the national team await him. The programme includes a mini tour of America and two qualifying matches for the 2010 World Cup. First, an important victory over Mexico; then a goalless draw against the United States at the New Jersey Giants' stadium. And then come the matches that matter: against Ecuador at the Monumental stadium and against Brazil at Belo Horizonte's Mieirão. The Albiceleste do not shine: two hard-earned draws.

Messi's commitments with the national team have finished; it is holiday time, time for advertising promotions and matches like the one he arranged with Ronaldinho on 28 June at the Monumental de Maturín in Venezuela, the second instalment of a charity match between Messi's friends and Ronnie's friends. A 7-7 result and a farewell to them being team-mates.

It is 2 July. Sergio Batista announces the list of the eighteen players who make up the national squad for the Olympics. Leo Messi is on it. It could be an end to the dispute. Julio Grondona, president of the AFA, also wants him there. 'Argentina will call up Messi in accordance with FIFA regulation, which states that he has to be with his national team at the Olympic Games. If I don't have Messi I don't have a team, and if he doesn't come and play with us, it will spark a precedent which will prompt other teams to ask for

their players and we don't want that to happen either. It is logical for him to play for Argentina, since Barcelona have him for the whole year. There are very few competitions in which Messi can play with his country.'

Sounds straightforward, doesn't it? But Barcelona have no intention of waving the white flag. 'We have read up on it, we have attended meetings with the AFA and, ultimately, the regulations will be adhered to. If the regulations favour us, Messi will play in the Champions League qualifier,' maintains Begiristain.

On 15 July, Barcelona is back in session, with Pep Guardiola and without Ronaldinho. The Brazilian only has to complete his medical before he can play for Milan. It is a transfer which allows him to go to the Olympic Games. Barça had refused, since Ronnie is over 23 and FIFA does not oblige clubs to relinquish players older than 23. But Berlusconi's club will relinquish him. 'He's so lucky,' Leo must be thinking, not knowing what fate has in store for him. 'The club will not talk to him about the matter, it's a negotiation between Barcelona and the AFA,' says his mother, Celia. 'And Leo won't speak, he won't ask. He just waits for their answer.' And for the moment he goes to St Andrews, Scotland, where Barcelona's pre-season begins. It is 21 July. Two days later, Leo should be in Tokyo with the Olympic squad: a friendly against Japan is scheduled for 29 July. But Barça have not agreed. They have proposed to the Argentine Federation that they will relinquish the player after the American tour and after the first leg of the Champions League qualifier. If the result is good and favourable, of course. Messi would miss the first three matches of the Olympic qualifying stages, but as long as Argentina qualify, he could be there for the quarter-finals. It is a proposition that the AFA does not want to consider. The most they will accept is that Leo will take part in the

Barça pre-season, and then join the national team before the first match. They will not entertain the possibility that Messi won't go to the Games. They think that Barça will not want to come up against them, FIFA and, above all, the player, who has always expressed his desire to participate in the Olympics.

On 23 July, Joseph Blatter makes his contribution to the drama. 'The relinquishing of players under 23 has always been compulsory for all clubs. This same principle applies for Beijing 2008,' says the FIFA president, adding: 'Obstructing the participation of players under 23 years of age in the final phase of the tournament could be interpreted as an attack on the spirit of the Olympics.' But this still is not the final word, since the PFL can refute this argument. 'There is no legal obligation to relinquish footballers. In contrast to the female football tournament, the male Olympic football tournament is not included in the international calendar of matches approved by FIFA for the 2008–14 period.'

The only one who suffers from this push and pull is Lionel. He is nervous and acts 'a little strangely', according to his team-mates. So much so that after a forceful tackle during a practice in Scotland, he ends up in an altercation with Rafa Márquez. Pep Guardiola has to intervene to calm the excitement and ask a bad-tempered Leo to end things once and for all. It is a minor incident, it's silly; nonetheless it affects the new Barça coach. Guardiola takes the boy to one side. He talks to him, he wants to know what's going on, why the bad mood, why he's unhappy. He doesn't want to see him like this. He wants him to be happy playing football with Barça. A few words are enough to make Leo confess. He says, loud and clear, that he wants to go to Beijing. Guardiola promises to do everything possible. And he starts to take a stand after the first friendly against Hibernian

(6-0 to Barça with a great goal from the Flea). 'In the end,' declares Guardiola, 'Leo is the one who is worst affected in this story. There are only two or three weeks to go, some are saying one thing and others are saying something else. Blatter will have to sit down and look at the regulations and decide if he's staying with us or going to the Games.' Despite the demands, FIFA's decision takes another six days. In the interim comes Barça's second friendly against Dundee United, with three Messi goals, as well as words from Joan Laporta, the Barça club president, who restates the club's position, the consensus solution offered to the AFA, and announces that in the event of a negative verdict from FIFA, Barcelona will 'turn to the legal guidance of the CAS (Court of Arbitration for Sport) so that our claims are taken into account'.

In short the tug-of-war continues. There is less than a week remaining until Argentina's debut at the Games and no one knows if Leo will be there. On the websites of the Spanish and Argentine newspapers, the polls appear in abundance: 'Should the national team keep waiting for Messi?' asks *Clarín* of its readers. Evidently tired of this soap opera, they respond with a resounding 'no': 70 per cent, against 29 per cent who are willing to continue waiting.

'What should Barça do about Messi? Should they let him compete in the Olympics, or try to keep him for the Champions League qualifier?' replies *El País* from across the pond a few days later. Seventy-three per cent think Messi should participate in the Olympics.

On Tuesday 30 July Leo's first words are heard. His total silence has generated all different types of response. Gabriel Batistuta, for example, defends him. 'He is doing the right thing by not saying anything, because after the Olympics he is going to go back to playing with Barcelona and the national team.' Maradona, on the other hand, attacks him.

'He has to decide for himself. This is the moment to be more of a man. It is a great opportunity to grow. Either way, Barcelona will wait for him. That's why they gave him the number 10 shirt: because they want him. If they gave it to him, it's not because Messi is a movie star, it's because he is a phenomenon, a great player.' And, on the other hand, there is his family, who do not know which path to take. Jorge Messi confirms it: 'There is a conflict of interest here in which the player is being put in the middle. And they are using my son as cannon fodder. You can't generate prejudice towards a 21-year-old footballer, you never know how it will end. It's crazy that the player should have to make the decision. It can't be the case that those who are in charge of managing the football cannot reach an agreement. We don't know what to do.'

Finally, before travelling to Florence, where the team are playing a friendly against the Purples (Fiorentina), Leo speaks his mind and says what he proposes to do. 'If FIFA says I don't have to go, I'm not going; if I have to go, I'll go, without waiting for the CAS, because if I wait for the CAS it will already be too late for my team-mates and the national selection staff.'

And a few hours later, FIFA says that Messi should go to the Games. 'The sole judge of the Comisión del Estatuto del Jugador, Slim Aloulou (Túnez), has ruled that the relinquishing of players under 23 for the Beijing 2008 male Olympic football tournament is compulsory,' announces the statement from Zurich.

The news is received with great relief from the Argentine camp. 'Luckily, after a lot of going backwards and forwards, it was resolved in our favour,' confesses Sergio Batista.

After the match against Fiorentina (3-1 to Barça), Pep Guardiola comments: 'We will survive without Messi. However, I have a feeling that we are a little bit stronger

with Messi. If he does not eventually return, we will ensure the team qualifies for the Champions League. And if he does return, we will welcome him back with open arms.'

There is a somewhat different response from the Blaugrana directors, whose opinion has not altered and who submit an appeal to the CAS. But in the meantime, instead of leaving for the American tour, Leo is off to China, promising to return if the CAS rule in favour of Barça.

In Shanghai, where he arrives on 1 August, Leo seems to recover the calm he had lost. He is laughing, and he finally seems happy during practice. He shares a room with Kun Agüero, as he did in the 2005 Under 20 World Cup. Thousands of PlayStation games, and *cumbia* music at full volume. The two get on well, they are relaxed, they let their hair down and do whatever they feel like. Checho breathes easily. The first time he saw Leo was at Barcelona, in the match against Catalunya. There were not many practices, and few with his team-mates, but fortunately he now has the chance to build up the group. For a while now, Batista has been thinking about where to position him on the field. 'I want Messi to come into the centre more, not be pinned to the touchline the way he is with Barcelona. I want him to generate more play, in front of Riquelme and behind Agüero,' he explains. Meanwhile, the Flea tells the press his dreams. 'For me, and for all the players, it would be really special to reclaim the title. We came here to win the gold medal. We'll take it slow and hopefully we can get it.' He denies that there is any problem between him and Riquelme (just before the World Cup qualifier against Brazil there had been rumours circulating of a dispute between the national number 10 and Messi). He maintains, although few believe him, that the relationship with Román has always been good. Regarding the controversy that kept him away from the national team, he explains: 'Batista understood me and

so did my team-mates, they had no problem waiting for me. I did what I had to do. I hope that this situation will not be an issue any longer.' And it won't.

On 6 August, on the eve of Argentina-Ivory Coast, the first group A match, the CAS rules in favour of Barcelona. 'The Olympic tournament does not appear on FIFA's official calendar, and there is no decision from the FIFA executive committee which establishes an obligation to make players less than 23 years of age available to their countries for this championship,' explains the tribunal's ruling. However, it then requests that the parties concerned find 'a reasonable solution with respect to the players who wish to represent their countries at the Olympic Games'. And how do the parties react? Grondona is the first to make himself heard: 'Messi is not going anywhere.' Sergio Batista confirms: 'He will be on the pitch tomorrow.' And Leo? He makes no statements about the ruling and it seems that, though he may have been willing to return to Barça, he has no intention of returning to the fold now.

'He has told me that he wants to stay with the squad and he asks Barcelona to be considerate of his position,' assures Checho. Begiristain does not seem to be considerate: 'It is our wish – with our fans in mind – that Leo Messi be with the club,' he says. Satisfied with Barcelona's legal victory, Laporta orders the player's immediate return. But first, Guardiola wants to speak to Leo. 'I want to listen to him, and we will make a decision,' he says, 'but I can't relay it without having heard from the player.' Then there is a long, intercontinental phone conference between New York (where Barça are concluding their American tour against the Red Bulls) and Shanghai. Leo Messi asks Guardiola – who, after Barcelona '92, knows what it means to win an Olympic gold – to help him: he wants to stay in China and participate in the Games. Pep promises to find a solution. No sooner said

than done. At the meeting, which takes place in a suite at the Saint Regis hotel, on the corner of Fifth Avenue and 53rd Street, he convinces Laporta and Begiristain. Messi is to stay in Beijing. But not without a few conditions. The first is that the AFA will take responsibility for medical insurance in case Messi is injured. The same clause that was demanded by Schalke 04 and Werder Bremen for Rafinha and Diego, the two Brazilians who were in the middle of a similar dispute between the clubs and the Brazilian Federation. The second is a 'personal agreement with Julio Grondona that the player will be relinquished from all the season's friendlies'. Guardiola is the one who announces Barcelona's decision to Leo. He calls him from the plane a few minutes before takeoff from New York. 'You're staying. Enjoy it,' he says.

On 7 August the Blaugrana expedition is on its way back to Barcelona. It falls to Begiristain and Guardiola to make the official announcement regarding the resolution of Messi's case. 'He found himself in a difficult position and he himself had expressed a desire to be with us for the pre-season,' explains the coach. 'But when he arrived in Beijing, he asked me personally not to request his return to Barcelona. I noted a lot of emotional tension. He has suffered brutal pressure, as has his family. I saw that he seemed very uncomfortable with the situation, and it also was not a good idea to bring him here if his head was in Beijing. Now, after this whole drama, the best thing is for him to play, to enjoy it, to be happy and for him to return content. The Barça fan-base knows that we have an extraordinary player and that he will do wonderful things when he returns. The people will be understanding towards him.'

Messi goes onto the pitch to face the Ivory Coast wearing the Argentine number 15 shirt. And he demonstrates why his presence at the Olympic Games was so important.

Towards the end of the first half, he receives a 45-yard pass from Riquelme, he picks up the pace and, almost from the penalty spot, places it delicately into the net. Five minutes from the final whistle, when the scoreboard seems stuck at 1-1 (Cissé responded to Leo's goal), the Flea takes a quick free kick with Román on the edge of the area and it takes a wicked deflection. The Elephants' goalie makes the save and Lautaro Acosta – who secured the team's qualification for the Games – then finds it easy to score the final goal to make it 2-1.

A few seconds from the end, Batista substitutes Leo and in doing so gives him the opportunity to be applauded by the Chinese crowd. They did it throughout the match and, when his picture appeared on the Olympic stadium screen, regardless of the fact that the Argentine national anthem was playing, a chant of 'Messi, Messi' began to pick up in the stands. He is one of the best-known sportsmen in the People's Republic of China. He sells well, from shirts to Pepsi Cola, and the children want to be like him. For the moment, let's leave aside his popularity, which grew exponentially during the Olympics, to the point that he joined FIFA's ranks as one of the best-known sportsmen, and at the end of the tournament will be chosen by the online users of MyBestPlay as the most favoured footballer of the Olympics, alongside athletes such as Michael Phelps, the swim king, or Usain Bolt, the fastest man in the world. Let's return to the match. Beneath the question of favourite footballers, which dominates the conversation, there is also a sense of happiness at the resolution of the conflict. This time it is Leo's turn to speak, and to thank Guardiola. 'He was a player and he knows how a player feels at those moments,' he says. 'He knew that I was in a situation that was difficult for me and he has supported me ever since he arrived at Barcelona, since the first day when I spoke to him. He has been outstanding,

and the truth is that I am very grateful.' With the chapter closed once and for all, his thoughts now turn to his friend Ronaldinho's Brazil, the other favourite to win the title: 'If we reach a final against Brazil, it will be much more difficult because Ronnie will be there. It is always great to win a final, and even more so against Brazil,' jokes the Flea, but before that, there is 'Australia, tough competitors, strong, who play well in the air and who will create a tricky match. It's going to be extremely difficult.'

It certainly is. Fifteen minutes from the end, the score at the Shanghai Olympic stadium still stands at 0-0. Argentina, at least in the first half, play better than in the debut match, they create chances, but Federici, the Australian goalkeeper, is difficult to beat. Then, in a few seconds, after various touches between Riquelme and Messi, Román plays the ball out to the left to Di María, who crosses into the centre and Pocho Lavezzi converts it. It's the victory goal.

On the other side of the world, two days after 12 August, a Messi-less Barcelona also win: 4-0 against Wisła Cracovia in the first leg of the preliminary round of the Champions League. The Blaugrana fears vanish. But let's go back to China. With their pass to the quarter-finals in the bag, the Albiceleste relocate to the Olympic Village in Beijing. Nothing fancy for the spoiled footballers, but lots of encounters. 'We were eating,' recalls Oscar Ustari, 'and we saw him arrive, queue for his food and sit down at the table. "Hi, I'm Kobe" (Bryant), he said to us. He spoke to us in Spanish, looked for Messi, and chatted to him for a bit. And we took the opportunity of taking a few photos. When it came to saying goodbye, he made the gesture of taking off his hat, looked directly at Leo, and said to him: "Messi, you're the best." We were in awe. Nadal (Rafa) also came over. When you're with Leo, you can't just cruise along, they stop you everywhere you go.'

But there are not only encounters with celebrities from all over the world. In Beijing they also have to face Serbia.

Checho rests Leo, keeps the already-cautioned Riquelme and Agüero on the bench, and lets the subs play. Seven changes, an overhaul which nonetheless leads to victory. 2-0 (a Lavezzi penalty and a Buonanotte free kick); nine consecutive Olympic victories (beating the record held by Uruguay for 80 years); first place in the group. The only ones who lost out were the 60,000 spectators who rushed to the Beijing Workers' Stadium to see Messi in action. During the first half they chant his name and when, at the end of the match, they see that the Flea is not coming on, they begin to whistle at the Argentine team. In the end, the coach has to justify himself. 'The people of China have to understand that we came here with an objective, that of winning the gold medal. It wasn't only Messi who didn't play today. Riquelme, Agüero and Garay didn't play either. I was thinking of the best for Argentina. If they were annoyed, it's bad luck. I hope they forgive me.'

The next fixture, also at the Beijing Workers' Stadium, is against Holland on 16 August. Maradona is also in the stands, to cheer for the national team, and for Kun, who is the boyfriend of his daughter Giannina. There is no room for mistakes. Leo knows it and puts on a show. Here is how *Clarín* describes it: 'How many wishes will be granted by this genie, who appears during the national team matches? If there were three in the original story, perhaps Batista's team will be left short of what they need from this magical figure who arrived from Barcelona and who did very well again today, with a fantastic goal and an incredible pass – to resolve a story that had become difficult and in which Holland was very close to stealing the dream of reclaiming the Olympic gold.' But what did the Flea do this time? He settled an extremely complicated match. Dodging around

one defender, dummying the goalie to leave him in the dust, and blasting it into the net before any desperate Dutchmen had the chance to intervene. 1-0. Then, in the fourteenth minute of extra time, he invents perfect geometry so that Di María can predict the course of a strong shot, a low cross, which secures the 2-1. And Argentina are to face Brazil in the semi-finals.

The *Clásico par excellence*, the anticipated final, the perfect occasion to avenge the most recent historic encounters (the defeats in the finals of the 2004 Copa América in Peru, in the 2005 Copa Confederaciones and again in the 2007 Copa América in Venezuela). The Olympic champions Argentina, against Brazil, who have never won the gold; it is the match that Leo dreamt of, although one stage earlier in the competition. And as if that weren't enough, there is the duel between Leo and Ronaldinho: two friends, two ex-team-mates, the talented youngster against the former Ballon d'Or winner, the present against the past, the current star against the champion who is looking to be reborn from the ashes. The list could go on and on. The debate over who is greater is wide open. Everyone has their own opinion. Even Kun gets involved: 'Lionel, nowadays, is better than Ronaldinho. He's the best player in the world.'

Messi avoids the topic, but he does not shy away from the avalanche of questions: 'I'm not one to make predictions, but Ronnie: remember the gold belongs to Argentina! My dream is the dream of the whole Argentine team. And more so now, for Ustari, for my friend [Oscar has been injured in the match against Holland and cannot keep goal for the Albiceleste]. It will be hard,' he says, 'it is always difficult against Brazil. We are both extremely worn out from the extra time in our quarter-finals matches. Brazil has an incredible team, but our team is immense. We are playing for the same thing, to see who gets the gold, and they won

the last final we played. I'm still cross about the final of the Copa América. Now it's our turn ...' And indeed it is Argentina's turn, but in a way no one had imagined. They quash, humiliate and make fun of Brazil. Agüero, with two goals and a hand in the third (he is fouled and Riquelme converts the penalty), and his celebrations – where he mimes putting a dummy in his mouth (Giannina is expecting a baby) – are all evidence of the weakness of Dunga's team and Ronaldinho's decline. 'Nowadays,' writes *El País*, 'the Brazilian is a false player, more given to pulling faces, cheerful chatter and other similar gestures, which are only an attempt to win front pages and the applause of a Chinese crowd who are novices when it comes to football. As much as he disguises his decline with lots of theatricality, the football he has left in him does not guarantee him a performance, except for when the ball is dead as he is: he still manages to take free kicks.' A cruel portrait of someone who was once the world number one. But even more cruel is the photo that appears in the media across the world the following day: Ronnie in his yellow number 10 shirt and captain's armband, finding solace, head bowed, in the arms of his 'little brother' Messi. Lionel is standing on tiptoes in order to console his idol. There is a lot of affection in that picture, but there is also a lot of melancholy. Without making a big impression, Leo has won that highly anticipated duel. He is happy. Ronnie only wants to hide, to disappear from the face of the earth. 'I'm sad, very sad,' he will say later. For him, this was the opportunity to be seen again in the world. He has failed. Leo, on the other hand, is making his way towards gold.

At twelve o'clock on Saturday 23 August (one in the morning in Argentina) at the National Stadium, nicknamed the Bird's Nest, the final of the Olympic Games football tournament begins. Opponent: Nigeria – just like in Atlanta

'96 and in the 2005 Under 20 World Cup in Holland. In the American Olympics, Nwankwo Kanu's Nigeria took home the gold after a 3-2 final, considered by FIFA to be one of the ten most memorable matches in a century of Olympic football. Argentine revenge comes in 2005, in Holland. And the protagonist, the one who defeats the Green Eagles, is Lionel: two penalties. Fifteen players from that final (including Messi and Kun) find themselves at the ground in Beijing. 'We're going to win, I have no doubt about it. 2-0 would be perfect,' prophesies Diego Maradona. It is not that easy.

The heat is so oppressive that after 30 minutes of the first half, Hungarian referee Victor Kassai calls a basketball-style timeout so the teams can cool down. A break that is repeated in the second half. The pitch is hard, dry and the Green Eagles leave no spaces uncovered. Messi and Agüero are alone up front. Their tiny runs with touches and dodges make no impression on the giant Nigerians. Riquelme is not having a good day. Midfielders Gago and 'Chief' Mascherano are working hard. The match is bad, wretched, boring, tiring. Until the 57th minute: there is a scuffle between an Argentine and an African, the ball rebounds towards the centre of the pitch, Messi recovers it, turns, and passes it perfectly, out deep, to Ángel Di María. The ex-Rosario Central currently at Real Madrid, the sensation of the Games, gallops away freely on the left. And on the edge of the area, in front of Vanzekin who desperately comes off his line, he is inspired to lift the ball softly with his left foot and send it lightly through the heavy Beijing air. The Nigerian goalkeeper can do nothing but get up and, motionless in the penalty area, watch from afar as the ball bounces into the net – a work of art that deserves the gold. Argentina return to the top after four years on the highest step of the podium at Athens. Messi, with his arms

around Kun, celebrates the fulfilment of the dream. He has triumphed over all the legal objections, over all those who didn't want to let him experience this fairytale. And he says it out loud: 'After everything that was said and discussed, it was worth coming.'

Chapter 31

Happiness

27 May 2009

Between Lexington Avenue and Fifth Avenue, Pakistani cab driver Happy Cabby offers customers his life philosophy: 'To make others happy, you must be happy yourself. That is where happiness lies,' he says, turning in his seat to face the passengers and tapping his head with his index finger. 'Yes, it all depends on you to make other people and the world happy.' Perhaps Leo has also felt this good news, conveyed over the noise of Midtown; one thing for sure is that the happiest year of his life began precisely here, in New York, on the corner of Fifth Avenue and 53rd Street, in the Saint Regis hotel suite, when Pep Guardiola convinced Laporta and Begiristain to let Messi stay in Beijing. Permission to participate in the Olympic Games has been without a doubt the biggest motivation for the Argentine and has created a special relationship between the Flea and the Blaugrana coach.

'Everything began over there in Beijing, with the gold medal. He has been happier than ever before,' says his father, Jorge. 'Yes, that's what Pep wanted, for him to get his dream.' 'I don't know … to me he seems very happy – I think we succeeded,' admits Guardiola. Indeed, the young manager was conscious of the fact that the key to the Flea being able to make the Barcelona camp happy was first to make him happy. And he has managed it. Txiki Begiristain,

sporting director of Barça, confirms it: 'If, when he sees you, he jokes with you, then he's happy, if he doesn't seem to see you and looks the other way, something's wrong. Leo has spent the whole year joking with me and with whomever he comes across.' And his team-mates say the same. 'He can only play his best football when he's happy and comfortable,' says Xavi. 'He has been happy,' adds Puyol, the captain, 'but I have also seen him angry. You have no idea what he's like when he doesn't win!' But this has not happened during the 2008–09 season, since Barcelona have won everything: La Liga, the Copa del Rey and the Champions League, the first Spanish team to win the triple. In addition, they have won the Spanish Super Cup and the European Super Cup. Leo has scored more goals than ever before in his professional career. Twenty-three in La Liga, the fourth-highest scorer after Diego Forlán, Samuel Eto'o and David Villa. And let's not forget the 5,000th goal in the Catalan club's Liga history, which Leo scores on 1 February 2009 in Santander against Racing. His second of the match, which secures a victory for Barça. Next up: six more in the Copa del Rey, the tournament's top goal scorer, and he only played 452 minutes (an average of a goal every 75 minutes), and two in the Spanish Super Cup. And nine goals in the Champions League, highest goal scorer in the European tournament. In contrast to the previous two years, he did not sustain even a minor injury in all his 51 matches. In addition to all that he garnered individual recognition. The Spanish coaches voted him the best Liga foreigner, over Forlán, Dani Alves and Kanouté, and according to the club coaches who reached the previous season's Champions League final sixteen, he was the best footballer and best forward of the continental tournament, beating Cristiano Ronaldo to the punch. It's true that the team's (spectacular) performance has helped him to win these trophies, but

ever since he put on the number 10 shirt, Messi has taken a step forward, he has taken up the mantle in the dressing room and on the pitch, he has given it his all, and done it all in an unassuming manner. 'Ever since I met him, at fourteen,' declares Blaugrana defender Gerard Piqué, 'he has always been the same. He has never thought of himself as the best, but he has always known that we all consider him the best.'

At the Grimaldi Forum in Monte Carlo – dressed elegantly in a dark suit, matching tie and white shirt – after having received the honour of best 2008–09 Champions League player, Leo comments: 'It has been an incredible year. I have thoroughly enjoyed it.' And to those who ask him what has been the most magical moment, he responds: 'There were so many wonderful moments that it would be impossible to pick one.'

Seeing as the champion does not know how to choose between so many happy occasions, we will give it a try.

27 May 2009, Olympic Stadium, Rome. Champions League final: Barcelona-Manchester United

Although Messi has one European Cup to his name, it has never felt like his. Because he was not there on the pitch on the evening of 17 May 2006 at the Saint-Denis stadium in Paris. The Flea was not granted permission to play by the medics, despite having repeated over and over that he was fine, that his thigh injury did not hurt any more. He watched the final, against Thierry Henry's Arsenal, from the stands. And during the moments of joy, the hugs and the celebrations, he shut himself into the dressing room in a huff. His friends Deco and Ronaldinho were the ones who got him out of there and tried to make him see that the victory belonged to him as well. Without much success, because to him you have to play in order to feel like a champion.

This time it is different. Leo knows it and feels it. He has been a decisive contributing factor in bringing Barcelona to Rome. With eight goals which make him the tournament's top goal scorer, ahead of Henry who has five and Berbatov, Rooney and Cristiano Ronaldo who have four apiece. Messi scores five goals in the group phase: two against Shakhtar Donetsk in Ukraine, to reclaim a match which had been an uphill struggle for the Blaugrana; another two against FC Basel: one in Switzerland, which ended up being a Barcelona attack-fest (0-5), and the other at the Nou Camp. The final one is against Sporting Lisbon. The Portuguese team suffered at the hands of Barça's goal-scoring ability when they were dealt a 2-5 blow on their home turf. And in the knockout rounds Lionel adds another three, all in front of the home crowd at the Nou Camp: one against Olympique Lyonnais in the quarter-final and two against Bayern Munich, among which he displays without a doubt his best football of the whole season. The Flea does not score in the semi-final against Chelsea. The Blaugrana hero is Andrés Iniesta with his heavenly shot in the 93rd minute, but it was Leo Messi who supplied the ball to the Blaugrana number 8 in the 'D'. At long last … after working day and night, the Barça number 10 has earned the right to be a team leader. The final pits the Liga champions and the 2008–09 Premier League champions against each other – two teams full of great players. Here are the teamsheets. Barcelona: Valdés, Puyol, Touré, Piqué, Sylvinho, Busquets, Xavi, Iniesta, Messi, Henry, Eto'o. Manchester United: Van Der Sar, O'Shea, Vidic, Ferdinand, Evra, Park, Anderson, Carrick, Rooney, Giggs, Cristiano Ronaldo.

Sir Alex Ferguson faces the final with his infinite experience, and Pep Guardiola, as the new sensation of the season. It is a match European football fans could only dream of, the best fixture possible, between two teams that put on

the best show out of anyone on the continent. And, as Leo declares, it is 'the most important game of my career'. He says it just before catching his flight to Rome. It is his first time in the Eternal City, but he doesn't like sightseeing – he is only going to the Italian capital to win. Although he says that 'they are the title holders, so if there is a favourite in a match like this – which there isn't always – then they are the favourites on this occasion'.

The media is promoting the match as the great duel between Cristiano Ronaldo and Leo Messi. They show each player's Champions League statistics and maintain that they are playing for the Ballon d'Or in Rome. It is a chance for the Flea to overtake a rival who beat him by 165 points in *France Football*'s Ballon d'Or vote on 2 December 2008, and who confirmed his place at the top by winning FIFA World Player of the Year on 12 January 2009. But Lionel doesn't see it that way. 'It would be reductive and disrespectful to two great teams, who are currently playing the best football. Two teams who have many other players who can be decisive.' In other words, there is no personal contest with Cristiano to see who is better. 'I am sure he thinks the same as I do: the important thing is the prize at stake for the team. One thing for sure is that whoever wins in Rome will be heralded as the best team in Europe.'

All true, but the two know that they are being watched by half the world. Cristiano Ronaldo, who, despite not having had a wonderful season, is longing to show that he is still number one, is really buzzing at the start of the match. In the first minute he takes a free kick from 35 yards. Five steps back as usual, rocking on his left leg, and the Portuguese shoots. A great shot. The ball spins, hitting Víctor Valdés on the chest, and he's unable to control it. In a final attempt to salvage the situation, Piqué anticipates the Korean Ji-Sun Park at the corner flag. Cristiano puts his head in his hands. Before Messi has

touched the ball, the white-shirted number 7 has given quite a performance: three shots and a yellow card for Piqué, who had tried to stop him with an obstructive foul. Manchester United's best play is coming from Cristiano's boots. In contrast, Lionel has yet to enter the game. His father, Jorge, sees it too: 'I saw that Leo was out of the game for quite a while, and only once we scored the goal I began to see him get more involved.' In fact, the Flea does not make an appearance until nine minutes after Eto'o has put Barcelona in front. He leaves the right-hand touchline, looks to move into the centre, and unleashes a cracking shot from 35 yards – gliding low just above the ground. Messi is playing as a dummy centre forward to force the Manchester United central defenders out of position – something Ferguson would later say 'surprised us and made it difficult for us to mark him'. It seems to be true, because every time the Argentine has the ball between his feet, he causes problems for the English team's defence. Barça begin to take control of the game and although it is not his best night and he only manages to infiltrate the forest of white shirts a few times, Messi is getting better and better. Manchester United's French left back, Patrice Evra – the man who won them the duel with Lionel in April 2008 (0-0 in the first leg, 1-0 in the return leg) – had already predicted it: 'Messi is "hungrier" and he is a better player now than he was a year ago.' He is right: 84 per cent of Leo's passes are on target. His angles are close to perfection, so much so that a veteran like Ryan Giggs says: 'When you see how they move you can't help but be amazed.' Then comes the 70th minute, when the Flea ascends to the Roman heavens. The smallest (it is worth noting that he is 1.69m) becomes the greatest.

The action: Xavi recovers the ball after a short rebound from the English defence, he heads towards the box, lifts his head and sends in a cross with spin – smooth and precise. With his back to the defenders, Messi goes up for it,

very high, and heads the ball in at the opposite post from where the goalie is. It's 2-0.

The explanation: 'When Xavi got the ball I got in position because I thought he would pass it there: I saw that Van Der Sar was a little off his line and I headed it.'

The photo: Messi suspended in the air, immobile, high, very high, leaning back. The ball, travelling on its arc, seems like it's going over the bar. In front, Van Der Sar, in yellow, watches it, open-mouthed, with a look of terror on his face. Close, very close, although out of focus, Rio Ferdinand, twenty centimetres taller than the Argentine, could do nothing to prevent that jump.

The precedent: Many people were betting on the number 10 scoring for Barça in the final. The bookies were offering very short odds. But few would have predicted a header. Up until that point he had only scored two. Pep Guardiola – who psyched up his players before the final by showing a clip from Ridley Scott's *Gladiator* – had been the only one to prophesy it. At a press conference in Santander on 1 February 2009, the day before the match against Racing, when asked if Messi needed to score more headers in order to become the best player in the world, the coach from Santpedor replied: 'I advise you not to test him because one day he'll score an incredible header and shut you all up.'

The curiosity: 'I didn't see my son's goal,' admits Jorge Messi, in the stands with his wife Celia, Leo's siblings and their respective families. 'At that moment I looked down, I don't know if it was due to nerves. I saw it afterwards on TV and I had honestly never seen him jump so high. But when did he take off his boot?' Because no sooner has his son come back down to earth – and before being inundated with hugs from his team-mates – than he does a lap holding up his new blue boot, as homage to Argentina. Meanwhile, the 20,000 Barça fans in the Olympic stadium chant his

name. At the end of the match, he is the first to be hugged by Guardiola – the man who has been so good to him. And what of the other competitor in the duel? Cristiano Ronaldo? He finishes the match powerless and wound up, he argues with Rooney, and receives a yellow card for a pointless foul on Puyol. Later, hurt, and already in his suit, he says: 'It wasn't a match between Messi and me, but his team was better than us, and he was too because he scored.'

The defeated pays homage to the victor. This time, Leo does feel that the cup is his. He kisses it, he hugs it, he adores it, he takes it on a lap around the ground, and he parties until three in the morning with his team-mates, friends and family. 'I feel like the happiest man in the world. It's like I'm dreaming, it's the most important victory of my life. I dedicate it to my family and to Argentina. This team deserves it after the great work they have put in all year,' declares Messi. Great work, and some marvellous football, exquisite, as recognised by the media across the world. But the front cover photos and the big headlines are reserved for the Flea. 'Messi, king of Europe,' runs the headline in *Corriere dello Sport*, the Rome sports paper; 'SuperMessi,' says the *Gazzetta dello Sport*; 'Messi and Barcelona on top of the world,' reads the headline in *La Nación* in Buenos Aires. Meanwhile, Buenos Aires sports paper *Olé* carries a picture of Leo with the cup, with the caption: 'Don't ask me to head it.' 'Marvellous Messi is too much for United,' reads the headline in *The Times*, which opts for the same photo as *El País.* A smiling Messi, pointing his fingers in the air, and a matter-of-fact headline: 'Messi is the best'. And no one argues.

2 May 2009, Bernabéu stadium, Madrid. The 34th match day of La Liga: Real Madrid-Barcelona

There is no contest; no possible comparison can be made. Two completely distinct worlds. Two different ways of

understanding football, but when they eventually come face to face, there is no league position that matters, and no run of winning results that counts. The cruel, numerical reality unfolds on the pitch at the Bernabéu: six goals against two – something that has never been seen before. The greatest humiliation in the Whites' history. The Blaugrana had never previously scored six goals at the Bernabéu; the result that came closest was 0-5 in 1974, when one Johan Cruyff played for Barça. And to think that before that sweltering Madrid night, Whites coach Juande Ramos and his boys thought they could win it. They were intending to close the gap, move within one point of Barcelona and joyfully sing their way through their last four Liga fixtures. Deep down they have reasons to be optimistic: they have come a long way since Barça beat them at the Nou Camp on 13 December 2008 (2-0, with goals from Eto'o and Leo, obviously), relegating them to twelve points. Despite an internal crisis which has affected the club, leading to Ramón Calderón's dismissal, the Whites have broken records: 52 points out of a possible 54, eighteen games without loss. In contrast to the Champions League (they were eliminated in the final sixteen 0-5 by Rafa Benítez's Liverpool), when it comes to La Liga they are still hopeful. True, this Barça team, together with Messi – who has already scored 21 goals in the championship – inspire fear. But when asked if he has thought about copying Chelsea manager Guus Hiddink's plan (implemented in the first leg of the Champions League semi-finals) the Real Madrid manager insists: 'I have no anti-Messi plan because taking him out doesn't guarantee anything. We have to try not to let Barcelona have a good day and work hard together as a team.' It is hard work that seems to bear fruit in the thirteenth minute, when Pipita Higuaín puts them ahead. But it's an illusion. The teams are worlds apart, because the men in blue-and-claret shirts

emanate football from every pore. They represent the beauty of the game in its purest form, the art of sophisticated play to the nth degree of potential. They play with ease, the passes are so precise and fluid it is as if they are in a training session. They ridicule the Whites. The white ball slides from side to side across the green carpet, bam, boom, until it finds someone who transforms it into an idea, into something magical, or simply into a chance at goal. Like Leo, for example, who lifts the ball lightly; it sails over Sergio Ramos, who tries desperately to reach it, and lands delicately at the feet of Henry, who puts it elegantly and efficiently past Casillas to finish. Good grief, where would Real Madrid be without 'Saint' Iker? The shots are coming from every angle and there are too many to count. It is a real nightmare for the Real goalie. Guardiola's men waste opportunities: out of selfishness, as is the case with Messi, who really wants to score against Madrid (in his previous three trips to the Bernabéu he has never once scored) and who fails to see his unmarked team-mate; or out of too much generosity, as is the case with Iniesta's yellow boots, which, after a duet of one-twos all the way up the pitch with the Argentine, do not seal the deal, and give the ball to the Flea who shoots at close range – blocked by Iker. But in any case, by the 45th minute there have already been three goals scored. After one from Henry, and one from Puyol, the captain, the half-time scoreboard is closed by Leo, who finally experiences the joy of scoring on the Whites' home turf. Xavi, the king of the night, steals the ball from Lass Diarrá in the middle. He offers it to Leo, who finishes it with a shot at the near post. The Bernabéu falls silent and the sandwich which is traditionally eaten in the break before kick-off tastes more bitter. The game recommences and it seems that Pep Guardiola's men do not want to be cruel to such renowned opponents. The Liga chasers bounce back

momentarily when Sergio Ramos heads in a Robben free kick to close the gap. But it lasts for a matter of minutes. The Barça players control the game as they please. And the goals score themselves: because Xavi, the 'doctor', creates ever more beautiful assists; because Iniesta makes one dribbling run after another; because Henry makes a laughing stock of Ramos and scores his second goal; because Messi is like a spirit who appears on any part of the pitch, wherever you least expect him. Casillas is not expecting him either, and finds himself on his backside, while the ball slides into the net. That makes five, and the kid from Rosario can run towards the cameras, holding his blue-and-claret shirt up between his teeth, showing the one beneath, which has a flower and the words 'Síndrome X Frágil'. For a while now, Leo has collaborated with the Catalan organisation that helps families who have children affected by fragile X chromosome syndrome (FXS) – also known as Martin-Bell syndrome. It is a genetic disorder passed down through families that can cause serious difficulties: from learning problems to diminished intellectual capacity. It affects one in every 4,000 boys and one in every 6,000 girls, and one in 250 women is a carrier without having any symptoms. It is not the first time that Messi is helping this organisation. In 2008 he was a patron of the book *39 historias solidarias alrededor del deporte* (*39 Stories of Solidarity in Sport*), written by Catalan journalists who donated the proceeds of its sale to the organisation. But this gesture of solidarity and this goal dedication is beamed around the world and tells millions of people about a genetic problem as yet under-researched. It is an example of how a ball in the back of the net can serve as something more than just a football result. But let's return to a game which has no precedent, because Barça are unstoppable. Gerard Piqué is a good example, he is majestic at the back – he doesn't make a single mistake

– and up front he manages to score the sixth goal, the goal that brings sadness. Real Madrid's Liga career is over. And no one will knock Barcelona off the top spot, since they are now seven points clear. And perhaps no one would have knocked them off even if the result had been different. But this match serves as a reminder of the show put on by Leo Messi and Guardiola's Blaugrana team throughout the entire season, in Spain as well as in Europe. And it closes a dark chapter for Madrid: the Whites just have to wait for the elections, a new president, or better still, a saviour (Florentino Pérez), who, with a few million, will rebuild this weak team, who up until this point had been champions. But there is something more: the 2-6 scoreline also tastes of revenge. The last time Barça visited the Bernabéu, on 7 May 2008, the players stood in two lines to form a walkway onto the pitch in order to honour Real Madrid, who had recently been declared Liga champions. It was a morbid match. And it finished in a resounding 4-1 defeat – a double humiliation for the Catalans. 'Before the match,' declared Leo to the *Gazzetta dello Sport,* 'we said we weren't thinking about getting "revenge" for the walkway from the previous year, but evidently, deep down, there was still a thorn in our sides which bothered us. More because of the result and the way in which we had lost than because of the walkway ... We removed the thorn brilliantly.'

13 May 2009, Mestalla stadium, Valencia. Final of the Copa del Rey: Athletic Bilbao-Barcelona

'Messi is the king' proclaims a yellow placard, which is being waved in the curve of the stadium where the Barcelona fans are sitting. No offence intended to Juan Carlos, king of Spain, who is watching the match from the stands, but the Barça fans are right. In his first final since he joined the Blaugrana first team, Leo is crowned king of the pitch. He

plays and he creates play, he scores and he creates goals. Nothing like Diego Armando Maradona did 25 years previously, on 5 May 1984, in the same final against Athletic. At the final whistle (the match had ended with the Bilbao Lions winning 1-0 thanks to a goal from Endico), Maradona aimed a kick at Sola and set off an impressive fight on the Bernabéu pitch. Practically all of the players were implicated in the battle. Maradona – who was appearing in his last fixture in a Barça shirt and was packing his bags for Napoli – wanted revenge over Athletic defender Andoni Goikoetxea, who had broken his leg nine months earlier. The result: an incredible punch-up and a three-month ban for six players. At that time the Golden Boy was 24, while the Flea is still only 21, but he seems more mature than Diego. He shows no sign of nerves and, together with Xavi, he is the central figure in the Blaugrana performance. He has a hand in three of Barcelona's four goals, which put paid to Athletic's dreams of winning their 24th cup. The Bilbaoans have the advantage, and they proudly resist until the second half when, just at the right moment, Messi appears. Leo makes a beautiful pass to Eto'o – the Cameroonian shoots hard across goal, Gorka Iraizoz responds, the ball rebounds freely. Keeping incredibly cool, the Barça number 10 goes for the shot and scores. It is 1-2 – the deciding goal of the match. The Flea's show continues: a perfect pass to Bojan, which he finishes like a pro to make it three. He also plays a part in the fourth: Leo provokes the foul, which Xavi converts with a fantastic free kick into the net. Then Messi looks for the pass that allows Eto'o to score – a reward for his self-denial throughout the entire match. And were it not for Gorka, who saves it with his foot, the Cameroonian almost would have made it. Barça win their 25th Copa del Rey. Mestalla is a scene of celebrations and Leo's name is the most chanted. And next day *Marca* writes:

'Messi hardly ever fails in this type of fixture, and yesterday he showed once again that he is the most decisive player of the Spanish Liga. The titles are beginning to rain down on this footballer who, without a doubt, will be the symbol of an era.'

23 August 2009, Nou Camp stadium, Barcelona. Return leg of the Spanish Super Cup: Barcelona-Athletic Bilbao

He didn't play in the first leg in San Mamés, but in the return leg, a week later, Lionel is on the pitch from the first minute onwards. Alongside him is the brand-new Blaugrana signing: Zlatan Ibrahimović, signed in exchange for 45 million euros and Samuel Eto'o's transfer to Inter. Without Leo, Ibrahimović and the injured Iniesta, Pep's team returned from Bilbao with a 1-2 result (goals from De Marcos, Xavi and Pedro) and the Super Cup almost in the bag. In reality it is a strange final, since Barça should have had to play against themselves, being both Liga and Copa del Rey champions, but the organisation has stipulated that they should face the Copa del Rey runners-up, Athletic Bilbao. It makes no difference, because in front of their fans, Barça are in fact playing Barça: although they are persistent and they put up a noble fight, the Athletic players are mere testimonial witnesses. The Flea is on hand again to make an impact and, as on other occasions, starts off slowly, but when he gets going he is lethal – when he passes as much as when he finishes. He starts off by wasting a face-to-face chance against Iraizoz, the Bilbaoan goalkeeper. He follows that up by setting up the new arrival (Ibrahimović) in a brilliant sequence, where the Argentine passes and the Swede controls it on his chest, before finishing it by shooting over the goalie. He sums it all up with a sensational move that breaks through the Lions' defence. Xavi passes to Ibrahimović, the striker backheels it to Messi, and the Argentine dodges past the central

defender with his left foot, in order to bounce the ball into the goalmouth with his right. He creates an impossible, fantastic goal – the goal of a real superstar. It is the advantage that has been a while coming, because throughout the first half, Barça have not been very precise when it comes to finishing. They had been lacking shots on target, but along comes Messi, who kick-starts the party with his incredible goal and finishes it up from the penalty spot in the 67th minute. After a confusing exchange that results in a foul on Alves – according to the referee – Leo places the ball on the spot and makes no mistake in getting it in the back of the net, to the right of Gorka. The game is already won, but before the festivities begin, Bojan is able to add his goal to the celebrations. It is Barça's fourth consecutive title. And it's not over yet.

28 August 2009, Stade Louis II, Monaco. UEFA Super Cup: Barcelona-Shakhtar Donetsk

'Leo left it to me. The assist was practically a goal, I just had to tap it in,' says Pedro Eliezer Rodríguez Ledesma, better known as Pedrito. He is a 22-year-old Brazilian player, and Barcelona's number 17. He arrived at Barcelona as a boy of fifteen, and is one of eight called upon by Pep Guardiola for the seemingly endless UEFA Super Cup match. The eternal reserves player just signed his first professional contract with Barça on 20 August; he is the striker who won the Champions League after only playing one minute of football and without even touching the ball. Well … in the 81st minute Pedrito comes on for Zlatan Ibrahimović and in the 115th, after a back-and-forth with Messi, he finds the perfect angle, the gap just by Pyatov's goalpost, in order to draw a line under a gruelling match and win Barça their fifth cup of the season. But in reality, and with great humility, the little Brazilian recognises that the credit belongs to Messi.

It has not been an easy match. The strategy designed by Mircea Lucescu, the sly dugout veteran, is working. The defence organised by the Romanian coach blocks successive attacks by Guardiola's men. They have to wait until half an hour into the game before seeing their first result. After a free kick, Leo, dribbling quickly and craftily, sees his shot blocked twice by the Ukrainian goalkeeper. But the Barça number 10 and his team-mates never tire of looking for the gaps, undeterred by the fact that Lucescu's men turn the counter-attack into their greatest weapon.

And here goes Leo Messi again, free kick just on the edge of the area. The ball is intercepted on its arc by the players in the wall. Leo and the other Blaugrana players protest. They demand a penalty. According to them, a defender has blocked the ball with his elbow. The first half ends and in the second half things are not much different. On the Stade Louis II pitch, in terrible conditions, the scoreline does not budge. The nerves are starting to show – so much so that after breaking away into the area only to end up in a tangle of opponents, Leo pushes a Shakhtar defender and finds himself head to head with Darijo Srna – an offence that earns him a caution.

There are five minutes of extra time remaining, five minutes until penalties, when Leo creates a brilliant pass to Pedrito. It is shot number 21 for Barça, and it is the victory shot. The Brazilian kicks it with his right while falling to the ground and sends this Barça team on their way to being legendary. It is the goal that brings Pep's team in line with Barça's five-cup team: the magnificent team made up of Ramallets, Martín, Biosca, Seguer, Gonzalvo III, Bosch, Basora, César, Vila, Kubala and Manchón. In the 1951–52 season, coach Ferdinand Daucik won La Liga, the Copa de España, the Copa Latina, the Copa Eva Duarte (named after Evita) and the Copa Martini & Rossi. It's a team that lives on

in the collective memory of the Blaugrana fans. Although, if truth be told, that group, led by Ladislao Kubala, won three titles on the pitch and the other two without playing. They did not play the Copa Duarte (which is today the Spanish Super Cup), since they were both Liga and Copa del Rey champions, and the Copa Martini & Rossi was the cup given to the team that scored the most league goals. By contrast, Leo's Barça have won all five cups on the pitch. All that remains is the FIFA Club World Cup, in December, to complete the set and break all the records. It will be the final chapter in the incredible Blaugrana saga.

But man cannot live on trophies and cups alone ... although, for Messi, football is very important. But first and foremost are his family, both present, and perhaps ... future. On this note, this year more than others, Leo has had his ups and downs. He has been extremely preoccupied with regard to the health of one family member (luckily everything has been resolved, it was a big scare and nothing more), but he has also been lucky enough to spend almost two months with his family. 'They were all here in Castelldefels, my uncles and aunts, my cousins, and it's always lovely when the house is full of family,' says Leo. And there's more: he has begun a romantic relationship. He admits to it on 25 January 2009 on *Hat Trik*, a Catalan TV programme. In front of the cameras, a boy asks him the most difficult question: 'Do you have a girlfriend?' And, after sticking out his tongue, he replies: 'I have a girlfriend and she's in Argentina. The truth is, I'm OK and I'm calm about it.' On 22 February, a month after his TV interview, he is seen in the streets of Sitges with his arm around a tanned girl with long hair. It kick-starts the race between the tabloids to find out the identity of the mystery girlfriend. She is the first official one after all the supposed squeezes attributed to him by the Argentine tabloids. Like the Rosario model Macarena

Lemos, before the 2006 World Cup, or eighteen-year-old Nerina, or the Argentine sex bomb Luciana Salazar.

Antonella Roccuzzo is a nineteen-year-old from Rosario, she is a Newell's fan, she studies nutrition and she is nothing like any of the fantasies concocted by the tabloids. 'I have known her since I was five, she is the cousin of my best friend (Luca Scaglia), and she's a Rosarina like me. I have seen her grow up and she has seen me grow up. Our families know each other, so I didn't have any doubts,' Leo tells Buenos Aires newspaper *Clarín* in May. He says that they have been in a relationship for a year. He has managed to keep it a secret because 'I'm discreet,' he says, adding: 'and if we hadn't decided to walk through Sitges during the carnivals, nobody would have known.' But the news is official and the two are photographed again in June in Buenos Aires, where Argentina are playing two qualifying matches for the South Africa World Cup. There is a family photo taken in the city streets, with Antonella arm-in-arm with Celia, Leo's mother. Marriage on the horizon?

No. 'I'm not getting married for the moment,' declares Leo. But the romance continues. We will wait ... Leo has all he needs in order to keep both them and future generations comfortable: on 18 September 2009, he renews his contract with Barcelona for the fourth year running. He will receive more than 10 million euros a year – the highest amount for any Blaugrana footballer, and his buyout clause is increased from 150 to 250 million euros. A new contract that will terminate on 30 June 2016, when the Flea will be 29 years old. The future is guaranteed. All that is missing is the cherry on the cake of the happiest year of his life: the Ballon d'Or and the title of best player in the world. 'A dream. The best you can achieve as an individual,' as he says in an interview with L'Equipe TV. 'Who is your favourite for this year?' they ask him. 'I hope that this year it will be my turn.'

Chapter 32

Third time lucky

1, 19 and 21 December 2009

Yes – this time, it is his turn. This time, the saying 'third time lucky' comes true. After coming third in 2007 and second in 2008, Lionel Andrés Messi wins *France Football* magazine's 2009 Ballon d'Or. And he wins it by a mile – Messi gets 473 out of a possible 480 points, more than double the score of Cristiano Ronaldo, the runner-up, who is awarded 233 points. Xavi Hernández comes in third with 173 points. Ninety of the award's 96 voters vote for Leo as their number one player; and with 98.54 per cent of the maximum number of points possible, nobody in the 54-year history of this prestigious prize has won it as convincingly or unanimously as Messi. Only Michel Platini, who won it in 1984 with 98.46 per cent of the possible points, has come close. It is a true triumph. According to the editor-in-chief of *France Football*, Denis Chaumier, there are three reasons for his success:

1. Messi's *coups de théâtre*, his dribbling, his acceleration, his efforts to destabilise the opposition, his talent, his creative spirit and his sense of teamwork, along with some of his goals, have made a profound impression throughout the year. His influence within football is still not complete, but what I find marvellous is the fact that the sheer joy and impertinence of his

presence on the pitch resemble those of a certain Maradona.

2. We shouldn't forget that despite his young age, Messi has been among the contenders for the Ballon d'Or several times. Clearly, modern football will not give its highest honour to a flash in the pan, even one as impressive as Messi.
3. Messi is champion of Europe, of La Liga with Barcelona, winner of the European Super Cup and the Copa del Rey, and with the Argentine side has qualified for the final stages of the World Cup. It is hard to imagine a more remarkable run of achievements.

All sides are united in agreement on Messi's records, performances, talent, class and professional career. The journalists of *France Football*'s international voting panel have all bowed to the Flea. Tributes have poured in from around the world: from Japan to Iceland, from Ghana to New Zealand, from Kazakhstan to England. Describing his reasons for voting for Messi, the *Daily Telegraph* journalist Henry Winter writes in *France Football*:

> Messi? Pure genius. He has a special relationship with the ball. He creates and scores goals, and works ceaselessly for the good of the team. To see him play is to witness a marvellous spectacle that greatly benefits the beautiful game.

It is 7.00pm on Monday 30 November 2009 when *France Football*'s representatives knock on the door of Messi's chalet in Castelldefels to deliver the good news. Leo has been awaiting this news with impatience and excitement, along with his girlfriend Antonella, his brother Rodrigo and his

niece and nephew. When the *France Football* director tells him that he has won the award he responds with his usual timid smile, but his eyes are sparkling.

The announcement comes at the end of a fantastic week for both Leo and Barça. On Tuesday 24 November, in the fifth match of the Champions League, the Blaugrana, with Piqué and Pedro, 'achieved an angelic victory over José Mourinho's Inter in a devilish match', in the words of *El País.* Up until now the task of getting into the last sixteen seemed a very difficult one for Guardiola's men, but now it is within their reach. Messi was unable to play in that match as he had sustained a muscular injury while playing Athletic Bilbao at San Mamés on the final match day of La Liga, but on Sunday 29 November he is in the starting line-up for the classic derby against Cristiano Ronaldo's Real Madrid. This is the fourth time that the two superstars have met. The Portuguese player, who has been out of competition for more than 50 days, shows excellent form in the 66 minutes that he spends on the pitch. He leads the Madrid attack, but misses the best chance that the Whites get. His shot is turned away by Valdés, and for the fourth time he fails to score against Barça. Messi appears very little in the first half; he does not create play and his contribution is not decisive. He plays in the hole, behind the forwards but without his usual craftiness. However, in the second half, after Ibrahimović puts Barça ahead with an unstoppable left-footed shot and Busquets gets a red card, the Flea is once again at his best. He receives passes, brings others into play, asks questions of the Madrid defence, helps neutralise their attacks and invents two or three ingenious pieces of play. He contributes a great deal to the team just when they need it most. In the 88th minute he is in a position to make it 2-0. Alves crosses it into the centre from the right wing and Lionel shoots point-blank, which the incredible Casillas

saves. It would have been a great pleasure for Messi to score his eighth goal against the Madrid keeper – his last one was a penalty in the friendly between Spain and Argentina on 14 November – but, as he says in his post-match interview, 'it was not to be, because of Casillas' great save. The most important thing is that Barcelona won.' And in reply to any questions about the Ballon d'Or, he replies: 'This afternoon Victor Valdés deserves the Ballon d'Or. He saved us.' This may be true, but Lionel has won his showdown with the 2008 winner of the award, Cristiano Ronaldo. The match was the perfect scenario for the baton to be passed on.

So, on this Monday in Castelldefels there is more than enough reason to celebrate. Wearing a green-and-white sweatshirt, Leo joins his family and the guests from *France Football* as they drink a toast to the boy who couldn't grow, and to his entry into the pantheon of world football. Afterwards, there is time to talk and to look at the front page – and 43 other pages – that the magazine has dedicated to this 'Young King of Football'.

The next day sees more front pages devoted to Messi, a huge press conference and interviews.

It is a time for reflection, for hearts on sleeves and for dedications. 'I cannot lie – I had a feeling that it could happen this year – but the results of the ballot surprised me,' says Messi in the Nou Camp press room. 'This prize is an honour; it is wonderful and very special, but I wasn't obsessed with winning it. I knew that if it was meant to happen it would, but either way I would keep on working in the same way as always,' he explains. Someone asks him how he feels about being the first Argentine player to win it. 'It's a great honour. Of course, under the modern rules Diego [Maradona] would have won it more than once – and Di Stéfano and Sivori both won it, albeit under different nationalities.' (We should remember that it is only since

1995 that the Ballon d'Or was opened up to any footballer who played for a European club, regardless of where he was from. Alfredo Di Stéfano, who was born in Buenos Aires, won it in 1957 and 1959 with Spanish nationality and Omar Sivori, who won it in 1961, did so with Italian nationality despite having been born in San Nicolás.)

And since Leo belongs to Barça as much as he does to Argentina, he does not forget how valuable the prize is to his 'home' team: 'The fact that I am the first footballer trained in the Barça youth academy to win this award really helps the "Barça project", and is very important for both the club and the people who work at the club.' As always, though, he thanks his family and his team-mates and dedicates the award to them. 'Without them, I would not have won it,' he says emphatically. He adds that if he had been on the voting panel, he would have voted for one of his team-mates: 'Xavi and Iniesta deserved this prize as well,' he says. He especially acknowledges Pep Guardiola, saying: 'The boss had a lot to do with it. I knew him from Barça B but had never had direct contact with him. I believe he is a very intelligent man with a huge knowledge of football, and that he has the ability to transmit this knowledge to others in the best possible way. He is a coach who recognises the human side of his players, and because of this they all love him. The titles we have won with him have been key to this award.'

The Barça coach replies: 'Leo is the rightful winner because as a player he is simply on another level. He has everything – he is tough, quick, scores goals even with his head [and who would dare to argue with this after the goal he scored in this way in the Champions League final?] – he understands the game and dominates all the records. But the difference with Leo is in his head, in his competitive spirit.'

And the boss is not the only one who is full of praise. On

1 December the whole world is talking about 'the boy who became a legend'.

The best footballer of 2009 is crowned on 6 December 2009 at 11.00am, on the set of the French football television programme *Téléfoot*. This is where Denis Chaumier hands over the golden ball trophy in person. But the day before the ceremony, Messi has a match to play against Deportivo de La Coruña, in the Riazor stadium. The Flea celebrates his prize with two goals and some spectacular play. The spectators in the old Galician stadium shout 'Messi, Messi, Messi!' At midnight, after a 3-1 victory, Lionel goes into the changing room for a quick shower, as a private plane waits to take him to Paris Le Bourget airport. His flight lands in the French capital at 3.15am, and a car transports him to the Hotel George V in the eighth arrondissement. It's now 4.00am, but Lionel doesn't sleep; he spends the rest of the night listening to music (to be specific, Don Omar and DJ Flex), watching TV and chatting with his brothers Rodrigo and Matías and his sister, María Sol.

At 9.30am, the Parisian victory tour begins. Messi parades round the city, wearing a suit, tie and make-up, and stops in front of the Eiffel Tower before going into the television studio, where he is greeted by his former Barça teammate Lilian Thuram. Then he is installed in front of the cameras for applause, speeches and finally the presentation of the trophy. After that there is a photo session with his family, friends and Barça president Joan Laporta, as well as people from the club, *France Football* and the French TV channel TF1. The official car picks him up and crosses Paris again, heading towards TF1's headquarters at Boulogne-Billancourt. But before Messi can have lunch in the Louis XIII salon of the Hotel George V and return home, he has to give one last press conference. It is now that Leo, sitting on a stool, confesses that he was a little bit impatient to

receive the award, to lift the Ballon d'Or. Because six days can feel like a very long time. And he also surprises those present by admitting: 'I would love to win it again; it would be magnificent to win one more.'

Well, the boy has a lot of faith in himself, but we'll soon see. In the meantime, Barça have other challenges ahead. The first: ensuring they go through to the Champions League final sixteen. A very difficult match awaits Pep's men in Kiev. It is below zero degrees and Shevchenko and his team-mates are still convinced that they can go through. It's true that the Blaugrana have two useful results: they could lose by a goal or they could need to draw, depending on what happens at the Giuseppe Meazza in Milan where Inter and Rubin Kazan are playing at the same time as they are. But the main objective is to qualify first in the group to avoid the English superpowers: Chelsea, Manchester United and Arsenal. 'It's forbidden to speculate,' declares Guardiola, demanding that his players respect team etiquette and aim only for the victory. It will not be easy, because Dynamo go ahead after two minutes at the V. Lobanovskiy stadium, due to an error in the Catalan defence. Everything becomes complicated in the worst possible way: the 2008–09 champions are only one goal away from being knocked out. But Barça do not fall apart, they keep the ball from the Ukrainians, they push ahead without stopping, until they manage first to equalise (thanks to Xavi), and then to claim victory. It is sealed by Leo with a fantastic goal from a free kick. They have been pounding on Messi continually. He had the opportunity to equalise early on, but he wasn't able to take advantage of the bad clearance gifted to him by Shovkovskiy, and in the scuffle ended up losing his nerve in the area. Direct free kick in the 86th minute. It is the Flea who steps up to the ball: majestic execution, left-footed shot hammered into the back of the net. What a shame that

four minutes later Almeida tackles him from behind – the ninth time he has been fouled – and he falls to the ground, injured.

'Anyone else in his situation could retire on the Ballon d'Or,' comments Pep Guardiola after the match. 'But Leo has an unmatched competitiveness in his soul, such ambition, that he gets angry and even in difficulty he wants another goal and he says: "I'm going for it." He goes right for it, straight ahead.'

The medical report states that Messi is suffering from a grade one sprain of his right ankle. He cannot play in the derby against Espanyol, and his participation in the semi-final of the Club World Cup in Abu Dhabi is threatened. On Saturday 12 December at the Nou Camp Leo is not playing, but he takes to the pitch to parade the Ballon d'Or in front of the 84,554 spectators. Celia, his mother, is there to present it to him.

An emotional moment and huge applause, before the long trip to Abu Dhabi, where Barça will face Mexican club Atlante in the semi-final on Wednesday 16 December, Atlante having just beaten Auckland City 3-0.

The photos and the TV footage from the United Arab Emirates show Messi on the beach, in blue swimming trunks and with a bandaged ankle, training in order to recover in good time. Leo and the whole of Barça are immersed in the competition, concentrating extremely hard on training in the lead-up to the game against Atlante, who are known as the Iron Colts. All predictions favour the Catalans far above the CONCACAF champions, but the Barça fans have not forgotten the two finals they lost in 1992 and 2006. They need to psych themselves up from the start. That's the plan, but things don't go their way. Barcelona are losing 1-0 after five minutes at the Zayed Sports City stadium. In the 35th minute Sergio Busquets equalises. Nonetheless Barça

cannot handle Atlante. The Mexicans are defending well and they take advantage of the few opportunities they have, while the Blaugrana make fools of themselves and seem to lose the thread of the game. There is nothing to do but call on Messi. The Argentine, on the bench, was not planning to play unless absolutely necessary. But Barça have stalled, and Guardiola makes use of him in the 53rd minute. 'I knew that Messi was coming on judging by the screams from the crowd. I knew that his presence could upset the balance of the match,' Atlante manager José Cruz will say later, 'but I wasn't expecting him to do it so quickly.'

One minute, just one minute, is all it takes Leo to turn the match around and dictate the outcome. The Argentine manages to lose his marker while making a diagonal run, Ibrahimović sees him, spins around and offers him a beautiful and precise shot out deep. The Flea does the rest: perfect control, perfect sidestep around the Atlante goalie and, of course, perfect shot. The ball sputters forward into the net. It is his first touch, and it is 1-2; the Mexican resistance is over; Barça has woken up; Pedro nets the third, becoming the only footballer in history to have scored in six different club competitions in one season; now the eleven Blaugrana players can dedicate themselves to delighting the crowd with kicks and touches. Pure virtuoso. The chances come one after the other and Messi allows himself the luxury of missing another head-to-head with Vilar, the Argentine goalie, whom he knows well from the Albiceleste. And, once again, Messi has been the genie. José Cruz explains it as follows: 'Without Messi Barcelona is the best team in the world; when Leo plays they are from another galaxy.' There is nothing more to be said.

Only the final remains, on 19 December; only Estudiantes de La Plata, the Argentine team who have eliminated South Korean club Pohang Steelers 2-1 in the semi-final.

They are the team of the bald 'Brujita' ('little witch'), Juan Sebastián Verón, who was Leo's mentor in the 2007 Copa América, the globe-trotter who has become the team's central figure and dreams of repeating the achievements of his father Juan Ramón 'La Bruja' ('the witch') Verón. In 1968 the Estudiantes striker led the 'Rat Stabbers', as they are nicknamed, to victory in the Intercontinental Cup, beating Manchester United at Old Trafford.

It is certainly a dream given the forces on the pitch, but it lasts 89 minutes – almost the whole match, almost a miracle. The Argentines find the goal and the advantage towards the end of the first half (37th minute), with a clean header from Boselli, who finds a gap between Puyol and Abidal to finish Díaz's cross. Barça find themselves in the worst possible scenario: a goal down, no goals of their own, Messi with a yellow card to his name and, above all, a team that is lost and can find neither gaps in midfield, nor decisive passes. All the gaps are blocked by the Rat Stabbers' *trivote* (a formation of three defensive midfielders). Messi is invisible and Henry is nowhere to be found; Ibrahimović battles on with little effect.

By contrast, Estudiantes know exactly what to do: kill the game, block the ball and any initiative from the Barça players and recoil into their shell, not conceding even the slightest chance to their opponents, using all the tools at their disposal (fouls, clearances, letting the ball go out, substitutions, little kicks) to waste time, to get to the 90th minute and win the cup they so desire for the second time. Barça do not give up, they show all their strength of character, all their determination, they try again and again until Xavi gets it in the box in the final minutes. Piqué passes to Pedro who heads the ball, which collides with the net. They have equalised. Extra time. And Barça have won, the Argentines know it. Their faces say it all – they cannot hold up any more,

they cannot stand up to little Messi, who plays as though he were playing in a playground; he scores with his chest, with his heart, with the emblem on his shirt. He anticipates his friend Juan Sebastián Verón, and in the 110th minute he finishes Daniel Alves' cross with that move which no one was expecting.

Why did he shoot with his chest instead of with his head? 'I was trying to play it safely. I saw that the goalie was unprepared,' Leo will explain the following day in an interview with *El País.* 'I thought it would be enough to put it in gently, just to the side of the area he was blocking. Luckily it turned out well.'

Simple as always, and as always the Flea looks up to the heavens and dedicates his goal to his grandmother Celia and to God for everything he has been given. After that there are only celebrations in the Blaugrana camp and tears from Pep Guardiola, who has been overcome by emotion for once. Leo is the first to hug him and thank him, but he does not forget his opponents. He goes over to shake hands with all the Estudiantes players one by one, 'because they played fantastically, because they're Argentine, because they were very sad'. Third time lucky. After the 1992 and 2006 defeats, Barça win the trophy for the first time in the club's 110-year history. And the team are crowned kings of the world. No team has ever won six titles in one year. 'Right now I don't think we have fully realised what we have achieved,' confesses Messi to *El Periódico.* 'It will be difficult for another team to match this and, as time goes on, we will value it more and more.'

Barça have climbed to the top of the world, and Leo reaches the top once again on Monday 21 December in a snow-covered Zurich.

A few minutes after 9.00pm, UEFA president Michel Platini steps up to the podium accompanied by FIFA

president Joseph 'Sepp' Blatter. Before he opens the golden envelope, one last look at the candidates for the prize. They roll the clip showing the faces of Cristiano Ronaldo, Andrés Iniesta, Kaká, Messi and Xavi.

Platini says he is very proud that all those nominated play in European teams. Then comes the most important moment, the announcement: 'The FIFA World Player 2009 is Lionel Messi.'

Third time lucky. Again. After coming second in 2007 and 2008, Leo is the number one. The Barça number 10 gets up from his seat, buttons his Ermenegildo Zegna jacket, adjusts his blue tie and goes up on stage. Michel Platini hands him the prize and invites him to speak.

> Good evening. First of all I would like to thank all the players who voted. It is a great honour for me to receive this prize, because it has been given by players from other clubs and other national teams, and that's really wonderful. I would like to thank – and share this with – my team-mates [here the camera pans to Iniesta in the audience], this is the best possible finish to what has been a magnificent year for Barcelona, for my team-mates, and for me. Thank you very much.

Leo's voice is shaking and he is smiling more than ever. He has won, and he has done it by a landslide once again: 1,073 points, three times as many as Cristiano Ronaldo, who is second with 352, Xavi is third (196), Kaká fourth (190) and Iniesta fifth (134). The managers and captains of 147 countries have awarded him an overwhelming victory.

'This is priceless, it's priceless,' declares Jorge Messi, who is accompanied by Celia, Matías, Rodrigo and María Sol. 'To win a prize, or for the team to win a title, those are things that are possible to comprehend. But to win everything at

once, that was inconceivable,' says the Flea's father. And, quite emotional, he explains: 'It's the perfect end to a perfect year – more happiness would be impossible.'

'Planet Earth surrenders to Messi', say the headlines the following day, but it still remains for Leo to conquer the heart of one particular country; his country, Argentina. Because 'it annoys them that he still isn't a "Gardel" when it comes to the national team'. Moreover, because although they have qualified, with difficulty, for the South Africa World Cup, the Flea has never shone with the Albiceleste. 'Because in the Barcelona shirt he is transformed, and in the Argentine one he is not.' Yes, it's true, in Argentina they accuse him of a lack of affection towards his nation 'as if his lesser performance were due to a lack of motivation rather than the popularisation of a player who, with the Albiceleste, has more chance of winning the lottery than receiving a decent pass. Maradona has imposed a Messianic model,' writes David Gistau in *El Mundo*, 'in which Messi, the child of another time, does not fit; furthermore, he left Argentina very quickly – as if immersing himself in a kind of popular idolatry.' They do not realise that the problem does not lie with Messi, but rather with the team. They see him as a foreigner, they write 'Messi is not Argentine', because he has given all he can to Barça, he has given it his all in Europe and, what's more, he has ruined Estudiantes' dream, which was supported by practically the whole country. Yes, Messi has a problem with Argentines, or better, the Argentines have a problem with Messi. Leo knows it and it bothers him that they say that he does not care about the Albiceleste. And there is nothing that angers him more than when they say that he is not Argentine. 'What do they know about my feelings?' he exclaims. But this year the problem can be resolved. At the World Cup. All that is needed is for Leo to do what he does best.

Chapter 33

Floods of tears

3 July 2010

It's the 89th minute. Germany are on the attack. Miroslav Klose's efforts lead to the final goal, bringing the scoreline to 4-0. From the opponent's half, Messi keeps running. He reaches the halfway line, pauses for a moment with his hands on his hips, then sags and leans his hands on his knees. He feels like crying. The Argentine number 10 has lost his spark – head down, at a loss, disbelieving. Klose runs past him, jubilant.

At referee Ravshan Irmatov's final whistle, Lionel heads down to the dressing room. Juan Sebastián 'La Brujita' Verón and Argentina's fitness coach Fernando Signorini try to console him, Diego Armando Maradona gives him a hug and a kiss – but he is inconsolable. It's the Pelusa who later emphasises what Leo's tears mean when speaking at the press conference. 'Anyone who claims he isn't proud to play for his country is just plain stupid,' he snaps.

'It was very hard to see Messi in such a state in the dressing room,' explains Signorini. 'Some people might think that he has no right to be like that as he has so much going for him in his life, but that's why I bring in boys like him. They're earning millions of dollars but they're in floods of tears in the dressing room – it shows just how much it means to them inside.'

That's how Messi's World Cup ends, with tears of

frustration, pain and a sense of powerlessness. He leaves South Africa feeling empty, without having scored a single goal. He has failed to live up to the hopes of the Argentine fans – the dream that he would rival Maradona's achievements in the 1986 Mexico World Cup. And he has failed to cement his reputation within the Albiceleste. He is leaving 'his' World Cup without having shown his true self. Messi the Ballon d'Or winner. Messi, Barcelona's brightest star. But now he is just another fallen star like Wayne Rooney, Cristiano Ronaldo, Kaká or Franck Ribéry. It's a sad conclusion to a story that began so differently …

Forty-seven goals shine like 47 jewels in the crown of Lionel's 2009–10 season. He has won the Golden Boot, the honour reserved for Europe's highest goal scorer. No one has come close to matching his achievements. He has left the strikers in the Spanish, English, German and Italian leagues in the dust. Gonzalo Higuaín has 27, Didier Drogba 29, Arjen Robben 23, and Antonio Di Natale has scored 29.

In La Liga, Messi has played better than anyone else and better than ever – he has beaten all his previous scores since he joined the first team six years ago. He is the top scorer, with nine double goals and four hat-tricks. And with 34 league goals he has equalled Ronaldo's 1996–97 figure. He has also broken a record at Barça HQ: he is the youngest player in the Catalan club's history to score more than 100 league goals, and he has outstripped strikers such as Rivaldo, Romario and Eto'o.

They are 34 important goals which help win the league. Barça takes the title on the final match day of the season thanks to a definitive whitewash – 4-0 against Valladolid with two from Messi. They have reclaimed the title after a duel to the bitter end with Cristiano Ronaldo's Real Madrid. The Blaugrana have racked up 99 points out of a possible 114, another La Liga record. They have fought a

lively, magnificent championship, scoring 98 goals and conceding just 24. They have beaten Florentino Pérez's Whites at both the Nou Camp and the Bernabéu. And Lionel has surpassed Cristiano Ronaldo, the 2008 Ballon d'Or, the most expensive player in footballing history and star of Florentino's team. The kid from Rosario has made it to the top, winning four league titles in six seasons. But above all, he has grown in maturity and has demonstrated an inner sense of calm as a person and as a footballer.

'He's no longer trying to make the play of the century every time he gets the ball. He passes it more and he mixes it up,' explains Tito Vilanova, Pep Guardiola's right hand man. 'He has grown as a team player. He does a lot more damage and it's much more difficult to stop him now.'

It has been a spectacular season for Lionel, with just two setbacks. The first is on 13 January 2010 against Sevilla at the Ramón Sánchez Pizjuán stadium. Barcelona are playing like a dream, at the top of their game, creating countless chances – but Palop blocks everything and they only manage to get one past him. Thanks to a first leg scoreline of 1-2 at the Nou Camp, Sevilla knock the Blaugrana out of the Copa del Rey. It's the first time Barça have let a title get away in the whole of Guardiola's reign. Messi is distraught. Words of comfort from his teammates and his Argentine friend Gaby Milito fall on deaf ears.

'A different person would have said, "Never mind, I'm the world champion, I've still got La Liga!"' explained Guardiola. 'But not him. He was the most upset out of everyone.'

The second setback occurs on 28 April 2010 at the Nou Camp. Following on from a fantastic defensive effort and a perfect game in Milan, José Mourinho's Inter succeed in knocking Barça out of the Champions League. The European champions are out in the semi-final and they won't be going to the much coveted final at the Bernabéu.

The comeback that the fans have been dreaming about is not to be. They are left with a consolation goal from Piqué in the 84th minute which does nothing to dent the 3-1 scoreline from the San Siro match. It is not enough to earn them their ticket to Madrid.

Barcelona's efforts are crushed by Inter's eleven men – and even by ten men after Motta's sending off. The same Messi who had scored four goals against Wenger's Arsenal has not managed a single goal against any team managed by Mourinho – Chelsea or Inter. His performance is not exactly noteworthy, but Guardiola still defends him. 'There is no reason to criticise him. They had six defending so he always had two men on him, regardless of whether he was in the middle or on the wing.' Defending the whole team, he says: 'They have nothing to apologise for after the game they've played. I'm very proud of all of them.' His message to the locals is clear: he is sorry he cannot lead them to Madrid and he promises to try again next year. But for now, he assures them that 'we'll pick ourselves up and carry on'.

And they do. On 16 May, the whole town chants, 'We are the champions, Barça are the champions.' During the title celebrations, Lionel grabs the microphone and yells, 'Come on Argentina, you sons of bitches!' The blue and claret fans clap and cheer. They want him to play well for his country. And so does the whole of Argentina.

'We've all dreamed of lifting the World Cup. Not because it makes you a more important player, but simply because there is nothing more beautiful in the world. I left the 2006 World Cup in tears after that defeat by Germany. I hope to leave South Africa crying too – but this time crying tears of joy,' declares Lionel at Ezeiza airport in Buenos Aires where he has touched down for the national team's training camp.

He adds: 'Playing with the national team is completely different from playing in Barcelona because of the lack of

time to train and practise. That's not to say that the international teams are worse – they're the best in the world – but we don't have much time to work, everything happens very quickly. Two days, and then a game. When we're all together, in a group and with plenty of time, then it's different. When we go to the tournament we'll keep ourselves to ourselves and stay calm and reserved. We're not the favourites, and that's good because that means we can create big surprises.'

This time, the Flea commands all the attention from the media as well as from fans from all over the world. Even the Cuban leader Fidel Castro, who has not appeared in public for four years due to serious illness, weighs in on Lionel's genius. In an article entitled 'On the Threshold of Tragedy' – dedicated to denouncing imperialist scandals in the United States – he writes that the Argentine striker 'is as quick as a bolt of lightning and fires the ball with incredible speed, with both his feet and his head'.

In Argentina, Lionel scores points in the eternal comparison with Maradona, despite the fact that many of his compatriots' hearts still beat for Diego. If Messi could be explosive for Argentina and lift the cup the fans have been dreaming about since 1986, then perhaps he would escape the Pelusa's shadow once and for all. Maradona-Messi, Messi-Maradona … the relationship appears to have found stability after all the back and forth, all the criticism and contradictory statements, and all the references to the Oedipus complex.

Since Diego's arrival in the Albiceleste dugout, Lionel has played eleven games and has only scored three goals. His worst moment with the team is on 14 October 2009, when he is accused of not celebrating Mario Bolatti's goal against Uruguay which seals Argentina's place in South Africa. His mother, Celia, has to intervene to defend her son. 'He is extremely hurt when people speak badly about

him. Why are they always out to get him? It really affects him and he finds it difficult to get over.'

And Lionel does not deal well with crises, as his Barcelona team-mates are well aware. But he gets no support from Maradona. Fed up, he calls the selector to tell him that he doesn't want to play for the Albiceleste anymore. Realising the gravity of the situation, Diego heads over to Barcelona. There, the two of them speak openly for the first time. The coach tells him not to worry, that things will be different from here onwards. And in that moment, the relationship between Leo and Diego is transformed.

Diego starts to indulge his protégé, and before the final pre-World Cup friendly against Canada, on Argentine soil, he affirms: 'I don't know what people think of Leo, but I can tell you what I think of him. I think he is the best in the world. And he's Argentine. I've already told the boys: "If Leo gets the ball, we'll have plenty of chances." I'm trying to get it into their heads that they're a team. And that we need Messi to play the way he does at Barça. Messi knows that his team-mates want him to be the cherry on the cake. He needs to lead them. We don't want him there as a soloist – not in training and not on the pitch. When we're playing, they can't pass it to me anymore … so if they don't pass it to Messi, then we're getting it wrong.'

The Pelusa looks out for him, he vouches for him, he confides in him, but at the same time he is cautious, in light of his own experiences. 'Messi has a lot more support than I had before the Mexico World Cup in 1986,' explains Maradona. 'But you just have to play the game. In Mexico I was on the attack, I was taking control of the ball and the team. I got things going and my team-mates followed me. I've explained it to Leo so that he can do the same in South Africa, and he gets it. We've talked about it a lot and I try to make sure he's okay.'

At the start of the training camp, he tells the group leaders to 'make Messi feel like the best'. And to ensure he is well taken care of, he puts him in a room with 'La Brujita' Verón – who was Lionel's mentor in the 2007 Copa América. The two players get on well. 'I keep an eye on them,' concedes Maradona in an interview with Argentine newspaper *Clarín*. 'La Brujita is a football buff – he knows a lot more than Leo. But they get engrossed in conversation and the Gaucho is enchanted, it's lovely to see.'

When Lionel speaks, it's clear that he is calm and content, ready to play and ready to make waves. And the first group match against Nigeria is fast approaching. At the pre-match press conference, Maradona gifts the media the following day's headline: 'Argentina is still a Rolls-Royce – but now it's driven by Messi.' And, as if it were no big deal, he tells him to be a fantastic leader and the best player of all time.

On Saturday 12 June at Johannesburg's Ellis Park, Lionel is the subject of a flurry of attention and compliments. He is the best in Argentina. He lights up the Albiceleste's game, he understands the needs of the team and he is the most active member of the Argentine attack. He does everything: he plays in the hole, he's on the wing, he's a striker, he puts in crosses. He creates the most chances in front of goal (wasted by Tévez and Higuaín), he is the most enthusiastic, and he takes the most shots at goal – eight. Four are on target, but the goals are denied by Nigeria's miracle-worker goalkeeper Vincent Enyeama, who also plays for Lille Olympic Sporting Club in France. His outstanding performance will later earn him man of the match.

'I have to thank God and Messi for this trophy, because my saves were the work of God,' Enyeama says afterwards. 'I believe in God and despite studying Messi's Liga goals extensively, I wouldn't have been able to do anything

without God's help. Secondly, I have to say that if I hadn't come face to face with the best player in the world, then I would not have received this recognition.'

At the end of the match, won by a header from Gabriel Heinze, Maradona rushes over to Messi and lifts him up in his arms. He squeezes him tight against his Tarantino-worthy suit and tie, and kisses him energetically. The Pelusa is the only manager in World Cup history to kiss his players after every game and every substitution, but his two kisses to Messi are a tribute, in recognition of what he has done for the whole team.

'Messi was on the ball all day. When he has the ball he has fun, and while he's having fun he entertains us all,' Diego remarks at the press conference later, while munching on an apple. The Pelusa is not the only one singing the Flea's praises. The Argentine and Spanish press are unanimous: Lionel has played better than the rest of the team and he has led his team to victory – a victory which should have been greater. The consensus is that the position in the hole behind the forwards that Maradona has created for the Rosarino is working well, and it is closer to the ideal formation used in Diego's own heyday. The problems in defence and midfield have not gone unnoticed by the pundits – and nor have the changes made by the selector, which created difficulties for the team in the final minutes. But at least they are through to the second round thanks to the victory – and Messi.

Argentina wakes up happy the following day. And on 13 June, accompanied by Gonzalo Higuaín, Lionel enters the press room in the Argentine camp in Pretoria with the same calm demeanour as always. 'It was a good match. I had a lot of freedom of movement and I was really well supported by my team mates. I had a lot more touches. I was

shooting from slightly further back than before, and I preferred that because I still had the option of going forward.'

The press ask him about the possible 'Messidependence' of the Argentine team. He replies: 'This team doesn't depend on me. On the contrary, I'm the one who depends on the midfielders getting me the ball.' As always, not a hint of superstar attitude. 'I'm just one member of the team,' he says, and it's clear that in this particular team he feels happy. 'I feel as comfortable here as I do in Barcelona,' he confirms, adding: 'I knew that without the pressure of qualifiers we would play better. I really enjoyed myself against Nigeria.'

Things have certainly changed, and the past is far behind now, as he explains to TyC Sports: 'In the national team I hadn't been myself. I wasn't playing the way I was at Barcelona, and it was noticeable. But I always had Diego's support and everything changed thanks to my team-mates' belief in me. I put the qualifiers out of my mind and I knew that we could start afresh at the World Cup. I had to take advantage of that. Now that I'm here I'm going to show everyone what I'm made of and I just have to keep doing that. I would love for everyone in Argentina to feel about me the way they do in Barcelona. I have to keep proving myself, but thank God I'm on the right track.'

So much so that even after the whole squad has had a chance to shine, it's clear that the Barcelona player is still the most valuable. No one has played better than the Flea. And the show continues. Against South Korea he excels in the hole, up front, and as general playmaker. Maradona positions him in front of Mascherano, the sweeper in midfield, and behind the battalion: Maxi, Tévez, Higuaín and di María.

The Flea organises the game, he gets the ball moving, he takes the free kicks and corners, and he gifts stunning passes to the strikers. He has a hand in each of Argentina's

four goals. He takes the free kick which Park Chu-Young puts in his own net; he crosses for 'Pipita' Higuaín's first goal; then he zigzags between the Korean defenders, shoots, Jung blocks the goal with his foot, his second attempt is just wide of the post but Pipita picks it up for his second goal. And to finish it off, he sets up the perfect assist for Kun, who then gives Pipita his hat-trick – scored right in front of the tournament organisers. Argentina goes from being condemned to ridicule to being one of the favourites.

According to Spanish newspaper *El País,* Messi is becoming 'another Xavi'. He hasn't hit the jackpot in terms of goals, but everyone is convinced that it will happen eventually, or rather, he'll get fed up with the status quo. The one who is most sure is Maradona. He is hoping that in the Greece match in Polokwane on 22 June he will see a similar performance to his own against the Greeks in the United States in 1994 – his last Albiceleste game before being sent home from the World Cup for failing a drug test. With the last sixteen almost within reach, Diego sends out his reserve team. But Leo is still playing because, explains the selector, 'to have a player of his level and to leave him on the bench would be a sin ... a sin against the team, against the crowd and against ourselves'.

The Pelusa has a big surprise in store for his number 10, which he tells him the day before in his room. Messi is overjoyed. He will be wearing the captain's armband for the first time. After a tough match hampered by the cold at the Peter Mokaba stadium in Polokwane, Argentina beat Greece 2-0 and claim their place in the last sixteen with three group-stage victories. The captain has endured the close marking of Papastathopoulos. The number 19 has stuck to Messi like glue the entire game. And whenever Lionel has managed to dodge away from him, he finds himself surrounded by another three white shirts. From the dugout, Maradona

is pained to see them continually fouling his student – he hates seeing him so held back. Only after Demichelis's goal, Lionel manages to burst free, find some space and show what he is made of. He leaves two men behind him and takes a fierce left-footed shot which hits the post. In the 88th minute he goes to the right, plays a one-two with di María and shoots towards the far post. Tzorvas blocks it, and veteran old-timer Martín Palermo takes advantage of the rebound to seal the game and make Maradona extremely happy.

On 24 June, it is Lionel's 23rd birthday. 'I have got to where I am today because of everything Diego has taught me,' he declares. 'I am flattered,' replies Maradona, 'but Leo is where he is today because he wants to be. You can see how happy he is. He's enjoying himself. He wants to play. To everyone who complained that Messi wasn't singing along and that he looked sad – who likes to lose? We lost in the knockout stages. Now everything has turned around and making Messi happy is something everyone is proud to do. Not least his team-mates.' He continues to sing his praises: 'At this World Cup, there is no one worth even 30 per cent of what Leo is worth. No one can match him.'

The last sixteen. Argentina versus Mexico, 27 June, Soccer City stadium in Johannesburg. Messi loses his bet with Maradona – he doesn't score a single goal. 'I have to score two against Germany or that's it,' jokes the number 10 at the end of the match. Argentina beat Javier Aguirre's men 3-1 with minimal effort, after Tévez opens with a goal which looks offside. 'I thought they were going to disallow it because they were looking at the replay, but luckily they ruled it as a goal,' says Messi, who set up the pass which the 'Apache' Tévez headed into the net.

It is not an easy game for Lionel. He looks uncomfortable. He is obliged to keep going back to the centre circle to get into the game. The Albiceleste midfield is not working

well and the Flea has to take charge, running too far away from the area where he could be doing the most damage. It once again sparks debate about the number 10's position, the midfielders, and Maradona's choice of formation. 'The national team has reached the quarter finals, but their best player is having difficulty shining just as he did in the first group match. Is he playing where he can make the best impact? Does he have enough support?' asks *Clarín.* The Argentine newspaper calls for changes in the midfield to free up Messi so that he doesn't have to run so far from the goal, because they certainly can't bench the best player in the world.

The Germany game is next. The German national team has beaten Fabio Capello's English team. Led by Joachim Löw, they are a well-oiled machine with a signature style of fresh and entertaining football, thanks to technical players like Müeller, Özil, Khedira and Cross. It's a team which evokes good and bad memories for the Argentines. The 3-2 win in the final of the 1986 Mexico World Cup, Maradona's tears after losing the 1990 final in Italy, and the defeat on penalties in the quarter finals in 2006. This time, there will only be bad memories. Germany crushes the Argentines' hopes with a definitive win, demonstrating fantastic teamwork. It is a collective triumph led by Schweinsteiger against Albiceleste individuals who have little more than dreams, enthusiasm and tactical disorder to show for themselves.

Maradona's tactical gamble, which had been hailed as revolutionary, fails Messi again and again, just when it matters most. It is fifteen minutes before he even touches the ball. He tries to organise and direct the play, but apart from a few runs which go nowhere, the odd tackle, and a couple of misguided shots, there is very little of note, except to say that Schweinsteiger and his team-mates have managed to stop him without having to foul him once. Stuck far away

from the goal, Lionel loses the ball twelve times and doesn't manage to get it back. He is despairing the fact that on the few occasions when he does manage to break free from the Germans, his team-mates don't manage to feed him the ball. He is left in no man's land, foundering fast.

His World Cup score sheet is dismal. He has played five matches, he has taken more shots than anyone – 30 times, twelve on target and two off the post – but he has had no luck. And that's not the worst part. Since the first match against Nigeria, his status has taken a beating bit by bit. Everyone had been making him out to be Superman, capable of anything, but against Germany he is just another footballer. Who or what is to blame for this disaster? Is it the players who didn't know how to respond and create a memorable game? Or was it the position behind the strikers that Maradona created which left Messi too far from the box? Or perhaps it was Diego's 4-1-5 formation in general – a daring move but useless against the Germans. In the end the lack of central midfielder gets the blame, as this would have created the best playing conditions for Lionel.

The following day, the headlines in the Argentine press tell the story:

> 'World Cup humiliation for the national team. The worst tour since 1974' – *Clarín*
> 'Germany crushes Argentina' – *La Nación*
> 'No goals or glory for Messi' – *Olé*
> 'Tears for Messi and Argentina' – *Perfil*

After the match, Maradona calls it 'the hardest moment in my life, a real blow'. But Messi says nothing, he can only shed tears. A few days later, a few lines appear on a Mandarin blog called Tencent apparently quoting Messi: 'I feel really awful, I want to go home. We played badly, we failed to live

up to everyone's expectations, and now we have to start all over again.'

When Barça team-mate Andrés Iniesta scores the goal which clinches Spain's first World Cup victory, Lionel is far away from South Africa. He is photographed by the paparazzi on the beaches of Rio de Janeiro with his girlfriend, not far from where the 2014 World Cup will be held. When it rolls around Lionel will be 26, the same age Maradona was in 1986 when he became king. Who knows ... perhaps that's when he will finally get his crown.

Chapter 34

Surprise

10 January 2011

Pep Guardiola's face is an open book. His expressions illustrate a moment in time better than a thousand words. Emotion, surprise or, who knows, perhaps the disappointment of one man or an entire country. The Barcelona coach is charged with opening the envelope to reveal the winner, despite the fact that *France Football* wanted Johan Cruyff to do it and FIFA's first choice was David Beckham. He pauses, then starts by saying 'Ladies and gentlemen' ... then he eschews protocol and switches into Catalan. '*El guanyador de la FIFA Pilota d'Or es ...*' He repeats it in Spanish: '*El ganador del Balón de Oro es ...*' and then finally in English: 'The winner is ...'

The cameras focus in on the three home-grown candidates – Andrés Iniesta, Lionel Messi and Xavi Hernández. An unprecedented trifecta in Blaugrana history, testament to the club's style and teaching traditions. Such a whitewash has not been seen since the late 1980s when Arrigo Sacchi's AC Milan did it twice in a row. In 1988 with Marco van Basten, Ruud Gullit and Frank Rjikaard, and in 1989 with van Basten winning again, alongside Franco Baresi and with Rjikaard again in third place.

Guardiola tears open the envelope, revealing the card. It is facing towards the audience, inadvertently allowing everyone to see the name. A moment of confusion ensues

while the gaffer turns it over, before finally announcing: 'Lionel Messi'. Days later, when the journalists ask about the rumours which had Andrés Iniesta tipped as the winner, Pep Guardiola replies: 'I think Leo is the best.'

On stage at the Zurich Palace of Congress everyone is surprised. No one was expecting it – least of all Lionel. Dazed and confused, the boy from Rosario gets up from his seat, buttons the jacket of his Dolce & Gabbana suit, adjusts his tie, sticks out his tongue like Michael Jordan after a great basket, and goes up on stage. Pep shakes his hand, gives him the trophy and a pat on the back and directs him over to FIFA president Joseph Blatter. Meanwhile, the cameras pan the audience for Lionel's parents Celia and Jorge, who are holding hands, as well as a smiling Sandro Rossell, Barcelona FC's president. The moment has arrived for the winner's speech.

'Good evening and thank you very much for your applause,' says Leo, gripping the lectern. 'The truth is ... I wasn't expecting to win tonight. It was already wonderful to be here with my team-mates, and to win it is even more exciting. This is a very special day for me and I want to share it with my team-mates and thank them, because without them I would not be here. I would also like to share it with the people I love, who have always supported me and are always by my side. And I want to share it with the whole of Barcelona and Argentina.' More applause, followed by a slideshow of the Argentine's best moments, congratulatory remarks, and a family photo with the runners-up.

Despite all bets being on Andrés Iniesta and Xavi Hernández as the favourites, Messi has won the 2010 FIFA Ballon d'Or. It is a prize which rewards the achievements of an individual during the preceding year, taking into account past record, influence on the team and fair play. This year, for the first time, the trophy which *France Football* created

in 1956 has been merged with the FIFA World Player of the year award, which the footballing organisation launched in 1991, meaning that this year Lionel has been chosen by journalists from all over the world, as well as the managers and captains of 208 national teams. The Argentine has been awarded 853 points (22.65 per cent of the vote), Andrés Iniesta 677 (17.36 per cent) and Xavi Hernández 637 (16.48 per cent). At 23, he is the youngest player to receive his second Ballon d'Or. Alfredo di Stéfano was 33 when he won it for the second time in 1959, Michel Platini was 29, Johan Cruyff was almost 26 when he won it, Ronaldo was 26 when he was crowned in 2002 after the Japan and Korea World Cup, while Marco van Basten won his second trophy before turning 25.

'Messi deserves it. He's the best, there's no doubt about it. I'm very happy, just being here is reward enough,' says Andrés Iniesta after the ceremony, although he seems disappointed to have missed out on the prize after coming so close.

'Anything is possible,' says Xavi, the bronze award winner. 'The truth is that none of the three of us knew who was going to win, but when Leo got it I felt that it was footballing justice because he's the best player in the world, he makes an impact in every match. It's not a big deal that I didn't win it. Individual prizes in football are always unfair, because it's a team sport. Raúl, Casillas and Puyol, for example, all deserve it and none of them have won it. At the end of the day, the prize has stayed in the family once again, with Barça and with *La Masia* – our youth academy.'

It's hard to believe that none of them knew who was going to win. But judging by Lionel's body language it must be true. The kid from Rosario has been perfectly calm at the gala during the lead-up to the announcement, much more so than he was at the same venue in 2009 when he

collected FIFA World Player of the Year. He gets into the festivities at the Hyatt Hotel with everyone else. He doesn't give the impression that he already knows the result of the votes. He is convinced that since Spain won the World Cup, one of their players will win the Ballon d'Or.

'I don't mind whether it's Xavi or Iniesta. Both of them deserve it,' he says. Unlike Real Madrid manager José Mourinho who knew beforehand that he had beaten Spain's manager Vicente del Bosque as well as Pep Guardiola to the best manager prize, Messi has no idea that he will be winning his second Ballon d'Or. He thinks there is no chance after his World Cup performance. Which is why, when he comes onto the Palace of Congress stage as a member of the 'best eleven of 2010' (Casillas, Puyol, Piqué, Lucio, Maicon, Iniesta, Xavi, Sneijder, Cristiano Ronaldo, Villa, Messi), he looks relaxed and nowhere near as nervous as he has on previous occasions.

It is only at 8.05pm when Guardiola announces his name that Leo realises that what he thought was unlikely has become reality. Father Christmas has brought him the present he wanted the most but didn't dare ask for. He is embarrassed to hold the trophy and he is almost apologetic to his team-mates in front of the cameras and microphones. On the private plane ride back to Barcelona, already having ditched the suit and tie in favour of a t-shirt, he lifts his champagne in a toast. 'I want to toast Xavi and Iniesta,' he says. 'Although I won, they deserve it just as much as I do. So this is for them.'

Surprises aside, it seems that none of the other candidates or winners objects to Messi's prize. José Mourinho, for example, explains: 'For me, Messi, Iniesta and Xavi are players on another level. And when a player on another level such as Messi wins, everyone should respect it. Obviously, I would have preferred Sneijder to win after everything he's

done in the past year, or Cristiano Ronaldo because he's one of my current players, or Diego Milito, but I have to respect the choice that has been made.'

Vicente del Bosque, who was tipped as the favourite for manager of the year, tells the journalists: 'Here nobody is a loser. It was very difficult to choose the best and I think that Mourinho deserves it just as much as Leo Messi.'

Real Madrid and Spanish captain Iker Casillas has a different opinion: 'I prefer to focus on the criteria required to award the Ballon d'Or ... the World Cup has always been extremely significant in these types of awards, except in the year after Spain's win. The least I can say is that we've been unlucky. All the Spaniards are feeling slightly incredulous. I would have liked Andrés or Xavi to win, but we'll keep fighting for them to win it one day.' (It is worth remembering that only one Spanish-born player has ever won the Ballon d'Or, Luis Suárez in 1960.)

The debate shows no sign of abating the following day. 'Spain is seething. It's gold for Messi and disappointment for Spain,' reads the *As* headline. And in its report, the Madrid publication notes that 'protocol generally dictates that the FIFA winners are chosen from the country that won the World Cup the previous year, but it has been ignored – it seemed like a foregone conclusion.' It later adds: 'Messi without Xavi and Iniesta is a lot less Messi.'

'Two giants [Messi and Mourinho] and a Spanish boycott,' complains the cover of *Marca*. 'Blatter deals Spanish football a slap in the face for the second time in a month. He denied us the 2018 World Cup in December, and now he has left Xavi, Iniesta and del Bosque trophy-less.' *Marca* has also launched a poll on its website: 'Was it fair for Messi to win the Ballon d'Or?' In fewer than twelve hours there are 80,000 votes – 68.2 per cent of which do not agree with *France Football* and FIFA's decision.

But it is not just the online voters and the Madrid sports media who are disappointed with FIFA. National newspaper *El País* also carries an article by José Sámano reflecting on the lack of silverware in Spain's coffers.

'Among the many ways of working out who was going to win the Ballon d'Or, South Africa 2010 should have been the best indicator. Not just because the World Cup is the best showcase for football, but because it was symptomatic of the three finalists yesterday. Messi has triumphed when he has played with Xavi and Iniesta, but he couldn't do it without them in Africa. The two Spaniards made it to the top without the Argentine's help. The two of them, Xavi as much as Iniesta, don't just symbolise an attractive ideology about the game the way that Messi does. They represent a national team that has been consistently successful during the last two tournaments. But it should be noted that since 1995 when the prize was extended to non-European players, in a World Cup year the winner has always been a World Cup champion: Zidane in 1998, Ronaldo in 2002, and Cannavaro in 2006. Maybe questions need to be asked about why Spain loses all the global sporting votes: the 2016 Olympics, the 2018 World Cup, the 2010 Ballon d'Or … It's a well deserved prize for Messi but it's an undeserved indifference towards Spanish football, a day Barcelona will not forget.'

If disappointment and 'nationalist' criticism prevail in Madrid, discussion over award criteria is also rife in Italy and France. And almost nobody agrees with the choice of Messi as winner. 'Messi? Nooo!' reads the headline in *Gazzetta dello Sport*, summing up the general feelings of the Italian press. For the tabloids, who had already crowned Andrés Iniesta as the winner, the Flea's second consecutive win is 'unbelievable' and 'unfair' because it 'doesn't reflect in the slightest' who the best player of 2010 really was. Turin

newspaper *La Stampa* writes that 'football has lost its way', since 'Messi has not won any titles of late'. Messi's 58 goals in the last season which helped Barça win their second consecutive Liga title and the Supercup against Seville seem to count for very little, as does the Argentine's brilliant start to the season (28 goals in 26 matches). All that matters is the World Cup and the Champions League.

More than calling Leo's abilities into question, the French and Italian media are keen to discuss FIFA's new formula. The first criticism began back on 26 October when the 23 nominations were announced. How could Diego Milito, a key player in Inter Milan's Italian league win and Champions League win, not have made the list? On the other hand, how could Asamoah Gyan (who played for Rennes and now Sunderland) be on the list with only three World Cup goals for Ghana?

And when the shortlist of the final three is announced on 5 December, the debate intensifies. The Italians don't understand why Inter's Dutch player Sneijder, winner of the triple (Liga, Champions League and Coppa Italia) and World Cup finalist with five goals during the tournament, has been left out of the running. (Later it transpires that if it hadn't been for the journalists' votes, Sneijder would have been the winner, with Messi in fourth place.) In any case, no one is expecting the Argentine to be on the winner's podium, everyone thinks it will be Iniesta, who scored the goal which clinched Spain's first World Cup title. But it isn't ... and the mutterings continue.

'It isn't a scandal,' maintains UEFA president Michel Platini, 'but in a World Cup year they should really have given it to one of the players involved. Like Paolo Rossi in 1982.' (The year in which Italy beat Spain.)

But in Barcelona they disagree. 'The undisputed number one doesn't need a World Cup in order to win the prize,'

insists *Mundo Deportivo.* 'Gold for Messi, glory for Barça,' reads the headline in *Sport*, emphasising that more than any individual player, there is one clear winner: Barcelona. The only dissenting opinion comes from weekly sports magazine *Don Balón*, which writes in its editorial: 'Few people doubt that Messi is number one, but in 2010, Xavi – if Iniesta will excuse me – deserved to be recognised as the chosen one.'

In Argentina, for once, there is no debate. All the newspapers sing Leo's praises. 'Messi is the best once again,' says *Clarín.* 'The world worships Messi,' writes *La Nación.* 'Messi is pure gold,' claims *Página 12.*

'*El secreto de sus oros*,' or, 'The secret of his gold,' reads the front cover of sports paper *Olé*, playing on the title of the well known Argentine film *El secreto de sus ojos* – *The secret in their eyes* – directed by Juan José Campanella and starring renowned Argentine actor Ricardo Darín.

'I didn't go to Zurich because I was afraid of witnessing an enormous injustice,' declares the president of the Argentine Football Association Julio Grondona. 'But in the end, the gap between first and second place was huge. I wouldn't have been able to bear it if Messi hadn't won.'

'If there had been three trophies, they would have given one to each of them, but there is only one and they gave it to the best. People will always complain, but let them talk,' reasons Diego Armando Maradona from where he is staying in Mar del Plata. 'Xavi always looks like he's in control, he plays with authority, but it's Messi who scores the goals. Yes, Iniesta scored in the World Cup final, he's a great player, fantastic, talented. I would want him in my team. But out of those three, I would choose Messi ten times over.' And when asked about the Spaniards' annoyance regarding Messi's triumph, the Pelusa replies: 'They might be the champions of the world, but we have the best player in the world.'

The day after the gala, responding to criticism over FIFA's decision and the feeling that the Rosarino has snatched the title away from Spanish football, Guardiola repeats Maradona's convictions that Leo is the best. 'How can anyone say they've been robbed by Messi?! Messi gives us so much,' declares the Barcelona manager. 'He allows everyone to sit down and enjoy themselves every weekend. He makes La Liga better and more respected. Could Xavi or Iniesta have won it? Of course, but Leo won it because more than 400 people voted for him. If people think it's unfair, it's just because they had a different preference.

'Look, this is an art – people sit down to watch a match and they say "That was a great match, and that one, and that one". At the end of the year they close their eyes and they remember a guy who gave them a hell of a show. And they vote. And there's no point in rehashing it all. Spain is the world champion, and they were represented by six players in the "best eleven of the year". How much more recognition for Spanish football could you ask for?!'

Despite having two such heavyweight advocates in his corner, Messi still has to speak out and explain to one and all that he has no reason to justify himself because has not 'robbed' anyone of anything, and he has done enough to merit lifting the trophy. He is speaking at a press conference, straight after a long *France Football* interview conducted at home just after the ceremony in Switzerland. He pays no attention to those who object to his win.

'It doesn't faze me,' he says. 'I have the respect and recognition of my team-mates and my fellow countrymen. All my colleagues are happy for me and that's the main thing. Spain should be happy because they are world champions and European champions and they have the best league in the world.'

Regarding his team-mates, he says: 'There is no jealousy between us. In the dressing room we are completely united. We are more than colleagues, we are friends. We know what relationship we have with each other, we know how well we all get on, we don't have to explain ourselves to anyone. Everything will continue exactly as before, and that's all that matters.' He adds that in his opinion Xavi and Iniesta are the best players in the world. He regrets not getting up and hugging them on the night after hearing that he had won the prize, but he explains that he had a panic attack and his legs were shaking. The press want to know how he feels about his new trophy. 'I'm very happy and very proud. Two Ballon d'Or awards at my age is fantastic. Or rather, I should say, unexpected.'

It's Wednesday 12 January 2011, and the Nou Camp is getting ready for the Copa del Rey quarter final against Real Betis. It's an opportunity to celebrate with the fans, to toast the trophy win with the Barcelona faithful. A gigantic Ballon d'Or made of golden balloons occupies the centre circle of the pitch. Leo, Xavi and Iniesta are on the pitch, listening to messages from their respective families being broadcast over the loudspeaker. Blaugrana captain Carles Puyol comes up to his number 10 and presents him with the trophy. Messi lifts the Ballon d'Or, waves to the crowd and poses for photographs while the coaches and staff give him a standing ovation. The entire stadium claps and cheers.

Eighty-five minutes later, the sound of 'Messi! Messi! Messi!' is even more deafening. The Flea has celebrated in the way only he knows how – with a hat-trick.

Chapter 35

Simply the best

28 May 2011

What can you say? What more is there to say about Leo after the final at Wembley? The only thing left to say is that Messi is simply the best. And it's unanimous. So much so that for once the English and Argentine media are in agreement, both using the word 'king' to describe him. 'God save the king' reads the headline in *Olé*, hopping on board with the current British love for royals, while the *Sunday Times* runs with 'King Messi reigns'. Back in 2009 when he had already been crowned 'King of Europe', a fan in Valencia was daring enough to try to confer on him the title of King of Spain – in front of King Juan Carlos himself.

At the home of English football, the Flea leads a wonderfully lively performance, exquisite and lyrical, and the Brits leave the ground convinced that they have just witnessed what can truly be called a beautiful game. A match to tell your grandchildren about. A performance rewarded with the man of the match title, presented on the pitch, a performance which exhausts all the media's best adjectives. It is so convincing that the *Guardian* compares it to Nándor Hidegkuti's performance at the same stadium, when he scored a hat-trick in Hungary's 6-3 victory over England in the autumn of 1953.

Above all, Messi has been a team player. He finds spaces and moves between the defence to strengthen Barça's

position and unravel Man United's game plan. He demonstrates his wide repertoire: quick runs, passes in from the touchline to get round the opponents, assists, and attempts at goal. He gives the Reds' defence a run for their money and he's Vidić and Evra's worst nightmare. 'To be honest, we've never been able to keep Messi completely in check, so we had fair warning,' concedes the Red Devils' manager Sir Alex Ferguson at the post-match press conference. 'We've never managed to close off the midfield enough to stop them in their tracks.'

During the first nine minutes the Flea, like the whole team, seems trapped on the line. He tries three times in a row to steal the play from Park … but on the fourth he comes out dribbling and Barça finally begin to implement their master plan. They destroy Manchester United, staying true to their signature style of quality, movement and exceptional class. Rarely has anything like this been seen in a Champions League final. 'We've never been given such a thrashing before,' admits Ferguson.

Lionel works with Xavi and Iniesta, and together the magic threesome begin to do some damage and take control of the ball, denying Manchester United any chances. Together, they delight the crowd with their creativity, precision and speed.

With a spectacular dodge to the right of Víctor Valdés, Wayne Rooney equals Pedro's goal and offers some short-lived excitement to the fans whose hopes are still high. But it is just an illusion which barely impacts what the Blaugrana have achieved in the first half and what they still have left to do. All they need to do is go back to building up momentum, passing back and forth and pressing their opponents. They just need to finish it off once and for all. And nobody can do that better than Messi.

Back again to the two midfield magicians. Xavi to Iniesta;

Iniesta passes it to Leo. A seemingly inoffensive pass. One of the 812 (726 good, 86 bad) racked up by Barça in the final. Leo is 35 yards from goal. Three touches, and before United's defender has realised the danger, he moves into the centre and closes in at 20 yards. Evra tries to get close, but he cuts past him and shoots. Clean, powerful. A left-footed shot from outside the area. On the last day of his long and glorious career, 40-year-old Edwin Van Der Sar sees the ball too late. He has no time to react. He dives and stretches as far as possible, but the ball ricochets off the ground and swerves into the net. 'I got some space, the goalie came out and luckily it went in,' says Messi later. It is not the most stunning goal the number 10 has ever scored for Barça, but he celebrates like never before. This is the one that puts Barça ahead just when they need it the most. The United fans' hopes are already melting away, even before David Villa later seals the deal with a perfectly timed arc which soars into the goal.

After his goal, Leo screams like a madman, he shoves away a microphone which is blocking his route to the corner flag, he kicks the advertisement boards, and if it hadn't have been for his team-mates catching him and hugging him, he would have been on his way to celebrating directly with the Blaugrana fans in the stands.

He has scored 53 goals in 54 games this season (31 in La Liga, twelve in the Champions League, seven in the Copa del Rey and three in the Spanish Supercup). He is level with Cristiano Ronaldo, who has claimed the title of top Liga scorer with 40 goals – a title which doesn't seem to matter much to the Flea. In terms of individual achievements, he places more emphasis on the various cups.

In the Champions League, he is in the lead: twelve goals, equalling Ruud van Nistelrooy's record. The Dutchman scored the same number with Man United in 2002–03.

For the third consecutive year, Messi is the top Champions League goal-scorer. In 2008–09 he scored nine, and despite not reaching the final in 2009–10, he was crowned top scorer with eight goals. The only others to reach the same heights were the German Gerd 'The Nation's Bomber' Müeller and Frenchman Jean Pierre Papin.

He has scored a total of 39 goals in his 59 Champions League matches, a fantastic achievement. And that's not all. He has finally broken a curse: in all the eight matches he had played on English turf, he had never once managed to score until now. 'Gaby Milito said that I was going to end my run of never having scored in England in this match – and luckily it happened. Scoring another goal in a final and helping to win an important title is really wonderful and I hope all the fans enjoyed it,' says the Flea later.

Twenty-three years of age, top Champions League scorer for the third time, not to mention winner of fourteen other titles. But statistics and trophies aside, it is worth noting that when it matters most, Messi is there when needed, he is always a game-changer and he always plays to the best of his abilities.

'He is the best player I have ever seen, and will ever see,' says Pep Guardiola after the final. 'We could compete at a very high level, but without him we wouldn't be able to play such a high quality game. We have demonstrated that we are capable of working very hard, we have talent, and we have Messi. He is a unique and irreplaceable footballer. I hope he doesn't get bored, I hope we can continue to make him feel comfortable and I hope the club continues to surround him with good enough players. I also hope that he can stay happy in his personal life, because when that happens Leo cannot fail.'

No, Messi has never failed and he has never been bored, not even for a single minute at Wembley or during the

entire 2010–11 season. It has been a year tempered by the eternal duel with Real Madrid and Cristiano Ronaldo. Five derbies, four of them in the space of a particularly eventful month.

The first encounter takes place on Monday 29 November 2010. It is a strange day for a Barça-Real match, but there are general elections in Catalonia on the Sunday, so it is better not to compound the politics with added drama. Adverts about the game have hailed it as the most closely matched *Clásico* for years, indicating the possibility of a transfer of power from Barcelona to Real Madrid. Why? Because, they say, Cristiano is better than Messi, because Özil is a genius, because di María and Benzema are the two best strikers. Because Mourinho is not Manuel Pellegrini, nor is he Bernd Schuster or Juande Ramos or even Fabio Capello.

The Portuguese coach is the one who was capable of crushing the Blaugrana's collective efforts from the Inter dugout just six months earlier, denying Guardiola and co. their ticket to the Champions League final in Madrid. He is the man chosen by the Real president as the antidote to the Catalan magic. A coach who, from the highest position in La Liga (unbeaten, and one point ahead of Barça on 32), questions Barcelona's successes and accuses the referees and rival managers of handing them all the power.

Classic propaganda from the Special One – a show of bravado that costs him dearly. By the end of a cold and rainy night at the Nou Camp, the goals number five and they could have easily been six, seven or eight without anyone calling foul play. The Whites have been tangoed in every direction. Cristiano Ronaldo's free kick from 45 yards which grazes the outside edge of Valdés's goalpost, and a shove against Guardiola after an offside decision – which creates a general commotion and an argument between the

managers – have all been long since forgotten. He leaves Barcelona without having notched up a single goal in the six games he has played against them.

Messi hasn't scored either, breaking a run of ten consecutive games in which he has scored, but he has been generous and helped set up goals three and four for David Villa with surgical precision. The Flea has ruffled Carvalho, Lass, Pepe and Sergio Ramos's composure, and after a senseless foul on the Argentine in the 92nd minute and a punch-up between Puyol and Xavi, the red card finally comes out. Ramos has lost control, which is not unusual in such a game of nerves, particularly when the Whites know that Mourinho's game plan is still under construction, his ideas still need fine tuning, and he still doesn't know how to beat his eternal rivals. Interestingly, this is the first time a team led by Mourinho has been beaten 5-0.

At the press conference, the manager assumes an air of calm for once. 'It is a very easy defeat to get over,' he says. 'It is not one of those games where we deserved to win and then lost, or where we continually hit the woodwork. There was one team that played well and another that played badly. You have to be good natured. When you win important titles then you have a reason to cry with happiness. When you lose like we did today you don't have a right to cry, you have to get back to work. We'll live to play another day.' But the Special One will have to wait until 16 April 2011 for his next duel with Barça, the first in a marathon of *Clásicos.*

From 29 November onwards Team Pep has retained its place at the top of the league. With sixteen consecutive victories they have beaten the record set by Real Madrid's 1960–61 team (which included Puskas, Di Stéfano, Gento and Santamaría) and they are eight points clear of their rivals. On 12 April, four days before their next Real derby, they beat Shakhtar Donetsk 0-1 in the first leg and 5-0 in

the second, to make it to the semi-finals of the Champions League where the draw dictates they will meet Real. The Whites beat Lyon in the final sixteen, and in the quarters they dispatched Spurs with ease (4-0 at home, 0-1 at White Hart Lane). So now, as well as the usual Liga derby, there will be two more in the Champions League semi-finals, the first leg on 27 April and the second on 3 May. And on top of that, the final of the Copa del Rey is on 20 April.

Let's start with the 32nd Liga match day, the last chance for Mourinho's team to get back into the race for the title. Eight points is a lot but who knows ... a victory for the Whites could help to bring down their rivals' morale and could have an effect on the remainder of the season. On 3 April Real Madrid suffered a devastating loss against Sporting which put them further out of reach – Mourinho's first home league loss in nine years. But the *Clásico* is another story. Mourinho has been preparing for this as though it were a stage production.

The night before the derby, he appears at the press conference in Valdebebas and does not utter a word. He lets Aitor Karanka, his second in command, do all the talking. He doesn't even greet the journalists and some of them leave as a sign of protest. In response to the Madrid manager's silence, Guardiola offers some praise of the opponent's game: 'I have never seen a team as good as this Madrid team. In four or five seconds the ball can go from Casillas to the opponent's goal. They are better and stronger than they were the last time we met, they shoot more, they pass more, and in the second half of the year they have spent more time playing as a team. They use a diverse range of tactics which makes them more difficult to control.' And with regard to the coach he adds: 'Mourinho is very powerful. He knows how to play a wide range of styles. We should watch closely because this dictates the way we attack and defend.'

The Portuguese's presence has intensified the atmosphere. He will undoubtedly be the decisive *Clásico* protagonist off the pitch. On the pitch, that role belongs to Messi. At this point in the season, the little number 10 has achieved a fantastic score of 48 goals in 45 matches. He is the highest scoring Barça player in a single season, beating Ronaldo Nazario's 1996–97 record when Bobby Robson was the coach. And he is ahead of rival Cristiano Ronaldo by thirteen goals. The Flea has also made eighteen assists as compared to Cristiano's seven and 43 successful runs against the white number 7's 34, but his contribution to the team is worth more than statistics. 'Messi gives us so much more than goals,' maintains Víctor Valdés. 'In the way he supports the team both in defence and attack. His hard work has a positive effect on everyone.'

Every time he plays he demonstrates more skill, better teamwork. He gets more involved in the action and he knows when to speed up the game and when to slow it down. 'He turns the mundane into the extraordinary,' explains Guardiola. But he has never scored against a team led by Mourinho and this will be his ninth game against him.

Penalty in the 52nd minute. Albiol brings down Villa in front of goal. He is sent off, and when it comes to the penalty the Flea doesn't miss. In the 82nd minute, rival Cristiano Ronaldo doesn't miss either. Another penalty levels the score – it's his seventh match against the Blaugrana and his first goal.

The score is 1-1 at the end of a weak and unpleasant match. Fearing another goal, Real put up a backline defence intended to block the opponent and create a struggle. It is a *Catenaccio*-style defence tactic worthy of the Italians. The only way to win is from set pieces or counterattacks. Despite having been ahead and having the extra man, Barça struggle

and don't know how to seal the game. It's a draw which still leaves Barça an arm's length away from their 21st Liga title, giving Real confidence in terms of what's to come. So much confidence that the fans at the Bernabéu celebrate the draw as though it is a win.

It's a rough match which has unleashed a string of controversies. The first is prompted by Mourinho, who criticises the referee at the press conference and paints a picture of a web of hidden powers which penalise any team he manages, be it Chelsea, Inter or Madrid. 'I'm tired of finishing every match against Barça with ten men. It was a very balanced game while we each had eleven. And then, as so often happens, with eleven against ten it's practically mission impossible against a team whose possession of the ball is the best in the world. Once again, I am witnessing unbelievable double standards on the part of the referees.'

Mourinho aside, there is another controversy which must be taken more seriously. This time it's Leo Messi in the spotlight, for kicking a ball into the stands. The ball runs away from him on the touchline, and instead of letting it go out, he sends it flying, hitting some fans in the crowd. The referee doesn't caution him, but the fans voice their disapproval. 'Are you crazy?' exclaims Pepe, rushing over to him. The fans are amazed, they cannot believe what they have just seen. What's going on with that Rosario boy? He rarely loses his cool on the pitch. Why did he pull such a nasty stunt?

The boy in question gives no explanation and he doesn't seem to apologise either. His team-mates come to his rescue. In his defence they cite the extreme tension on the pitch, Leo's sense of frustration in the face of Pepe's close marking, and they highlight the Real midfielder's five fouls against their number 10 without so much as a booking. These recurring themes will be heard again and again as the soap opera continues.

It's 20 April, the day of the Copa del Rey final in Valencia. The game at Mestalla stadium breaks down into three distinct parts: in the first half, Madrid play superbly; in the second half, Barça shine; but in extra time it's Cristiano Ronaldo and Mourinho who are the winners. The Portuguese number 7 gets round Adriano and nets a powerful header after a curling cross from di María. It's the winning goal, clinching the cup for Real for the first time in eighteen years.

And where was Messi? 'He was desperate. He tried to get things going from wherever he happened to be in the attack, but with no luck,' says *El País* in its evaluation of his performance. 'His zigzags invariably landed him in the clutches of the Real players. The Flea was controlling the play far too much – in the first half the team hardly passed the ball at all. After the break everything changed and the deep passes to Pedrito were excellent. Unfortunately, the solitary goal was ruled offside. In the end, he took advantage of his position as a leader, trying to control the play too much, and this allowed Real Madrid to make a comeback.' It is a fair assessment, and it is also the first defeat in a final for Barça under Guardiola.

Seven days later, it is the first leg of the Champions League semi-finals. In the press conference at the Bernabéu the day before, Pep Guardiola loses his rag. Mourinho has sent him some message or other about the quality of the refereeing at the Mestalla match and the choice of referee for the semi-final, and Pep explodes, ranting for more than two minutes. This is unheard of for the coach. 'Since Mr Mourinho has addressed me in such familiar terms and called me "Pep", I'll call him "José",' he begins. 'At 8.45 tomorrow evening, we have a game to play. He has already been winning all year off the pitch. Let him have the Champions League. He can take the trophy home with him. We will be playing, whether we

win or lose. Normally, he wins because his career is guaranteed. We are happy. With our little victories, which everyone admires, we are happy. In this room, he's the bloody boss, the goddamn master. He knows more than everyone else put together. I have no desire whatsoever to compete with him.'

The next day, Lionel Messi is the master on the pitch, but at the press conference it's Mourinho once again. Two successful plays, and two goals by the Argentine, bringing down a Real Madrid team which has resorted to conservative tactics and possessive guarding of the area. Right from the start, the Whites move to block Messi's game, but they don't make any attempt to play their own. So much so that after a quarter of an hour, Cristiano Ronaldo is signalling desperately to his team-mates to move out of their positions so that he can play with them, and so that they can create chances for him. At the end of the first half, he is the one who creates the most dangerous opportunity for Real. He launches the ball from far out, creating plenty of difficulty for Valdés – difficulty matched only by a shot from Özil later in the game. But at this point, Ronaldo's attempt is their only chance worth mentioning.

At the other end, Messi is playing as deep as midfield, being kept far away from the box where he can do the most damage. He keeps himself busy with runs and dodges which go nowhere. But things change in the 60th minute when Pepe falls with full force onto Dani Alves's leg. He is immediately shown the red card. He can argue all he wants, but German referee Wolfgang Stark will not be deterred. And two minutes later he has no qualms about removing José Mourinho from the dugout either. Expelled for his over-the-top reaction.

Barça now have eleven men against Real's ten, and Leo is able to get into the opponent's area. In the 77th minute, buzzing between white shirts like a careless wasp around

the edge of the area, he takes a shot. It's deflected, Xavi retrieves it and passes it out to Afellay on the wing. The Dutch midfielder makes a run and crosses it in towards the penalty spot. Messi gets there first, beating Sergio Ramos to the ball. He taps it into the goal with his toe and it's 1-0. Ten minutes later the Flea completes his encore. This time it's magnificent: he leaves the centre circle, passes to Busquets who passes it back, he sets off on a slalom leaving Ramos behind and breaking free from Albiol, changes direction, gets into the box, dodges past Marcelo and before Ramos can catch him he finishes it off in spectacular style.

Game, set, match. He is certainly the master of this particular match. Once again, Mourinho outdoes himself in the art of provocation, determined to dominate the press conference. 'Real Madrid is out of the Champions League,' he says. 'We will go to the Nou Camp with our pride intact, with total respect for our footballing world, albeit a world which every so often makes me feel a little bit disgusted. We will go without Pepe, who didn't do a single thing wrong, and without Ramos, who didn't do anything wrong, and without the coach, who is not allowed to be in the dugout … with a scoreline which is practically insurmountable.

'And if by chance we score a goal over there and we get a little closer to staying in it, I'm sure they'll quash us all over again. My question is, why? Why aren't other teams allowed to play against them? I don't understand it! If I told the referee and UEFA what I think about what has gone on here, my career would be over immediately. I don't know if it's because they're patrons of UNICEF, or because they smile more sweetly, or because Villar [president of the Spanish Footballers' Association] has so much clout within UEFA. The fact is that they have something which is very difficult to come by – power.

'Why was Pepe sent off? Why weren't Chelsea given four

penalties they deserved? Why was van Persie sent off? Why was Motta sent off? Where does this power come from? Their power should be due to their footballing talent. That they *do* have. They should win because of that. It must taste very differently to win the way that they win. You have to be really rotten to enjoy that kind of win. Guardiola is a great manager, but he has won a Champions League that I would have been ashamed of winning. He won it thanks to a scandal at Stamford Bridge. And this year he'll be winning his second thanks to a scandal at the Bernabéu. That's why I hope that one day Guardiola has the opportunity to win a Champions League with integrity. Clean. He deserves it.'

Mourinho has put on quite a show. He has launched into a tirade which will again cost him dearly. On 6 May, UEFA's Commission for Control and Discipline fines him €50,000 and decides to suspend him for five matches. One has already passed, on 3 May – the second leg of the Champions League semi-finals at the Nou Camp – Mourinho is not even in the stands. He watches the match on TV from his hotel room. And he witnesses his team being more daring and ambitious than in the other derbies. They have Barça on the back foot and in the first quarter of an hour they manage to keep them firmly in their own half.

But little by little Barça start to chip away at their usual game. Messi finally comes face to face with Casillas, who miraculously manages to block three attempts in five minutes, to keep his team out of danger. Messi doesn't manage to score this time, but he is running all over the shop and keeping up the pressure. He provokes a warning against Carvalho and yellow cards on Xavi Alonso and Adebayor. He is fouled twelve times and he looks absolutely shattered. With or without the goal, he has been the definitive player in a match which ends in a 1-1 draw and sends Barça on their way to Wembley.

While the Blaugrana are celebrating the end of an exhausting month, the Whites are complaining about referee bias and that network of hidden power which has once again favoured their rivals. They protest about Gonzalo Higuaín's goal which was disallowed due to a supposed foul by Cristiano. Everyone, from Karanka to Iker Casillas, seems to have learned Mourinho's tirade by heart. 'This is Mission Impossible 4,' asserts Cristiano Ronaldo. 'Barça have a great team, but there is something else going on here. I don't want to suggest any kind of corruption, but it bothers me.'

Amid all the chaos, Messi is happy to be carried along by the atmosphere at the Nou Camp. And just when it seems like the excitement is about to become too overwhelming, Pep Guardiola comes over and envelops his star player in a bear hug.

It's time to celebrate once again on 11 May. At the Ciudad de Valencia stadium, Barcelona win their third consecutive league title with a 1-1 draw against Levante. 'It has been a very tough year and we have worked extremely hard against Real Madrid, our biggest rival,' comments Lionel. 'We have experienced some very difficult circumstances but we always know how to come out on top.'

But when he is handed the microphone at the Nou Camp celebrations on the Friday, he yells: 'It is wonderful to celebrate another Liga title, but I'm saving my comments for the 29th, when we get back from London. Then I'll tell you how I feel!'

And he is true to his word, one day early. He is at Wembley with the ball at his feet. He cheers when, in a noble gesture, Carles Puyol offers his captain's armband to defender Eric Abidal so that the Frenchman he can wear it as he lifts the trophy. It's a fitting tribute to a man who has just overcome liver cancer. Diagnosed in March, he underwent surgery and has returned in order to play at the home of football.

Messi is laughing as he hugs the cup, holding up three fingers for three European trophies. And he tells everyone that it has been a match they will never forget.

'Today we were the best and we deserved to win. It is incredible what this team has achieved. Right now, I don't think we know what's hit us. We just want to keep winning things. Now it's time for a holiday. Or rather, I'm going to the Copa América. But when we get back, we'll pick up from where we left off.'

Chapter 36

A thwarted dream

16 July 2011

Goalie goes right, ball goes left. No wasted chances from Argentina's number 10. He's the first to step up in the penalty shoot-out and he has had to wait several minutes for Uruguay's Muslera to get in position, but the attempts at distraction have not put him off. In fact, it's local boy 'El Apache' Tévez who misses. He's third up and Muslera blocks his shot. And Uruguay have knocked Argentina out of the Copa América on their home turf – a cup that should have been theirs for the taking. Sixty-one years after Uruguay's 'Maracanazo' in the World Cup against Brazil, the Sky Blues have done it again on enemy ground. It's a victory for a mature, solid, well-organised team, playing clean, simple football. A team who will go on to beat Paraguay in the final at River Plate's Monumental stadium in Buenos Aires on 24 July.

Just as in the 2006 World Cup, Leo Messi is on his way home after a penalty shoot-out. On that occasion it was at the hands of Germany, and he didn't even make it onto the pitch.

In the quarter-finals in Santa Fe, against the Uruguayan 'Charrúas', the Flea sends a perfect cross to Higuaín, which the Real Madrid player heads in to level the score after Pérez's early goal. Messi has played well in the first half. The second half and extra time have been more touch-and-go,

and he has been pushed to his limits. He scores his penalty in the shoot-out but, as in the 2010 World Cup, he has not scored during open play in any of the four matches. It has been sixteen official games since he made his mark. He has come close, but not close enough. Having donned the captain's armband after Mascherano's sending off, Leo is the first to go over and console little Carlos Tévez, saving his own tears for the privacy of the dressing room. For the Rosarino, his team-mates and the country as a whole it is 'the same pain as always', says Mascherano. Another 'national failure', reports *Olé*.

Argentina have not won an international tournament since 1993, when they beat Mexico in Ecuador in the final of the Copa América, with Coco Basile in the dugout and Ruggeri as captain. The Flea was just five years old. This time everything seemed different, as though history wouldn't repeat itself. The Albiceleste had a chance to triumph at home, led by the best player in the world. And Argentine football had a chance to redeem itself after the furore caused by River Plate's relegation into the second division for the first time in its 110-year history, and its fans' violent rioting at Monumental.

This time things felt different because the Flea was desperate to win at home, and he had finally begun to feel comfortable with the national team. He had won Olympic gold with Checho Batista in Beijing, and since the coach took the helm Leo has scored four goals in seven games, whereas under Maradona he only managed three in sixteen. Meanwhile the papers, TV stations and online pundits have finally warmed to him – although they have no qualms about splashing his alleged late-night partying in his Puerto Madero apartment all over the news.

And the fans now feel more of an affinity with him. It began in September 2010 at Monumental, when Messi led

the charge against new world champions Spain, and the entire crowd chanted his name for the first time. By the final friendly before the Copa América, against Albania, the relationship had been cemented.

'I was always seen as controversial in the national team,' says Lionel. 'I come over after winning everything with Barcelona, and the whole world recognises my achievements, but I had yet to win over Argentina. I began to feel it the other day against Albania, and I hope everything turns out well.'

Unfortunately it doesn't turn out well – it doesn't even start well. The team kicks off the 34th Copa América on Friday 1 July against Bolivia at La Plata. It ends in a draw – 1-1 after a late goal from Agüero – but it might as well be a loss as far as Argentina and Messi are concerned.

'That wasn't what we were expecting. We had to win. But there's another match very soon and we can't drive ourselves crazy. Now we just have to work on improving our game, and we absolutely have to win our other two matches,' says Lionel. 'We tried everything, but some things just didn't go as we wanted. It was an anomalous match.' Leo is named man of the match, but it's not enough. He receives the trophy reluctantly, without a smile. 'It grates on him, he doesn't like to lose,' says a source close to him.

The media finds fault with everyone, from Batista to the players, who put on a pretty poor performance. An Argentina 'lacking in appetite', who 'did everything backwards'. The squad is described as 'still too inexperienced'. But no one gets quite as much stick as the Flea. 'Leo was lost between a sea of legs. He didn't lead, and his performance was miles away from what he is capable of,' writes *Olé*. 'Leo was everywhere and nowhere,' claims *La Nación,* adding that, in terms of his teamwork, 'he was never comfortable, and only shone through in occasional bursts. He played an

uneven game.' The unexpected hero was substitute Kun Agüero, who rescued the match in the 76th minute.

On Wednesday 6 July against Colombia in Santa Fe, Argentina need a win, one way or another. But they can't get past the 0-0 draw, and in the end it could have been worse. Argentina are not putting up much of a fight. The best chances fall to the Colombians, who can't quite believe what a weak, pathetic team they are facing. Checho's strategy is not working. Playing the younger squad members, à la Pep Guardiola's Barça, is somewhat wishful thinking. The five-man midfield is overcrowded, the ball doesn't flow, the wingers aren't getting up front and the strikers aren't attacking. Meanwhile the defence is full of holes and goalie Romero has to fend off countless shots.

And Messi has barely made an impact. In the first half he has had just three touches, because no one is getting the ball forward, and the coach has told him not to drop back looking for it. All he has to show for himself is a glorious pass to Lavezzi, right in front of Colombian goalie Martínez. But the Napoli player misses. In the second half it's much the same story. Things improve a bit when he can work with Gago and Agüero, but the chances are not flowing. The team and the fans are starting to get fed up.

Messi has two scuffles with Nicolás Burdisso. The Roma defender criticises the Rosarino for not marking a Colombian winger, he retaliates, and the dispute continues into the dressing room. Mascherano and Tévez are also vocal about the team's weak performance. And in the Santa Fe stands, the crowd has had enough. The chants have descended into referencing players' mothers and invoking Maradona as the country's saviour. As the match finishes, they dismiss Argentina with a collective whistle – the worst possible insult.

The press are not much better. Their patience has run out – along with Batista's grace period. They talk of

a 'ridiculous' and 'directionless' team. And Messi's performance for his country makes him seem like something of a Jekyll and Hyde. His success at club level, coupled with his shortcomings in Argentina, reignite the debate about his dependence on Barça. Clarín writes: 'The Flea was also to blame for Argentina's bad night. Why? Because it's not just the coach who relies on him to lead, it's his team-mates as well. And things aren't working out for him because there's no Iniesta or Xavi there to make him feel like he's at Barça.'

These are difficult times for the Ballon d'Or winner. He has to endure public criticism, as well as the abuse from his usual detractors. They accuse him of not singing his heart out during the national anthem, of not shouting and celebrating as Maradona would have done, of not knowing how to carry the team … and one Uruguayan player even jokes about slaughtering him in the upcoming match. In response, Jorge Messi goes on Radio 10 to defend his son.

'Diego is unique and he has a different personality to Leo. My son is finding his own path and I don't know what people think "carrying the team" means. Does that mean insulting or shouting at your team-mates? That's not Leo. But he is still very strong, although not everyone sees it.' Jorge is convinced that there is jealousy and that the press are throwing fuel on the fire of an already difficult situation. He says Leo 'is taking it very badly. It's the first time they've booed him and he wasn't expecting it. It's very hard for him.'

Diego Armando Maradona is going through a particularly tough time. His mother is in hospital fighting for her life, but he still wants to defend the Argentine number 10. 'I'm going to visit my mother, and I just can't believe all these idiots I hear on the radio, tearing him to pieces. At any moment, Leo can give it his all without any problem. I say that because I know him. Because he's all about the

game and he loves the Argentine shirt. We have the best in the world, an exceptional kid ...' He pleads for Messi to be patient: 'I want him to stay calm. Before the 1986 World Cup, I played some bad matches. It was a disaster, I was criticised by 80 per cent of the journalists. And after the World Cup there wasn't a single one who didn't want to hear from me. So I can understand what it's like. He has to stay calm and talk to the coach, and say, listen, put someone in who I can work with, who can pass, so we can destroy the opponent.'

Between all the back and forth, it's time for the decisive match: Argentina versus Costa Rica on 11 July in Córdoba. The crowds at the Mario Alberto Kempes stadium are committed to the cause. They have put their grievances aside and have thrown themselves behind the team – and Messi in particular. They treat him like an idol, chanting his name the entire match, and showing their support. 'Messi, we believe in you', says one banner. 'Leo, thank you for everything, forgive us for not being more supportive', reads another.

On the fourth anniversary of his incredible goal against Mexico in the 2007 Copa América in Venezuela, Lionel finally turns it around. It's a fantastic performance – one of his best with the Albiceleste to date. He single-handedly quashes the Costa Rican 'Ticos' and leads Argentina into the quarter-finals with a resounding 3-0 win – two goals from Kun Agüero, the second thanks to a Messi assist, and one from Di María, also set up by Messi. The Flea has done what everyone asked of him: he has taken responsibility under the most difficult of circumstances, he has dominated possession, created chances for the strikers and transformed himself into the leader the nation was hoping for. And he has silenced his critics with his abundance of talent.

The following day *Olé* weighs in on his performance:

'There is only one Messi and it's this one: the one who gets thousands of shots on target, is unstoppable on the right, gets in position for the pass, coaxes a performance out of his team-mates and receives the kind of standing ovation that makes Mario Kempes stadium feel like we could be in Catalonia.'

Batista's changes have worked well for the number 10. The goalie and Mascherano stay put, but the shifting of Gago, Di María, Higuaín and Kun Agüero have created a team better suited to Messi. And he has enjoyed the reception from the fans as well. In the post-match press conference he even asks for the microphone and offers a rare twenty-second sound bite. 'I want to thank the people of Córdoba for how they have treated all of us, particularly me,' he says. 'I hadn't yet experienced any of that affection because of our recent performances. We started off badly, but we've made it through in another Cup and we – more than anyone – want the best for Argentina.' But Messi has more to say than just a few thank yous. In the press conference before the Uruguay classic, he finally gets his feelings off his chest: 'No one likes to feel screwed over.'

The discord between Messi and Argentina has melted away. The Flea finally seems to have found what he was looking for, and what he already had in Barcelona: support and affection. But the dream lasts just five more days. It will be shattered into a million pieces by the end of the Uruguay match. At least this time no one can blame Messi for the elimination, and he avoids the scepticism and negative commentary about his abilities on the pitch. This time the finger of blame is pointed at the coach, and there is even talk of the decline of Argentine football. But it's of little comfort to Leo. Another thwarted dream, another disappointment.

The only thing he can carry with him to Rosario, where he is spending a few days with his family, is the affection of

the fans. When the Uruguayan fans were chanting 'Messi is Spanish!' the home crowd were responding with 'Messi, thanks for being Argentine!' The people love him and believe in him. 'Messi + national team + fans = World Cup 2014', reads one banner. And that's something Leo has been dreaming about for a long time.

Chapter 37

Ace of cups

14/17/26 August 2011

During the summer he had been spotted on a yacht as it ploughed through the waters of Formentera, south of Ibiza, lounging on deck sporting a scruffy beard and a touch of sunburn. Photographers whizzed past on jet skis, snapping him as he holidayed with girlfriend Antonella and teammate Dani Alves.

Eight days later, on 14 August, he is back on the pitch at the Santiago Bernabéu for the first leg against Real Madrid in the Spanish Supercup. No summer training, no friendlies or tours abroad … just five days of intense work are enough to get Leo into shape.

After the Copa América defeat, Leo has not been allowed to let the grass grow beneath his feet during the summer. His personal trainer Juanjo Brau has tried to help him ward off injuries and exhaustion and stay fit. The number 10 has regained muscle tone and speed, and recovered from the mammoth 55 matches of the previous season. He is ready to play – and win – as usual. But at the Bernabéu, Real are in control – unheard of in a *Clásico* for at least the last five years. They are certainly getting a lot more possession than Barça.

Pep's team are missing Puyol, and injury niggles have kept out Xavi, Busquets and Piqué – three crucial players for getting the ball moving. Valdés is forced to pull off a

miracle save against a stunning Benzema header. But he is powerless when the Frenchman dances up the right wing, dodges away from Abidal and crosses to Özil who scores with a left-footed touch. Barça have stumbled and the defence is feeling the pressure. Spurred on by Guardiola, Iniesta starts calling for long passes, trying to get the ball moving before it can be intercepted by the ruthless Özil–Benzema duo.

In the first half-hour, Messi only makes one deep pass – to David Villa, behind Sergio Ramos's back. It's a great chance until the referee rules it offside. In the 36th minute he tries again. Villa has a beautiful opening just outside the box. Ramos is on him, he goes one way, and as the Real player turns to follow him, he sends the ball sailing just under the bar, out of Casillas's reach.

The equaliser stirs up the crowd and energises Leo. He's on the attack again ten minutes later, taking advantage of disorder in the Real defensive ranks, and is fouled by Thiago. New signing Alexis Sánchez steps up for the free kick and aims it towards Leo, who controls it. Khedira launches himself towards him, thinking Carvalho and Pepe won't be enough to hold him back. Messi collides with the German giant but stays on his feet and retrieves the ball. Pepe stumbles as he tries to switch direction, leaving the Flea free to take on Casillas and score. Barça have taken the lead. Xabi Alonso will later equalise, but Mourinho and the fans are far from satisfied. They have put on the better performance but have nothing to show for it, thanks to the little Flea.

The first trophy of the season will be decided at the Nou Camp on Wednesday 17 August. Once again, despite Mou's men dominating, they are no match for Messi. This time he does a Xavi, timing his pass perfectly to create a chance for Iniesta. The hero of the South Africa World Cup beats Spanish team-mate Casillas hands down.

Keen to make an impression on enemy turf, Cristiano Ronaldo tries to revive Real's performance. He equalises five minutes later to make it 1-1, before whacking one into the crossbar. Real are back in the game, but can't seem to take the lead. The potential is there, but they aren't converting their plays into chances. Meanwhile, the soloists shine – particularly Messi. He gets a back-heel in the box from Piqué and has no problem creating a gap, outrunning Cristiano, and taking down Casillas.

An equaliser from Benzema seems certain to take the match into extra time, but Leo turns the tables yet again, scoring the third to secure the Supercup and help Guardiola equal Johan Cruyff's record of eleven titles. This time the assist comes from ex-Arsenal captain and Barça debutant Cesc Fàbregas, and Adriano. With three minutes to go, Cesc passes to Leo, who sends it to Adriano on the right wing. He crosses back to centre, and the Argentine appears out of nowhere to shoot and score.

The match ends with a scuffle as Marcelo receives a red card for a foul on Cesc, Özil and Villa come to blows and Mourinho pokes Guardiola's assistant Tito Vilanova in the eye. At the post-match press conference, Mourinho claims not to know who Vilanova is.

On 25 August in Monaco, Messi collects another prize, newly created by UEFA to recognise the best player in Europe. He wins with 38 votes to Xavi Hernández's eleven and Cristiano Ronaldo's three. Thanking those who voted for him, Leo says: 'I keep these prizes in my house, but I still have space to add one more.' The following day he can add the UEFA Super Cup, after he scores against Porto.

It's his first Super Cup goal. He takes advantage of a slip by Guarín as the Colombian tries to pass it backwards, not realising Barça's number 10 is right behind him. It's a lucky break – all Leo has to do is get past Porto goalkeeper

Helton to net his 184th goal. He has scored against the Dragons, the team against which he debuted with Barça on 16 November 2003. He goes on to help Cesc make it 2-0, rekindling the partnership that was formed years earlier in the youth academy under Vilanova.

The Super Cup takes Messi to a total of seventeen titles: five Liga wins, three Champions League trophies, five Spanish Supercups, one Copa del Rey, one Club World Cup and two UEFA Super Cups. And seeing as he wants to keep on winning, he will have to make space in the Castelldefels cabinet for more trophies. Trophies like the 2011 Ballon d'Or.

Chapter 38

Hat-trick

9 January 2012

No surprises in store when Brazilian legend Ronaldo, recently recovered from Dengue fever, opens the envelope containing the name of the 2011 Ballon d'Or. No upsets this time.

Lionel Messi wins the trophy for best player in the world for the third year running, equalling the tallies of Michel Platini (1983, 1984, 1985), Johan Cruyff (1971, 1972, 1974) and Marco van Basten (1988, 1989, 1992). He has entered the hall of fame. No one has ever won this type of hat-trick at the age of 24.

On hearing his name the Flea hugs Xavi, seated beside him in the Zurich Congress House, and goes up on stage. He is wearing a black bowtie and waistcoat and a wine-coloured velvet jacket – Dolce & Gabbana, as always. He seems much more relaxed than the previous year, when the excitement was overwhelming. He greets Sepp Blatter and hugs Ronaldo, whom he met in the summer through Dani Alves. He takes the trophy from UEFA president Platini, before going over to shake hands with Ruud Gullit and journalist Kay Murray, who are presiding over the evening's festivities. He has no need to improvise his speech this year, unlike last year when he wasn't expecting to win. He hasn't written any notes, but he has thought about what he wants to say. No need to lean on the lectern to control his shaky legs this time either.

After thanking the voters, his Barça team-mates and the Argentine squad, he reserves a special mention for the Blaugrana number 6. 'Very importantly, I want to share this Ballon d'Or with my friend Xavi,' he says. 'This is the fourth time we have attended this gala together. You deserve it too. It is a pleasure to be by your side, here and on the pitch.'

'That was unexpected,' says Xavi. 'We are very good friends. He's a great person, but expressing his feelings is difficult for him. I am very grateful – that was a wonderful gift. What Leo has achieved is worth more than any prize.'

Clutching his trophy, Leo comments after the ceremony: 'I never dreamed I would win even one Ballon d'Or, let alone three. I mean, it's incredible and an honour, although I would never have achieved any of it without my magnificent team-mates. That's why I shared it with Xavi. I hope we'll be able to keep it going for years to come, although it's a challenge. The most important thing is to maintain the level we're at now.'

Brazilian player Neymar comes past with his well-coiffed hair. The Santos star has won Goal of the Year for his spectacular shot against Flamengo. He looks at Leo, starstruck. He has already aired his views about the Flea and Barça after the final of the World Club Cup on 18 December, which finished Santos 0, Barça 4. 'Today we have been shown what playing football really means,' he admitted. And midfielder Ganso added: 'I have seen the two best players in the world: Messi and Xavi. You can't play when you don't have the ball. And getting it off those two is impossible.' Messi scored two, Xavi one, and the whole team lit up Japan, drawing admiration and compliments from rivals and critics.

It's much the same story in Zurich. Sir Alex Ferguson, who receives the Presidential Award for his contribution to football over 25 years at Manchester United, spares no praise when it comes to Messi. 'Great players would play

in any generation. Lionel Messi could play in the 1950s and the present day, as could Di Stéfano, Pele, Maradona, Cruyff,' he says. 'Lionel Messi without question fits into that category.' Paying tribute to Pep Guardiola, who has been named Coach of the Year, the Scotsman says: 'The Barcelona team at the moment is by far the best team, and we experienced two years of it. Sometimes in football you have to hold your hands up and say "they're better than us". It's not a crime and it's not a weakness or lack of belief in my own team, it's a statement of fact.'

José Mourinho and Cristiano Ronaldo are not at the gala. Real Madrid are playing Malaga the following day in the Copa del Rey. Mourinho comes third behind Guardiola and Ferguson in the best coach stakes, with 12.43 per cent of the votes. Cristiano has pushed Xavi into third place for the Ballon d'Or, with 21.6 per cent to the Spaniard's 9.23 per cent. But he is no match for Messi, who has received 47.88 per cent of the votes. The Real number 7 is back in the top three after a year of absence – a testament to his 40 Liga goals, which won him the European Golden Boot and helped Real to defeat Barça in the final of the Copa del Rey. But there's no beating the Flea.

Leo has now won five of the big titles and reaffirmed his number one status in the 10 December *Clásico.* He didn't score in his ninth visit to the Santiago Bernabéu, but he left grinning from ear to ear after Barça schooled the favourites in a 3-1 win, while Cristiano also failed to make his mark. After the match, Mourinho mentions the number 7 when defending his team: 'In every match there are details that make all the difference. At 1-0 we had the opportunity to make it 2-0, and under normal circumstances we would have done, because Cristiano is a fantastic player and he always scores.' Under normal circumstances Ronaldo is a goal-scoring machine, but he is dwarfed by Messi and Barça.

Naturally, the duel continues. But for now Leo is enjoying the party with his parents, team-mates and Antonella. His future lies ahead of him, as Platini says: 'Messi is a killer player, he is strong and he will achieve many things. He is young, we have to let him work out his career path before we can know where he will end up. I don't know if he will overtake me, but he has many years ahead of him in football and he will continue to win many things.'

Two days later in an interview with *France Football*, Messi challenges Platini: 'Me? A killer?! That seems a bit strong. I prefer to focus on mental strength, because you have to work hard to maintain that level. Every day it gets tougher, more competitive. I'm not a machine. When I hit a bump I have to work on it.' Reflecting on the future, he says: 'I'd be happy to give up the Ballon d'Or for the next two years if we could be the best in the world. Winning it in 2014 would be amazing – that would mean Argentina are world champions. That would be the greatest thing ever.'

Chapter 39

Record

7 January 2013

'It hasn't been my best year.'

Hard to believe, but true. Leo Messi is at the Ballon d'Or pre-gala press conference on 7 January in Zurich, explaining why he is not satisfied with his 2012 performance.

'There were other years that were better, where we won many more titles,' says the Argentine. He is dressed in a grey jersey, seated next to the golden trophy, in front of an army of journalists. The Copa del Rey, Barcelona's only 2011–12 title, was a bit of a consolation prize. The titles that count have gone elsewhere: Real won La Liga and the Spanish Supercup, Chelsea triumphed in the Champions League, and São Paulo's Corinthians took home the World Club Cup.

Nonetheless, 2012 has been a crazy year for the Flea, full of success and new records. It began on a cold rainy night in Zurich on 9 January, where he won his third Ballon d'Or, and continued in La Liga with five goals in two games, against Real Betis and Malaga, having already scored two against Osasuna earlier in the month. In February he scores ten, including four against Valencia, helping Barça to a 5-1 win at the Nou Camp. When asked about his performance, he says: 'What's important is the team, not my goals. Today we played well, that's what is important, that's what makes me happy.'

Sixteen days later he goes one better in the Champions League final sixteen against Bayer Leverkusen. Pep's team have already won 3-1 in Germany, and the return leg seems set to be an easy ride. But the Flea doesn't care if it's a cinch. He's not bothered if it's a friendly or an official match, a challenge or a done deal, a Sunday or a Wednesday, rainy or sunny, home or away. He approaches it with the same intensity as ever, the same desire to score and win and put on a great show. It's the 26th minute on 7 March: long pass from Xavi, Messi controls it on the left and shoots. Bayer goalkeeper Leno barely moves as the ball slams into the back of the net. Goal number one.

A play with Iniesta in the 43rd minute lands the Argentine just to the right of the box. He latches onto the ball and heads towards the centre, dodging past five defenders. After four touches he finds a gap and sends it flying to the right of Leno. Goal two.

Ball from Fàbregas in the 50th minute, controls it with his left, shakes off Schwaab, and shoots with his right, his weaker foot. It's a perfect ball, and another crushing moment for the goalie. That's three.

Fifty-fifth minute. He retrieves a ball that Leno let get away from him, and shows no mercy. He crosses the ball from the left just out of the German goalkeeper's reach to make it four.

In the 84th minute Seydou Keita passes and Leo shoots with his left, towards the right-hand corner of the goal. Once again, it's out of reach, and Messi brings his tally up to five. What a performance. The last person to score five in a European Cup match was Danish footballer Søren Lerby in the 1979–80 season for Ajax against Greek club AC Omonia – and no one has done it since it became the UEFA Champions League.

'He's on another level,' says a dejected Robin Dutt, the

Bayer Leverkusen coach. Meanwhile, Wayne Rooney tweets that Messi is 'the best ever', and Argentine team-mate Javier Mascherano tells Catalan radio station RAC1: 'In terms of football, Leo is a killer. He goes out onto the pitch to round up his prey. That's his greatest skill – he loves to play and he doesn't care who he's up against. He's competing against himself – he has reached that level. He seems like more of a golf player than a footballer because every day he's aiming to reduce his handicap. Messi dominates the game, whereas for other footballers, the game dominates them.'

The Flea scores thirteen goals in March, which will end up being his most prolific month of 2012. Aside from the Bayer Leverkusen match, he also scores against Racing Santander, Sevilla, Mallorca and Athletic Bilbao. On 20 March, in the 29th Liga match day against Granada, he scores a hat-trick and breaks another record. With 234 goals in 315 games, he has become Barcelona's all-time leading goal-scorer, beating striker César Rodríguez, who played in the 1940s and 50s and scored 232 in 348 games.

But the next month takes a turn for the worse. On 21 April at 8pm, Barcelona are playing Real Madrid. For the first time since the 2008–09 season, the Whites have made it to the end of the season ahead of the Blaugrana. They are four points ahead, 85 to Pep's 81, enough to confirm their Liga win at the home of their rivals, and end the run of an incredible team who have won La Liga three years in a row. This is Barça's last chance to pull it back. It's *Clásico* number 184 and it's neck and neck: 86 wins each and 12 draws. Naturally, everyone is talking about Ronaldo and Messi. 'It's not about two teams, it's about two players,' proclaims the *Sport* editorial. The two star players have carried their teams. Each has scored 41 goals in 32 Liga matches, including six braces, five hat-tricks and one four-goal match for the Flea. 'You've never seen anything like it. Never has La Liga had

two such phenomenal players,' says *Sport.* Tonight they are playing for La Liga, the top-scorer position, the Golden Boot and the Ballon d'Or.

But tonight is Cristiano's night. He scores the winning goal to make it 2-1 in the 73rd minute, shortly after an equaliser from Alexis, putting an end to Barça's attempted comeback. Mesut Özil gets the ball from Di María in front of the halfway line and crosses deep towards Cristiano. The number 9 breaks away from Mascherano and heads towards Víctor Valdés. He sends the ball to the right, beating the Barça goalie at the near post. It's an incredible shot, and Cristiano celebrates by running towards the Barça fans, signalling for them to calm down, mimicking the gesture Raúl once made towards them. 'Calm down, calm down, I'm right here,' he shouts, only too aware of what the goal symbolises.

Cristiano has scored once again at the Nou Camp, playing a crucial role in breaking Real's three-year drought. And as far as the Madrid press are concerned, he has dethroned Messi. The Argentine has been unrecognisable. On his home turf, in a derby that he had dominated from the very first encounter, he has barely made an impact. He is a shadow of his former self. He had scored in the previous ten Liga matches, but against Real he has drawn a blank. In the first half he doesn't even take a single shot – unheard of for him. After the first half hour he makes a great pass to Xavi, and in the second half he makes a run that ends up leading to Alexis's goal, but that's it. He doesn't get into the box, he doesn't shoot, he doesn't dribble or create great plays with his team-mates, he doesn't put the pressure on his opponents. He looks uncomfortable. Mourinho's game plan has kept him at bay, and it's a match he would probably rather forget. At the post-match press conference, Pep congratulates Real Madrid on their victory and on their Liga title. 'We kept trying until the very end, but it wasn't to be.'

Barça are now trailing Real by seven points and all hopes of winning La Liga are over. Only the Champions League remains within their reach. Three days later, on Tuesday 24 April, they face Chelsea at the Nou Camp. In the first leg at Stamford Bridge, a goal from Drogba broke their concentration and they lost 1-0. Now it's time for the rematch. Everyone is looking to Messi, who has never scored against the Blues in all his seven encounters against them. He needs to break his drought in the home leg so that Barça can go through to the final in Munich, for the third time in four seasons.

In the 43rd minute Iniesta scores the second thanks to a pass from Messi, and Barça seem to have taken control. The Blaugrana are leading 2-0 against ten men after John Terry's sending off – they have fought back after their first leg defeat. But their jubilation is short-lived. Two minutes later, on the stroke of half-time, Lampard's pass finds Ramires, who breaks away from Busquets and Puyol before getting it past Valdés. Once again, Chelsea have proved they only need one chance in order to score.

When the game resumes, Drogba fouls Cesc in the box and the referee gives the penalty. Petr Cech spreads his long arms to defend his goal, as Messi steps up to the penalty spot looking serious. He knows this is crucial and he has already failed once against Cech in the first half. In fact, he has never beaten him. He shoots. Cech throws himself to his left. But the Flea has aimed too high and the ball rebounds off the crossbar. He has missed – at the moment when it mattered most. It's the third penalty he has missed out of the thirteen he has taken all season, and his eighth miss out of 34 for the first team. It's a major blow for both Messi and Barça.

There is one final chance, in the 83rd minute. Leo moves into the centre and takes a shot from outside the area. It's

a powerful strike that rockets to the goalie's left. But Cech just manages to get a glove to it and deflect it off the post. Barça are not feeling lucky tonight. It's Fernando Torres who gets the final word. In the 92nd minute, El Niño goes up against Valdés to make it 2-2.

Barça's 81 per cent possession and 47 shots on target are worthless. With just four shots Chelsea have scored three goals, and their defensive play has carried them into the final. Leo Messi buries his face in his shirt. It has been his worst night for some time. It doesn't matter that he is the Champions League top goal-scorer for the fourth year running, equalling Gerd Müller's 1970s record. And it doesn't matter that with 56 goals, he is the second-highest Champions League goal-scorer ever, after Raúl's 71. Or that he has equalled José Altafini's 1996–97 record of fourteen goals in one tournament. Barça are out – they won't get to defend their title in Munich.

'He is as deflated as everyone else in the dressing room, but let's not blame Leo,' says Cesc. And Guardiola adds: 'We are only here thanks to him and I want to thank him more than ever for what he has done for us. I'm sure it will be a tough time for him, but that is the beauty of this game. Sometimes you cry and sometimes you get to laugh.'

The Champions League is over, and La Liga is decided on 13 May. Real have won it at Bilbao with two games remaining. They have 100 points, ahead of Barça on 91. Messi failed to score against Real Betis on 12 May, but his total for the season stands at 50. He is the top scorer, ahead of Ronaldo, who has 46, and Atlético Madrid's Radamel Falcao, who has 24. And he has smashed Cristiano's 2010–11 record of 40. But all these goals have not brought Barça any closer to any titles. Their only consolation is the Copa del Rey.

On 25 May, in front of a 55,000-strong crowd at the Vicente Calderón, Marcelo Bielsa's Athletic Bilbao – who

have performed spectacularly against Manchester United, FC Shalke 04 and Sporting Lisbon – seem distracted. On 9 May they lost the UEFA Cup in a cruel 3-0 beating by Atlético Madrid in Bucharest. They are about to get the same treatment at the Calderón. Two minutes in, Pedro takes advantage of a rebound to score the first, in the 20th minute Messi gets in on the action, and five minutes later Pedro puts the final nail in the coffin.

Leo ends the 2011–12 season with 73 goals: 50 in La Liga, three in the Copa del Rey, fourteen in the Champions League, three in the Spanish Supercup, one in the UEFA Super Cup, and three in the World Club Cup. And Pep rounds off his four seasons as Barcelona coach with his fourteenth trophy. The most trophy-laden coach in the club's history announced his departure on 27 April, two days after the Champions League defeat. His assistant Tito Vilanova will step in from 30 June.

'I'm all worn out, I need to re-energise,' the Santpedorian tells a mass press conference, as he explains his reasons for leaving. In the audience sit captains Puyol, Xavi, Iniesta and Valdés, along with Cesc, Piqué, Busquets and Pedro. Leo is not there. But that afternoon, when all sorts of rumours are already circulating, he makes a statement on Facebook: 'I want to thank Pep from the bottom of my heart for everything he has done for me, professionally and personally. As I am feeling particularly emotional, I decided not to attend the press conference. I wanted to stay away from the media because I know they look for the pain on the players' faces, and that is something I have decided not to show.' The Flea does not want to be seen crying in public. But that morning during training, Leo hugged Pep and broke down after he informed the squad of his decision to leave. He embraces him again after the final of the Copa del Rey when the team dedicate their latest trophy to him.

Guardiola is on his way to New York to enjoy a year's sabbatical with his family. And Leo is also off to the States to join the Albiceleste. On 9 June, while Europe is focused on Poland and Ukraine for Euro 2012, a not-so-friendly friendly is taking place between Brazil and Argentina at the MetLife Stadium in East Rutherford, New Jersey. The Flea puts on a spectacular performance: two goals in the first half and one at the end to seal the 4-3 victory. The final goal is particularly impressive: a 50-yard run in from the right wing, followed by a left-footed shot into the top-left corner, beating goalkeeper Rafael. It's a superb goal, his 26th with the national team, making him the country's fourth-highest goal-scorer after Gabriel Batistuta (56), Crespo (35) and Maradona (34). And on 16 October against Chile in the World Cup 2014 qualifiers, he will score his twelfth goal in nine matches with Argentina, equalling Batistuta's stellar achievements in 1998 and taking him to 31 goals.

There is no doubt that things have been going much better for the Flea with the national team since the arrival of Alejandro Sabella, ex-coach of Estudiantes de la Plata, who took over in 2011 after the Copa América. Leo is wearing the captain's armband, he is enjoying far more freedom of movement and he can count on an abundance of talent in Di María, Agüero and Higuaín. He has finally been able to prove his worth to his country. And he is happy: 'The Argentine team has changed. We have been getting the results we wanted, we haven't lost, and above all we're playing well,' says Leo. 'We have a good dynamic and we just have to keep growing.' Brazil–Argentina is the final fixture before the summer break: sun, sea and sand in Mexico's Riviera Maya, Miami and Ibiza await him, disrupted only by friendlies with friends.

It's back to work in August for the *Clásico*: Real Madrid–Barcelona in the Spanish Supercup. On 23 August the first

leg at the Nou Camp finishes 3-2 to Barça, thanks to Pedro, Xavi and a Messi penalty. In the 85th minute, when it looked likely to end 3-1, a Victor Valdés error enabled Di María to make it 3-2, leaving it open for the return leg. The decider is on 29 August at the Bernabéu. By the ninth minute Real have already scored their first. Pepe sends in a long pass, Mascherano can't get to it, and Higuaín beats Valdés with a shot between his legs. And Cristiano scores the second after another Barça defensive error, this time from Piqué. Once again, Valdés has to watch as the ball flies between his legs.

Messi has been in the background during the first half. But after the break, he scores from a free kick, unexpectedly throwing the game wide open once again. Barça are a man down after Adriano's sending off and they seem weaker and more uncertain than usual. But they are still creating chances. Real are struggling, but they manage to hang on thanks to Casillas – and a shot from Messi that misses by a whisker. It's their first title of the season.

They will face each other little more than 40 days later, this time in La Liga at the Nou Camp on 7 October 2012. It's early in the season, but already it's a crucial game. After just seven matches, Barça are already eight points ahead of the Whites. Mourinho's men need to close the gap. Just one defeat could ruin their championship prospects. Leo has already scored ten: six in La Liga, two in the Champions League and two in the Supercup – but none in the last three matches. Cristiano is on twelve, including eight in the last four matches. Another interesting statistic: Leo has scored fifteen goals in the 21 *Clásicos* he has played, just three shy of Di Stéfano's historic record.

With Tito Vilanova in the dugout, the Argentine has strengthened his leadership, increased his participation and improved how he reads the game. He has shown greater insight and capability of creating new strategies and

plays with his team-mates. He has also learned how to look after himself better and ration his efforts. Word in the dressing room is that he is calmer, more mature and more at ease chatting to the coach. He is still the same Leo – he gets frustrated with David Villa against Granada for not looking up and missing a chance – but he knows how to handle things better. He even goes on Barcelona TV to explain his disagreement with Villa, and to say that he is not a 'little dictator' or a ball hogger. As ever, the only thing that really gets to him is losing.

And there's no fear of that happening in this *Clásico.* Messi and Cristiano put on a stunning performance in an intense match that delights the 400 million live TV viewers. They are both on form in front of goal. The Portuguese gets one past Valdés in the 23rd minute, with a sharp shot that tucks in at the left post. The Argentine replies in the 31st. Pepe fails to clear a cross from Pedro, the ball lies dead momentarily, and the number 10 shows Casillas no mercy. And he keeps up the pace in the second half. Xabi Alonso fouls him on the edge of the area, and the referee spares him the red. Leo retrieves the ball and takes a left-footed free kick, clearing the wall and beating the goalie with a beautiful strike to make it 2-1. Five minutes later Cristiano silences the Nou Camp. After a pass from Özil, he dashes away from the defenders and finishes it cleanly. 'Messi and CR7 show with their doubles why they are from another planet', reads the *Marca* headline the following day. It ends 2-2, and there's everything to play for in La Liga.

The month ends with another individual trophy for Messi's cabinet at Castelldefels. On 29 October he receives his second Golden Boot as the 2011–12 top goal-scorer in the European leagues, with a total of 100 points. Cristiano is second with 92 and Arsenal's Robin van Persie is third with 60. He is awarded the prize by 1960 Ballon d'Or winner Luis

Suárez Miramontes at Barcelona's Antigua Fabrica Damm. *Marca* director Oscar Campillo goes up on stage to present Messi with the 'mini Golden Boot' – a little golden bootie and dummy, presents for Leo and Antonella's baby, who is due in a matter of days.

At 5.14pm on Friday 2 November, at Hospital USP Dexeus near the Nou Camp, little Thiago is born. The Flea's sister María Sol is tasked with informing the world of the new arrival. Half an hour after the birth, she tweets 'Welcome little Thiago!!' Messi is a father. He had accompanied Antonella to the maternity ward at 9am, to a suite on the seventh floor where the whole family could have the maximum possible privacy. Jorge, Celia, Matías, Rodrigo and María Sol had arrived around 3pm – along with the media. Leo is by Antonella's side and assists with the delivery. Everything goes well and both mother and baby are healthy. At 6.20pm, Leo posts on Facebook: 'Today I am the happiest man in the world, my son was born and thanks to God for this gift! Thanks to my family for the support! A hug to everyone.'

Leo has excused himself from training to be there for his partner of four years, but the following day he is starting in a Liga match against Celta Vigo. He is particularly psyched up for the game, as he wants to dedicate a goal to Thiago. As he revealed at the Fabrica Damm: 'I will do something special when I score the first goal, but then it'll be back to normal.' But as much as he tries, he doesn't score against Celta. The dummy tucked into his left sock stays put. 'We tried to help him as always, particularly today, but it just wasn't happening,' says Pedro. Iniesta adds: 'It would have been lovely for him and for all of us, but he'll have another chance on Wednesday.'

On Wednesday 7 November Leo scores in injury time at Glasgow's Celtic Park, and sticks his thumb in his mouth

in tribute to his son. When asked why he chose such a low-key celebration, he explains: 'The goal didn't really do much [Barcelona lost 2-1]. There will be other chances to dedicate goals to him.' Plenty of other chances. On Sunday 11 November against Mallorca in La Liga, he is able to celebrate two goals, a victory and the birth in the way that he wanted. And on Sunday 25 November against Levante, he wears a wristband that reads 'I love you Thiago', which he kisses after scoring each of his two goals.

On Wednesday 5 December Barcelona are playing Benfica in the final match of the Champions League group stage. It's an inconsequential match as the Blaugrana are leading Group G and are already through to the final sixteen. The only thing up for grabs is the record for top goalscorer in a calendar year. In 1972 Gerd Müller scored 85 across all competitions. Lionel Messi has scored 84. Tonight could be his night. 'Everyone is talking about it – except Messi,' says Vilanova. Barça have asked UEFA's permission to congratulate the Argentinian on the scoreboard if he breaks the record by scoring two goals. UEFA have said no, but have asked for a media appearance instead. Leo starts the match on the bench. He comes on twelve minutes into the second half to play for half an hour – his chance to beat the record. The Barcelona coach denies this was the reason for bringing him on, saying it was agreed he would play the 30 minutes as part of his weekly training.

A pass from Piqué in the 85th minute puts Leo in front of goalkeeper Artur. He tries in vain to dodge past him, and the goalie knocks into his knee. He keeps going, spins and shoots, but the ball ends up in Artur's hands. Messi falls to the ground clutching his knee and writhing in pain and is eventually stretchered off in front of an anxious crowd. His team-mates, coach and fans all look worried. The last time Messi was seriously injured was in March 2006 against

Chelsea, when he tore a muscle in his right thigh. There are fears this could be something similar. On that occasion he was out for eight matches, including the Champions League final against Arsenal in Paris. But it is nothing more than a scare. The medics report he has bruised his left knee, and will be able to play again as and when it goes down.

The following day, at a press conference as part of a promotion for Turkish Airlines, Leo recalls what went through his head at that moment. 'I feared the worst because of the pain. I finished the play and took a shot because I thought it would be the last ball I touched for a long time. Luckily it was just a bad hit.' He is asked if he will play Betis in Seville on Sunday. He doesn't know, but he doesn't seem too worried, and he's certainly not concerned about Müller. 'It's not a particular obsession of mine, although it would be nice to beat a very longstanding record.'

On Sunday 9 December in Seville he is back on the pitch. With two stunning goals he helps defeat Betis and topple Müller's record. He doesn't take the ball home or make a fuss, heading off the pitch as though nothing has changed. Afterwards he says: 'Of course it's wonderful, it's a great record. I'll try to score another one to make it that little bit more difficult for the next person to beat. As I have said many times, anyone can break a record. It's very nice, but the victories that help us get ahead of other teams are far more important.' Asked whether he felt nervous before the match, he replies: 'You were the ones talking about the record, not me. I was very calm, I wanted to play after the scare I had the other day. I was lucky enough to beat it, but let's not focus on that, let's focus on Córdoba, our next fixture.' That's it. Onwards and upwards.

Messi and Müller have little in common apart from their goal-scoring abilities. The German is 1.76 metres, 84 kilograms, while the Argentine is 1.69 metres and 67 kilograms.

Leo is an all-rounder, while Gerd was king of the box. After Messi breaks the record, a German newspaper seeks out Müller to try to bring them together. But the former Bayern Munich player has been unwell and declines the invitation. But he praises Messi from Germany: 'I held that record for 40 years and now the best player in the world has broken it. I'm delighted for Leo Messi – he is incredible, a footballing giant, and a really nice, modest guy.'

Meanwhile, the Madrid press write that the record doesn't belong to Messi, but to a footballer named Godfrey Chitalu. Born in 1947 in Luanshya, Northern Rhodesia, he played for Zambia and later coached. On 27 April 1993, an aeroplane crash off the Atlantic coast of Gabon tragically claimed the lives of eighteen Zambian players, the country's football association president, and three technical staff, including Chitalu, then head coach of the national team. In 1972, the same year as Müller's record haul, Chitalu scored 107 goals across the league and the Zambia Cup with his club, the Kabwe Warriors, as well as the Africa Cup of Nations and other international games with Zambia. There is even a photo of him posing with the ball to mark his incredible tally. The debate is thrown wide open, and the Football Association of Zambia tries to reclaim the record for its star.

Over in Brazil, Flamengo insist that Zico scored 89 goals in 1979, and there is no shortage of people who maintain that Pelé racked up 110 in 1961. The Argentines are quick to mention striker Luis Artime, who excelled with Independiente, River Plate and the national team in the 1960s and early 1970s, and who, according to Uruguayan statistician Eduardo Gutiérrez Cortinas, netted 148 in a single year. In the end, FIFA doesn't recognise any official record for Chitalu, Zico, Pelé, Artime – or Messi. 'It doesn't matter,' writes Santiago Solari, ex-River Plate, Atlético

Madrid, Real and Inter player in *El País*. 'Leo's record has been a good excuse to relive historic moments and discover others.' All that matters is that Messi's goal-scoring continues.

On 18 December, Barcelona announces that it has reached an agreement to renew Messi's contract. The Flea's prior contract was due to expire in 2016, but he has renewed until 2018, by which time he will be 31. It is said his annual salary will increase to 16 million euros.

On 22 December against Real Valladolid, Leo scores his 91st goal in 69 matches. He might be little, but he has become a goal-scoring giant. He has scored 80 with his left foot, eight with his right, and three with his head. Fourteen were penalties, seven from free kicks. He has scored in every competition, and has helped Barcelona to no fewer than 53 points. He has equalled or beaten one record after another.

But there is one more to go.

On 7 January 2013 in Zurich, Lionel Messi becomes the first player in footballing history to win a fourth Ballon d'Or, the accolade recognised as rewarding the best player in the world. He overtakes legends and three-time winners Johan Cruyff, Marco van Basten and Michel Platini. Barça's number 10 has received 41.6 per cent of the votes, beating Cristiano Ronaldo's 23.68 per cent and Iniesta's 10.91 per cent. The Flea's 91 goals have counted for more than Cristiano's Liga or Supercup victories with Real, or Iniesta's UEFA Euro 2012 trophy with Spain.

Just before 8pm, 2006 Ballon d'Or winner Fabio Cannavaro opens the envelope, as the cameras focus in on the three finalists. This time Messi has brought along his father and brothers. Antonella, Thiago, his mother Celia and sister Marisol are watching on television at the Arroyo Seco country resort by the Paraná river in Rosario. Leo awaits the verdict in his black and white polka dot Dolce

& Gabbana jacket – quite a talking point. (The Spanish press will later publish his photo alongside one of Diego Armando Maradona in Seville in the early 1990s, wearing a similarly polka dotted suit.) There is a brief moment of suspense, before the former Italy captain proclaims: 'Lion Messi'. Andrés Iniesta turns to congratulate his team-mate, while Cristiano looks disappointed. During the applause the Flea goes up on stage, looking emotional. Cannavaro hands him the Ballon d'Or and Sepp Blatter congratulates him. The number 10 rests his trophy on the lectern while he makes his speech.

'Good evening. In truth … it's incredible to be able to take home this trophy again. To win it for a fourth time in a row is truly amazing. I want to thank and share it with my Barcelona team-mates, particularly Andrés. It is an honour to train and play with you every day. To my Argentine team-mates, to those who voted for me – captains and coaches … I don't know what to say, I'm very nervous. I want to thank my family, my friends and last but not least my wife and my son, who is the most beautiful thing God has given me. Thank you very much.'

A standing ovation for the record-breaker. After he comes off stage, Leo says: 'I didn't fall. I am very happy. As I said, I couldn't get the words out because of the emotion and the nerves.' He says he had no idea: 'When we arrived, all three of us considered ourselves winners.' And he admits he voted for Iniesta, Xavi and Kun Agüero. 'Of course I could have voted for CR7, he's an incredible player. But I prefer to vote for my team-mates.' In any case, as Ronaldo says: 'We don't compete on an individual level, it's all about football.' Leo agrees: 'He's right, we only try to do the best we can so that our teams win.'

He continues to thank people for the award, and shares it with coach Vilanova, who has suffered a relapse of the

cancer in the parotid saliva gland that was first operated on in November 2011, as well as defender Éric Abidal, who has just had a liver transplant. 'I hope they recover as soon as possible. It has been a tough time, and seeing them here tonight makes us very happy, it's the greatest reward they could have given us.'

And while Messi pays tribute to coaches and team-mates, they are all talking about him. Spain's Vicente del Bosque, who has beaten Mourinho and Guardiola to the Coach of the Year award, is in no doubt as to who is the best. 'Messi is the greatest, full stop. He would play well anywhere, with anyone, he's a street player, a "trickster", as we used to say back in the day. And I'm not one for getting nostalgic.'

'There is nothing more to say,' says Piqué. 'We just have to enjoy having him and hope he stays with us until he retires, so that we can keep winning many titles together at Barcelona.'

'If he keeps it up,' muses Iniesta, 'he'll win again next year.'

Chapter 40

Messidependence

19 May 2013

Dummy in the mouth, little Thiago in his arms: that's the abiding image of Leo Messi during the festivities as Barça celebrate their Liga victory.

It's 19 May and Barça have just completed the formality of beating Valladolid to receive the 2012–13 Liga trophy. There's not much of a buzz. It's late, it's raining and there have already been plenty of celebrations, including an open-top bus parade through the streets of Barcelona on 13 May, which drew more than 500,000 fans. The Blaugrana's 22nd Liga title has particular sporting significance. They have dominated the championship from beginning to end. They went top on 19 August after their first match of the season finished 5-1 against Real Sociedad – with two Messi goals – and they have not strayed from the top spot the whole year. They sealed their win no fewer than four match days before the end of the season. No one has maintained a lead like that for the whole year since Real Madrid in 1987–88, and Barça themselves in 1984–85. No one has been able to get anywhere near Tito Vilanova's team at any point during the season.

Real were trailing right from the start. On 19 September, on the fourth match day of the season, the Blaugrana's victory over Getafe and the Whites' defeat at Sevilla put Barça eight points clear of their rivals. And the Blaugrana were

already breaking records: best-ever start to the season in Liga history with thirteen wins and one draw in fourteen matches, followed by a best-ever first half of the season: eighteen wins and just one draw – at the Nou Camp against Real – and 55 points out of a possible 57 at the halfway stage. They later went on to get 100 points, equalling Madrid's 2011–12 record. In the face of an unstoppable rival, José Mourinho had already given up on La Liga. Third in the table on 13 January, Real were already eighteen points behind, and Atlético Madrid, in second place, were trailing by eleven points. Barça practically had it in the bag.

But then came a difficult spell. On 19 January they suffered their first defeat at the hands of Real Sociedad in San Sebastián, and Vilanova left for New York to undergo chemotherapy for his throat cancer. He would not return until 2 April. Assistant coach Jordi Roura was left in charge – or, as some would have it, the dressing room would just run itself. In the second half, they would suffer setbacks against Real Sociedad, Valencia, Real Madrid, Celta Vigo and Athletic Bilbao, and in the end there would be a total of two losses and four draws. They would go on to miss out on twelve points and concede 40 goals. But it doesn't matter, because the cushion from the first half means Barça stay top and it's only a matter of time before their win is official.

On 6 April, Éric Abidal comes on for Gerard Piqué for the last twenty minutes of Barça's match at home to Mallorca. He has not played in an official match for 402 days, and underwent a liver transplant necessitated by a tumour the previous April. He helps to win the biggest match of his life 5-0 and gets a standing ovation from the Nou Camp fans. Sadly, the club decide not to renew his contract at the end of the season. He wants to continue playing, but the club only offers him a technical post.

At midnight on 11 May Real Madrid draw with Espanyol at the Cornellà-El Prat stadium to hand Barça the title, and their fourth Liga win in five years. Tito's involvement has been decisive. He has made a visible impact, and there was a clear difference when he was in the dugout, compared with when he had to go to New York. It is also something of a personal victory for him over the past and the memory of Pep's successes – not to mention over a rival as unsettling as José Mourinho.

Meanwhile, Messi is enjoying life as a happy father. On 6 February he renews his contract, taking him all the way through to 30 June 2018. In March he debuts a tattoo on his left calf muscle, depicting his son's name and handprints. And now, he can put his sixth Liga medal in his trophy cabinet. No one can deny his contribution has been decisive. The number 10 has scored 46 goals in 32 games. He hasn't topped his 2011–12 tally of 50 Liga goals because he missed three matches due to injury. But he has succeeded in setting an astonishing number of records. He scored four against Osasuna on 27 January, taking him to a total of 202 Liga goals and making him the youngest player to break the 200 mark. Telmo Zarra, who held the record from 1951, was 29 years and 352 days old when he scored his 200th goal with Athletic Bilbao, four years older than the Flea. The Liga win means the Argentine is also the youngest player to win twenty titles with Barça.

Leo had already broken the record of most consecutive goal-scoring Liga matches – eighteen. And on 30 March against Celta Vigo at the Balaídos stadium, he goes one better by completing a set of nineteen consecutive goal-scoring matches, against every single Liga team – a total of 29 goals in that time. No one in the history of La Liga can lay claim to these sorts of statistics. Brazil's Ronaldo scored twelve in ten matches with Barça in 1996–97. 'It's not a record people

have ever heard of. That's how rare it is,' comments assistant coach Roura after the Celta Vigo game. Leo, captain for the first time in an official match, plays it down as always. 'I don't place any importance on it, it's not my main goal to break records,' he insists.

Nonetheless, it seems his insatiable thirst for goals will barely leave him any records to break. With 24 away goals he beats Cristiano Ronaldo's 2011–12 tally for most Liga away goals scored in a season, and he overtakes Dani Güiza's 2007–08 record of fourteen goal-scoring Liga away matches by scoring in fifteen. He finishes with a tally of 21 consecutive goal-scoring matches, a footballing world record. He had already overtaken Teodor Peterek, who scored in sixteen matches in a row in 1937–38.

Last but not least, he is now neck and neck with two greats: Alfredo Di Stéfano and Diego Armando Maradona. On 1 April he scores at the Bernabéu to equal Di Stéfano's record of eighteen *Clásico* goals, and on 5 May against Real Betis, he reaches goal number 345 – the amount netted by Diego in his entire career. The Pelusa scored 345 goals in 679 matches – 311 in 588 matches at club level and 34 in 91 games with Argentina. Leo has scored 345 in 457 matches – 313 in 378 with Barça, and 32 in 79 with Argentina.

These are crazy figures. And everyone's already talking about what comes next, the few records left for the breaking. For now, let's leave aside individual achievements and focus on Leo's contribution to the team. With 60 for Barça across all competitions, he has scored 40.5 per cent of the club's goals. It's an impressive figure, which serves to highlight the chasm between him and the club's other top strikers over the years. Eto'o, Ronaldinho, Henry and Ibrahimović never enjoyed this sort of prominence. And nor do those who currently play up front: David Villa has scored a total of fifteen, Alexis Sánchez eleven, Cesc thirteen and Pedro ten. If his

team-mates' performance has receded in recent years, the Flea's has continued to improve spectacularly: from 24 per cent of the goals in 2008–09, to 38.6 per cent in 2011–12, and now to 40.5 per cent.

'We have moved from Messi's "Barçadependence" to Barça's "Messidependence",' says Evarist Mutra – friend of Guardiola and club board member in the days of Núñez and Joan Laporta – in *El País.* It could not be more true – and not just because of the goals. It wasn't long ago that the pundits were insisting Messi's success relied largely on the performances of Xavi, Iniesta, Busquets and Dani Alves. And Messi himself repeatedly reinforced the notion – 'My good luck was ending up in this Barça team'. But the number 10's dominance is now abundantly clear. His presence or absence, his contribution, good or bad, have impacted every match, result, team-mate, opponent and fan.

The most striking example is against Paris Saint-Germain, in the second leg of the 2012–13 Champions League quarter-finals. In the first leg at the Parc des Princes, Leo had scored a goal and sustained a thigh strain, something he hadn't done for years. He is substituted by Cesc at half time. Barça are winning 1-0 at this point, but in the second half, led by Ibrahimović, Carlo Ancelotti's team manage to hold them to 2-2. The return leg is looking more difficult, and the fact that Messi might be out for three weeks has the entire town on tenterhooks. He is out of the starting line-up at the Nou Camp on Wednesday 10 April. He is on the bench biting his nails until Vilanova lets him go on in the 62nd minute. Their agreement is clear – if he's not needed, he doesn't go on. The Flea gets thirteen touches, makes two good passes, runs 2,828 metres, finishes off PSG – who up until that point had been tormenting Barça – and helps take them through to their sixth consecutive Champions League semi-final.

'One leg is enough for Messi', proclaims the *El País* headline the following day. And Ramón Besa writes: 'There is only one footballer in the world who can come onto the pitch to sort out a dire match like that. Even injured he is decisive in a game as demanding as a Champions League fixture. There is no doubt about the power and ascendance of Messi. The number 10 knocked out PSG and took Barça through in one fell swoop, with one play, one touch and one shot – one pass, one chance. Everything about him is unique, even his selective, cautious performance yesterday. After dominating for the first hour, the French gave up when they saw Messi coming. Battered and bruised, the Blaugrana felt invincible for that half hour, thanks to their number 10.'

Journalistic hyperbole? Not according to the Flea's team-mates. 'Everything changed with Leo,' claims Iniesta. 'He's the best, his presence alone helped to turn the match around,' adds goal-scorer Pedro. 'Leo came on and they got scared,' says Piqué. And Dani Alves adds: 'He has that power. His presence can change the mood of the match.'

It's not the first time the number 10's performance has influenced the mood of a match, and it won't be the last. One need only think back to the return leg of the Champions League final sixteen match against AC Milan in February – a difficult one for Messi and Barça. The first leg at the San Siro had been a fiasco, with the Blaugrana seemingly incapable of penetrating the Black and Reds' defence. They endure a tough 2-0 defeat. Messi is unable to beat goalkeeper Abbiati – he doesn't seem present. Seven days later, an on-form Real Madrid, led by Cristiano Ronaldo, destroy Barça 3-1 at the Nou Camp, knocking them out of the Copa del Rey. Once again Messi is barely there. On 2 March it's the same story in La Liga as Real win 2-1 – the first time they have beaten Barça at the Bernabéu since the

2007–08 season. Leo scores the goal and equals Di Stéfano's record, but the historic detail is hardly important at that moment. Everyone from Spain to Argentina is wondering what is going on with Barcelona and Messi.

Olé journalist Marcelo Sottile maintains that 'Barcelona seem dejected. Today we have seen at least eleven unanimated faces, very little individual flair, not much in the way of tactics from the dugout, and even a lacklustre effort physically – tired legs and sad faces – in trying to change the rhythm or fight back against Milan or Real, who have beaten them with plenty of well-organised football. Leo came up short in that respect, the fire was out, he wasn't able to break out of the mould, but he also didn't have anyone to work with. Today it just wasn't possible.'

There is talk of a Barcelona with a tormented soul, of a sad, frustrated and isolated Messi, disconnected from a team that is a shadow of its former self. So much so that, as always happens in such situations, there are even rumblings of this being the end of an era, the twilight of a team that conquered the world with its beautiful football. So the Milan return leg on 12 March is feted as a crucial encounter, a chance to evaluate how the Blaugrana – and Messi – are faring. And to hope for a comeback.

'This generation has not pulled off that kind of historic, epic recovery. This team has never really done it over the past four or five years, but this is our chance,' says Xavi Hernández. 'We are going to give it our best shot, but we're aware of the difficulty ahead, and to be 2-0 down is the worst position to be in, going into the home leg.' The midfielder is convinced everything will be different at the Nou Camp. And he's a pretty good prophet: the comeback kicks in not a moment too soon. Leo's spark is back. He levels the score with a brace in the first half-hour, and Villa and Jordi Alba go on to make it a sensational 4-0, taking them through to

the quarter-finals. Thankfully, it has not been a repeat of the time they played Mourinho's Inter in the Champions League semis, or their match against Chelsea in 2012.

And it's all down to the number 10, hailed by the Italian press as extraordinary, monstrous and other-worldly. They compare his first goal, from a position surrounded by five Milan players, to Maradona's against Greece in the 1994 World Cup in the United States. A left-footed swing sends the ball flying into the corner, leaving Abbiati no time to react. And don't even start on the Catalan press. Playing on the election of the Argentine Pope Francis, *Mundo Deportivo* runs with the headline: '*Habemus papam.* Messi is the new pope.' Everything seems to have returned to normal. Or, as Italy's *La Repubblica* newspaper puts it: 'Barça's extraterrestrials have returned.'

But no one could have foreseen the bad luck coming Leo's way when he gets injured in Paris on 2 April. From that moment onwards it's agony for the Flea and Barcelona. He misses two Liga matches, but plays just enough to knock out PSG. After tests the following day, the club medics are satisfied that his injury has not worsened, and 'he will follow the recuperation guidelines set by the medical team'. He will not play Zaragoza or Levante in La Liga. 'I hope to play in the semis,' insists the Argentine, to the relief of the team and the fans.

Barça have drawn a tough opponent in Bayern Munich for the Champions League semi-finals – a strong, solid team, full of individual and collective talent. Both Barcelona and Bayern have been key protagonists in the last four Champions League tournaments. They have each played in two finals, with opposite results: Barça won in 2009 and 2011, while Bayern lost to Inter in 2010 and Chelsea in 2012. The last time the German and Catalan teams faced each other, in the quarters in 2009, there wasn't much contest:

4-0 at the Nou Camp and 1-1 in Munich. But a lot has happened since then. Bayern will be coached by Pep Guardiola from the 2013–14 season onwards, and they are having their moment in the European spotlight. They have reinvented their game, they have a talented squad, they are capable of varying their tactics, and they have top-flight players such as Robben, Ribéry, Mario Gómez and Thomas Müller. They have demonstrated their prowess with a record number of goals and points in the Bundesliga.

This time Bayern are the favourites. Away from home against Milan and PSG, Barça have shown themselves to be defensively fragile and lacking their usual aggression, speed and liveliness. In addition, the team is not on form – they seem to have lost the sparkle of the first half of the season, and there are serious doubts surrounding key players. Messi is the biggest doubt. Everyone is waiting to see what will happen with the Argentine, who has been out for twelve days. No one knows for sure how he is doing.

On Tuesday 23 April, Leo is in Vilanova's starting line-up at Munich's Allianz Arena. He is on the pitch, but he barely plays. The match stats show that he had one shot on target, made 57 passes and touched the ball 76 times in the whole match – his lowest figures for the entire season. He tried to set off on a run eleven times, but only succeeded twice. It's not only the statistics that attest to Leo's weakest Champions League performance, it's the feelings of all the football lovers who watch the match. The top goal-scorer of the last four tournaments is merely a bystander in this fixture. Messi doesn't seem like Messi – or else Bayern are holding him back. They outstrip him, along with the rest of Barcelona. It ends 4-0, and there are no viable excuses.

The gates of Wembley are closing on the Blaugrana, and the fans are reminded of one of the team's worst defeats: the 1994 Champions League final against Milan in Athens.

In the press area after the match, Dani Alves is quizzed about Barça's Messidependence. Annoyed, he answers: 'As ever, whenever we lose that's what people talk about. It's not a question of whether Messi plays better or worse, or is more or less decisive. We all lost. Leo is the best in the world and obviously he is decisive for us, but that's nothing new. It has always been like that.' Technical staff spokesman Jordi Roura also comes out in defence of the Argentine: 'Leo has made a huge effort to be here today, he has done everything he could.'

Despite their efforts, the debate continues the following day. Many ask whether Leo was in the best condition to play. His father Jorge says he seemed well, and that the medical team's regime had been going smoothly. Medically, the number 10 seemed fit enough to play, but the fact that he didn't play his usual game was evident. The return leg awaits, but another comeback seems impossible, and discussions resume over whether the team needs to change it up and reinvent itself if it wants to retain its place at the pinnacle of the footballing world. Leo is doing his best to heal, in the hope of being able to pull off the unlikely comeback. He comes on for a short time on Saturday 27 April against Athletic Bilbao at the San Mamés stadium, replacing Xavi in the 59th minute, and manages to turn the game around with a spectacular goal and an assist for Alexis to make it two. But the Lions pull it back in the 90th minute, postponing Barça's opportunity to be hailed Liga winners.

Regardless, Messi looks to be feeling good and back on form. And he will be able to play the Champions League semi-final against Bayern on 1 May. The number 10 is enthused about the idea of going out onto the pitch. He writes an optimistic message on Chinese social network Weibo: 'Preparing for the comeback'. His presence seems to generate more of a feeling of certainty. 'Let's hope to see

plenty of involvement from Messi,' says Piqué on the eve of the match. If there is any chance of a recovery from such a poor result, it is with a great performance from the number 10. But the bombshell is dropped just an hour before kick-off – a blow to his team-mates, a surprise for his opponents: Messi is not playing. He will be on the bench. 'It was a relief that he wouldn't be playing,' confesses Bayern midfielder Javi Martínez. 'Without Messi it's a different story. He is fundamental to Barça,' says coach Jupp Heynckes. Without Leo, the team will go on to lose 3-0.

But what has happened to the Argentine? 'In fact, there was a risk of him doing further damage. He didn't feel comfortable, he didn't think he would be able to help the team in that state,' explains Tito Vilanova. And Alves confirms: 'He told me that he felt some strange sensations after the Bilbao match. Something wasn't quite right. He tried, but he just wasn't ready to play.' Vilanova admits he put him on the bench 'in case we needed to risk bringing him on at the end, but there was no point risking it after that first goal from Robben'.

Barça's Champions League ends with a 7-0 defeat on aggregate. It's a horrendous outcome that will go down in history – a defeat that would have seemed unthinkable even a short while ago. The press call it a shameful elimination. And it forces the club to think again about the future of the team.

Meanwhile, there is the small matter of La Liga. On 5 May Real Betis descend on the Nou Camp. In the 54th minute the Green and Whites make it 2-1, and Barça are not in any state to find an equaliser. The stadium is quiet, and suddenly the season looks like it might turn sour. But then Messi appears from the dugout and starts to warm up on the touchline. At that moment everything changes – from the mood in the stands and the mentality of the

players, to the result. Villa equalises, Messi nets two, and is disappointed when the goalkeeper denies him a third. Yet another display of the Argentine's voracity for goals, and Barcelona's Messidependence.

A week later, on 12 May at the Vicente Calderón, they sweep aside Atlético Madrid to be crowned La Liga champions. Leo is back in the starting line-up, nineteen days since he last started in Munich. After just over an hour's play, he heads off the pitch without asking for any medical assistance, leaving his team a man down. All three substitutions have already been made, and Barça are 1-0 down. He heads directly to the dressing room, and only exchanges a couple of words with the bosses after re-emerging in a tracksuit.

'Leo came off because he was having some trouble in the injured area that has affected him in recent weeks,' Vilanova tells the post-match press conference. 'He had begun to feel some strange sensations. Tomorrow we will do some tests to see if he will be out for days or weeks.' There are plenty of questions about this mysterious injury that has caused the Argentine to play in irregular bursts ever since 2 April. Vilanova explains: 'It might seem difficult to understand the way in which we have managed Leo's injury. It's not easy. In fact, he never felt completely fine, and we put him in or not, depending on his form on each occasion. Before the match he was fine, and he came to training as usual during the week. He wasn't bothered when he was playing, right up until the point when he came off. As you know, muscular injuries can flare up without warning.'

Those 67 minutes against Atlético Madrid are to be the last Leo will play in the 2012–13 season, as he turns his attention to making a full recovery and attending publicity commitments. On Friday 31 May, just a day before Barça's final Liga game against Mallorca, he heads to Buenos Aires to meet the rest of the Albiceleste, to focus on the

forthcoming qualifiers for the 2014 World Cup. Earlier, he had expressed his thoughts about the arrival of Neymar Júnior at Barcelona. 'He would be a fantastic addition,' he tells Qatar's Al Kass sports channel. 'He is a player who offers a very different individual style.'

There is already talk about whether the Brazilian will play alongside Messi, whether the two are compatible, whether it would get a bit crowded with two superstars, whether a Brazilian and an Argentine can get on well, whether Messi will be the king and Neymar the prince … and how many goals might be scored by what could become the most lethal pairing in football history.

Chapter 41

Barcelona

Conversation with Leo Messi

Twenty-six years are very few. The past is just over the shoulder, the future still seems far away. It is soon, too soon, to weigh things up and it is difficult to look forwards to see what the coming days will bring. But you can always try. Leo Messi agrees.

Sitting at a desk in a lounge in the bowels of the Nou Camp, he seems almost like a schoolboy who is about to do his homework in class. A mobile on the table is his only aid.

Let's begin.

What are the most difficult moments you have endured in your life?
'Moving country from Argentina to Spain. I left my hometown, my friends, my people. The first few years here were tough. There were times when my father and I were in Barcelona and the rest of the family was in Rosario. We were suffering. I missed Matías, Rodrigo, my little sister and my mother. I used to cry alone in my house so that my father wouldn't see.'

And the happiest moments?
'The birth of my son Thiago.'

And in your professional life?
'The titles I won with Barcelona and with Argentina.'

And the Ballon d'Or trophies?
'Winning one Ballon d'Or was incredible enough, so imagine what it was like to win four in a row. The individual awards make the people I love happy, they make up for the sacrifices that my family has made. But the titles which make an entire town or country happy are worth much more. It's incredible, incomparable.'

But now you are the king of the world.
'I'm the same guy and I'm lucky to be part of a great team.'

Could you possibly have imagined what the last few incredible years would bring?
'I would never have predicted all this. Not in my wildest dreams did I think that things would turn out so well.'

Let's go back to the past: what is your first good footballing memory?
'It was at the beginning, at Grandoli, we were playing in the Afi league against Amanecer. They said they were the best, the champions. My whole family was in the stands. And I scored four goals, one of which was very good.'

Why do you love football so much?
'I don't know. I first took a liking to it as a child, like all children do, and I still enjoy it a lot. For me, playing ball is one of the most beautiful things in the world. And before my son came along, it was the most important. I will always enjoy this wonderful game.'

How did you acquire such confidence with the ball, how did you learn all those tricks you know how to do?
'By spending every moment with a football. When I was little I would stand all on my own on a corner and kick the ball around continuously. But I don't study certain moves. I

don't invent feints, or anything like that. I just play the way it comes out. I don't think about it.'

Who was the one who determined your love of football?
'My grandmother Celia took me to the ground the first time. She was a very important person, very special to all of us. She was such a good person. I remember Sundays at her house being something of a party. My brother Rodrigo and my cousin have been role models. And my father also supported me a lot.'

Has it been difficult to get to where you are today?
'All kids want to be footballers, but in order to make it you need to work hard and make a lot of sacrifices. And you have to go through some very tough times, like when I decided to stay in Barcelona … It was my decision. No one forced me to make it. My parents asked me many times what I wanted to do. I wanted to stay in the youth academy because I knew that that was my chance to be a footballer. I was very responsible from a very young age.'

How have the growth problems and your height affected your development?
'I was a child, I didn't really have any idea of what was happening to me, apart from the injections in my legs every night. But, being smaller, I have learned to control the ball better on the ground, be more agile and faster than the bigger players in order to keep the ball.'

Which games throughout your career conjure up the best memories?
'That one against Chelsea in the Champions League, the derby against Real Madrid when I scored three goals and, of course, the final of the Under 20 World Cup and the semi-final against Brazil in Beijing.'

The most beautiful goals?
'If I had to choose now, I would say the one in Rome and the one against Estudiantes.'

And the one against Getafe?
'True, that one was also great.'

Is the one against Getafe the best goal you have scored in your life?
'Yes, it could be, but there were a couple of others when I was little, when I was ten or eleven years old and played for Newell's, which were similar. We have them on video at home.'

At around that age, when they asked you who your favourite player was, you responded: 'My brother Rodrigo and my cousin Maxi.' Have you ever had a football idol?
'No, I have never had a favourite player, or an idol. When I got a bit older I started to like Aimar, I admired his playing style. When I played against him at Valencia, I finally got to ask him for his shirt.'

And Maradona?
'He's the greatest.'

Did you see him play during his stint with Newell's in Rosario?
'I was very young, I was six years old. I went to a match the day that Maradona made his debut. But I don't remember it.'

Is it true that your father bought you a video of Maradona's best moments?
'I have seen Diego's goals many times, but I don't remember who gave me the video.'

What do you make of it when everyone compares you with Maradona and maintains that you're his successor?
'It makes me very happy. It's an honour, it's wonderful to be compared to one of the world's greatest players. But I don't like comparisons. I will work hard, and when I finish my career, we'll see.'

It's the most obvious answer. Let's move onto another topic.

What advice did Maradona give you?
'He told me to keep doing what I'm doing, always to enjoy football and to look after myself, because it's a short career and if you want to improve throughout it and make it last as long as possible, you always have to be in good shape.'

Let's leave him aside and go back to the Getafe goal for a moment. Some people say that that goal changed you. Is that true?
'It could be that previously I played more respectfully, I was more inhibited in front of my team-mates, and bit by bit I was starting to go out there and play the way I like to play.'

Everyone talks about the way you play ... How would you define it? Try to answer, even though it's a question you hate.
'It's complicated talking about oneself, it's better to let others do the talking. What can I say? That I like to be behind the strikers, create opportunities, find the goal whenever I can.'

What is your best skill?
'Maybe my variation of pace.'

Another tiresome question: about tension. It seems strange that you virtually don't feel it.
'When I go onto the pitch I am not interested in the opposition, nor in who's marking me. I try to do well, enjoy myself and make a good contribution to my team.'

FC Barcelona?
'I have been here for thirteen years. I feel happy here. They took a chance on me when I was thirteen, I wanted to make it into the first team and I did. I wanted to win many titles with this team and I did. But I never forget that I am just one person, without the help of my team-mates I couldn't do anything.'

The Argentine team?
'Wearing the national shirt is something really great. Although I live thousands of miles away, I would like to be at all the games and bring a lot of happiness to my people. What a shame that it wasn't to be in South Africa.'

Unfulfilled goal: would you like to play football in Argentina?
'I would enjoy playing for a club in my country. But that's a while away …'

The telephone rings.

Pause.

It is a glorious day outside. Clear skies and an almost summery temperature, although according to the calendar it is winter. The grass gleams a shiny green. At the edge of the pitch, the tourists are taking a break in their tour of the stadium in order to pose for photos with life-size cardboard cutouts of their idols. A Japanese couple arrive. They choose Messi and she is delighted because she is the same height as him, she can put her arm around his neck.

Inside, the phone call has finished. We can return to our conversation.

How do you find living with fame?
'I don't think about that. I think about being able to keep on playing, that's what I like the most. I live the same life as always. The only thing is that if I want to go out with my family in Rosario, I can't.'

Doesn't it bother you when people stop you in the street, asking for autographs, photos, kisses?
'No. There are people who spend hours waiting just to have a photo with me. It's only fair to give them some time.'

Is it true, as those who know you well say, that the fame has not gone to your head?
'It's true. I have my feet firmly on the ground and I never forget where I came from.'

And the money hasn't changed your life?
'It's the same as always. We're not people who waste money on luxury items.'

Do you like the advertising?
'I enjoy it, I like doing it.'

Changing the subject, let's talk about your first mentors.
'I learnt a lot from Guillermo Hoyos [his coach with the youth B team], he was very important to me. I did everything I could to move up the ranks.'

And your life mentors?
'My father, my family, my brother Rodrigo have always advised me and helped me in every way possible.'

You made a special dedication – 'I love you, Dad' – the day you scored your first goal on Argentine soil, at the Monumental stadium with the national team.
'I had promised, and he deserved it.'

What is your relationship like?
'Very good. We have spent a lot of time together here. We're mates, we're friends, although we have our ups and downs. Sometimes, he gets worried over little things, he starts to bother me and it annoys me …'

Do you argue over contracts and investments?
'He always consults me, but he handles everything. I play the football.'

And what does your father think of the football?
'Ever since I was little, after a match, he tells me, "you played well" or "you played badly", but he doesn't get involved in the rest …'

What do you enjoy most in life aside from football?
'Being with my family and friends.'

Try to picture yourself in fifteen or twenty years' time. How do you see yourself?
'Living in Rosario with my family … always close to my family.'

Family means everything to you, doesn't it?
'I owe a lot to my parents and my siblings. If they are OK, so am I.'

Let's take a test: here are some of the questions La Capital *asked you when you were thirteen years old. Let's see how you've changed. Favourite book?*
'Maradona's book (*Yo soy el Diego* [*I am the Diego*]), I started it but I never finished it. I'm not much of a reader …'

Eight years ago you said the Bible. Are you religious?
'I don't practise, but I believe in God.'

Are you superstitious?
'No.'

Favourite CD?
'Argentine *cumbia* style music, but I don't know which group to choose.'

Favourite film?
'*El hijo de la novia* [*Son of the Bride*] and *Nueve reinas* [*Nine Queens*]. Ricardo Darín is my favourite actor. My grandmother looked a lot like the protagonist in *El hijo de la novia,* she used to do things that she also does and she also had Alzheimer's.'

Aims?
'To win many more titles.'

You really like winning.
'When you win it makes you happy, when you lose you always feel bad and you spend your time thinking about where and how you went wrong. Ever since I was really little I have never liked to lose.'

A dream?
'To be world champion with Argentina.'

The phone rings again: it's Jorge, his father.

They are expecting him home for dinner. The whole family has come from Rosario: Celia, María Sol and his uncle and aunt, Claudio and Marcela.

In tracksuit trousers and a white hoodie with trainers, Leo Messi walks through the stadium hallway to the lift which leads to the car park. One last goodbye before he heads home, to his family.

I wonder what delicious things Celia and aunt Marcela have made today?

Chapter 42

A turbulent season

17 May 2014

Leo Messi arrives at the courthouse in Gava, a small municipality around 20km outside Barcelona, and is greeted with cheers and applause from dozens of ardent fans. One even calls out 'Messi for president!', while the occasional shout of criticism is well and truly drowned out. The Barça star responds with a thumbs-up. He is smiling and seems relaxed in a dark suit and white open-necked shirt.

It is just before 11.00am on 27 September 2013 and Lionel is here to answer questions regarding three alleged counts of tax fraud between 2007 and 2009. The television cameras zoom in towards him to capture the moment. Both Messi and his father are accused of concocting an elaborate financial scheme to defraud the taxman. The authorities claim they transferred the footballer's image rights into shell companies registered in tax havens including Belize and Uruguay. They allegedly drew up 'licensing or service contracts between these companies and others registered in convenient jurisdictions', such as the UK and Switzerland. The prosecutors say this enabled them to avoid tax payments on earnings from the player's various publicity deals with companies such as Adidas and Banco Sabadell, as well as FC Barcelona itself. It is alleged that they have made more than 10 million euros, of which 4.1 million is owed in unpaid tax.

The defence's strategy is to save Leo by allowing his father to assume responsibility. Jorge Messi is also due before the judge today. He has arrived just before his son, wearing rather a different expression: serious and distant, head bowed, eyes hidden behind sunglasses. As expected, he insists that Lionel had absolutely nothing to do with the management of his image rights and tax issues. His aim is to resolve everything as quickly as possible. 'It is clear there is little desire to defraud and a great desire to clear up all the details with the Inland Revenue,' explains Cristóbal Martell, the Messis' lawyer.

The following day the Barça number 10 is injured in a match at the Almería ground. Lionel scores an incredible goal in the 21st minute, but is substituted five minutes later due to a muscle strain in his right leg. The Blaugrana go on to win 2-0 to maintain one of the club's best ever starts to a Liga season, but it's bad news for Messi: he will be out for three weeks. This is his second injury since the beginning of the season. On 22 August he was injured during the first leg of the Spanish Supercup against Atlético Madrid and ended up missing the next Liga match. It was the same issue then, except in the left leg – the same as the injury he sustained back in April in a Champions League match against Paris Saint-Germain. In August he was back in time to play the return leg of the Supercup, and help Barcelona win their first – and what was to be their only – title of the 2013–14 season. Of course, at this point, no one could have imagined that Barça, much less the Argentine superstar, were about to have their worst season in years.

At this early stage, it all looked so promising. Barça were league leaders and Leo was still scoring despite not being entirely fit. Plus, the media were claiming that he had been gifted the manager of his choice in Gerardo 'Tata' Martino, much as Leo denied having anything to do with it. Little was

known of Martino in Europe before he was brought in to take over from Tito Vilanova. He comes from Messi's home town, and he has played and coached at Newell's Old Boys. Just to fuel the conspiracy theories, Leo's older brother Matías tweeted about the arrival of the new coach even before the club's official announcement. 'Welcome Tata! Hope everything goes well and we continue on a good path. Thanks Tito! God bless you!'

From the moment he set foot in the Catalan city, Martino met with distrust from a fair few Barça fans, as well as the press. It wasn't that he didn't have a good track record – he had just won the Argentine championship's Torneo Final with Newell's, and as Paraguay coach he had qualified for the 2010 World Cup and reached the final of the 2011 Copa América, where they lost to Uruguay. But he's not a local, and his appointment is viewed as a sop to Messi: a quiet and inoffensive boss for someone who is extraordinary both on and off the pitch. Messi is footballing wizard, but he is also a master of eloquent silences, and those around him need to know how to read him in order to get the best out of him. Some pundits said Tata's appointment confirmed that Leo is 'the real power behind Barça'. His arrival was also interpreted as a way to make up for bringing in the next Brazilian star, Neymar Júnior, whom club president Sandro Rosell had gone to great lengths to sign.

Three weeks after the injury at Almería, it's time for Lionel to get back on the pitch. Martino has put him on the teamsheet for the Osasuna match at El Sadar, although he'll be starting on the bench. He comes on for Xavi in the 69th minute, but his shots are just as off target as those of his teammates. Barça can't get past a 0-0 draw, breaking their run of eight consecutive victories. Leo makes up for it on 6 November in the Champions League, scoring two goals against AC Milan to make it 3-1 at the final whistle

and put them through to the last sixteen. Officially he has recovered, although during the match he is seen massaging his muscle several times. Four days later his worst fears are confirmed as he is injured again against Real Betis. He has only been on the pitch for twenty minutes when he asks to be taken off. His left leg is playing up again and this time it's serious – not just a sprain but a break. He will be out until after Christmas.

In the face of scant information from the Barça camp, the rumour mill goes into overdrive. Some recall that before the arrival of Guardiola, the player suffered a catalogue of injuries due to his diet – reportedly fizzy drinks, chocolate and too many Argentine barbecues – and his habit of not warming up fully before playing. Others speculate that there could be a psychological reason behind so many physical injuries. There is also talk that Messi's relationship with Juanjo Brau – who up until now has been his main physiotherapist and one of the people at the club who knows him best – has supposedly disintegrated. The Barça goal-scoring machine is out of order and everyone is trying to come up with an explanation, however far-fetched.

Leo, as sparing as ever with his words, responds in Argentine newspaper *Olé*: 'This injury happened because it happened. There is no strange explanation and no reason to go looking for one. One knock or awkward movement, and I get injured.' He says the press are responsible for 'a whole lot of conjecture', insists his diet is 'the same as always' and announces that he intends to play again 'as soon as my body is ready'. His sick leave means he won't have the opportunity to score on the tenth anniversary of his debut in a Blaugrana shirt. But much to the relief of his millions of fans, he declares he is 'almost pain free' when he arrives to collect the Golden Boot for being the highest goal-scorer in a European league on 20 November.

Once again he indulges his penchant for eccentric fashion – undoubtedly brought out by his sponsorship deal with Dolce & Gabbana – in a black velvet jacket covered in enormous tapestry flowers. Certainly not something he would have worn back in the day.

At the end of the month, the Barça number 10 returns to his home country to recuperate. He is being overseen by two medics from the Argentine national team, although the club have also sent over one of their trainers. Even sporting director Andoni Zubizarreta has flown over to observe his recovery. No effort is too great to ensure Leo is back on his feet as soon as possible to spearhead the team's attack, which is why he has been allowed to go home. He has always clung on to his roots despite having lived half his life in Spain, and it's important for him to be surrounded by his loved ones.

It is thought being away from Barcelona will curb the media frenzy. No such luck. In fact, Barça's own economic vice-president stirs up yet another controversy in his absence by opposing the renegotiation of Messi's contract. 'I don't know why we should have to do it again. We have no reason to offer a better contract every six months,' he tells Catalan radio station RAC1. Leo does nothing to hide his irritation: 'He doesn't know anything about football. He wants to manage Barcelona as if it were a company, and it isn't. Barcelona is one of the greatest teams in the world and it deserves to be represented by the best directors.' He insists that neither he nor anyone in his entourage have asked for 'any raise or renewal'. That's the end of one controversy ... for now.

Of course, there is another one just around the corner. On 16 December *El Mundo* leads with the shock headline: 'Messi's father investigated for laundering drug money'. The Civil Guard suspect that charitable 'Friends of Messi' matches could have been targeted by big-time drug traffickers as a way to launder money. The player's family strongly

deny the accusations, and the investigators confirm that their inquiry does not centre on Jorge.

As far as those at Barcelona are concerned, it's yet another provocation intended to destabilise the club. The president thinks there are dark forces at work behind all these scandals surrounding his star player – not to mention recent arrival Neymar, whose transfer is being scrutinised by the courts for suspected fraud involving 9 million euros. 'The Barça leadership have had to put up with this for years. Of course it makes you stop and think, but I still want to do this. It's just a coincidence, nothing more,' declares Sandro Rosell. But shortly afterwards, on 21 January, he resigns his post over the Neymar case. It's the end of a president elected with the most votes in Barça history, not to mention a lifelong fan. His father was the club's director general during Agustí Montal's tenure, and he himself went to his first match at the Nou Camp at the age of nine. As vice-president to Joan Laporta (2003–10) he succeeded in bringing in Ronaldinho, and in the top role he enjoyed some of his most glorious years, despite constant controversies.

Leo could go either way with regard to this latest upset. Rosell may not have taken as good care of him as some of his predecessors, and there have even been rumours that he wanted to sell the star. But Leo has always been able to count on him for support, at least in public. That much was made clear during contract renewal talks, after it came out that Neymar was earning more than the Argentine. Rosell insisted that 'Messi has to be the highest paid player in the world because he is the best in the world'. Perhaps in an attempt to quash any notion of rifts within the Barça camp, newly promoted president Josep Maria Bartomeu assures the world that Messi is 'saddened' by Rosell's departure. 'It has affected him. He has known him for thirteen years,' he tells North American network beIN Sports in an interview.

It's an unfortunate situation for Messi at the worst possible time. He is just back in action after missing eight matches, and his first outing is a Copa del Rey first-leg match against Getafe. He starts on the bench, but comes on in the 73rd minute when Barça are already winning 2-0. He gets a standing ovation from the Nou Camp crowd, and returns the favour by scoring two more. 'He's back with a vengeance,' Tata had warned before the game. Afterwards, he adds: 'Messi's career is like a film script. What happened here tonight is just another scene in his Barça career.'

The stats are impressive: in 30 minutes he has made 36 touches and nineteen good passes, had four shots on target and scored two goals. Tito Vilanova, visibly weakened following treatment for cancer, is watching Leo's performance from a hospitality box. The result is somewhat eclipsed by the poignant memory of what is to be the former coach's last public appearance.

On 12 February the team makes it through to the Copa del Rey final after beating Real Sociedad. But instead of celebrating, they are preoccupied by a recurrence of Leo's vomiting problem. Although it has happened a few times, he never has to come off the pitch. He simply doubles over, throws up and continues playing as though nothing has happened. In fact, he goes on to score the goal against Real Sociedad. Nonetheless, it's clearly not healthy, and the media and fans are keen to know what's going on. 'I don't know what it is. I have had thousands of tests,' he insists. 'Sometimes it happens before a match. I retch, I end up almost being sick, and then I feel better.'

Tata's first explanation about what happened at Anoeta is that the player is suffering from flu-like symptoms. He had 'a blocked nose and was all bunged up'. But a few days later he acknowledges that it is strange. 'I'm not the expert, I don't understand it,' he says. 'The specialists haven't been

able to put their finger on it, but let's not dwell on it unnecessarily, because it's not impeding his ability to play.' But not everyone is convinced, and there are murmurings once again about the state of the Argentine's health. Some suggest the vomiting could be due to the growth hormones that Leo took until his teens, although the endocrinologist who administered the treatment rejects the possibility of residual effects. Some say it is due to stress caused by nerves during a match, while others think he is overexerting himself. The mystery remains unresolved, although that certainly won't stop the conspiracy theories.

Ten days later, on the very same pitch, Barça lose their Liga lead after being trounced 3-1 by Real Sociedad. The Argentine nets the consolation goal, but even he isn't immune from criticism this time. Something isn't working in Tata's team. Their play just isn't convincing, and the Messi–Neymar partnership isn't clicking. They have played together so rarely because of all their injuries, and when they do they are lacking in chemistry. The Argentine has only received three assists from the Brazilian, all back in September. And Neymar has not received a single one from Messi in return. The team is barely recognisable from the exquisite, trophy-accumulating Barça of recent seasons. Nor does Messi look like the same player.

Doubts surface once again … Is he saving his efforts for the World Cup? Could he be putting his national team before the club that has given him everything, including countless trophies? It hardly matters that he scores a hat-trick in a 7-0 Liga win over Osasuna and repeats the feat in a 4-3 victory over Real Madrid the following week. As far as the fans and press are concerned he is no longer the boy wonder. His commitment is under scrutiny, and with it, all of Barcelona's activities. Even La Masia, the club's world-renowned academy that has nurtured generations of talent,

is under the microscope. FIFA accuses the club of infringing article 19 which relates to youth recruitment, and bans it from signing new players for twelve months. Barcelona succeed in delaying the ban through appeal, but the club is still being hounded on all sides.

On the pitch the team suffer two significant blows: they are knocked out of the Champions League in the quarter-finals by Atlético Madrid (2-1 on aggregate), and they lose the final of the Copa del Rey 2-1 to Real Madrid at Mestalla. Their last chance for a trophy comes down to the final Liga clash of the season, against Atlético Madrid. Martino's men need a win, but the best they can manage is a 1-1 draw. Messi gives a mediocre performance, and Barcelona close out their worst season in a long time.

Leo ends the season with no Ballon d'Or for the first time in five years (Cristiano clinched it this time, although the Argentine still made headlines with his three-piece red suit), no top goal-scoring honour in La Liga (beaten by the Real star once again), and very little love from the fans. It has been his most difficult season since he arrived at Barça. He has broken Telmo Zarra's record of being the highest goal-scorer across all national competitions, and he is the club's top-scoring player of all time, but that's nothing for a footballing genius who is used to winning everything.

He is off to Argentina on 19 May, but not before he signs his new contract, his seventh since he came to the club. His net salary will increase from around 13 million euros to 20 million. Despite the pay rise, he warns: 'If they don't want me or have any doubts, I'll be happy to leave.'

Meanwhile, the various legal proceedings are just as turbulent as his emotions. The case against him and his father for tax fraud is ongoing, although they have made a voluntary contribution of 5 million euros to the Inland Revenue, which would reduce any eventual fine they could incur if

found guilty. In addition, the 'Friends of Messi' matches are under scrutiny once again. In June, *El País* reveals that the Civil Guard is investigating the Lionel Messi Foundation's financial records in the belief that some of the proceeds of charity matches may have ended up in some of the footballer's offshore accounts. Separately, there are fresh allegations that the matches may have been used by drug traffickers to launder drug money – although there is no suggestion that the Barcelona player or his teammates who participated had any knowledge of this. And as if that's not enough, various NGOs claim they never received the charitable donations they were promised.

Chapter 43

History's revenge

13 July 2014

'I don't care about the Golden Ball, I wanted to lift the World Cup.'

Leo Messi doesn't bother to hide his disappointment from the media. For nearly 120 minutes he was within reach of realising his dream of becoming world champion with Argentina. But just when the whole world was convinced that the Brazil 2014 final was heading for a penalty shootout, a surprise goal from Mario Götze has brought Leo back down to earth with a bump. Germany have done it yet again.

The *Mannschaft* are longstanding rivals of the Argentines, and they certainly know how to crush their dreams. They did it in humiliating fashion in the quarter-finals in South Africa in 2010, and they did it on penalties on German soil in 2006. The last time the two teams faced each other in the final was in Italy in 1990, and the Germans waited until the last possible moment to clinch the trophy on that occasion too, with a controversial penalty, converted by Andreas Brehme in the 86th minute. It was revenge as much as anything. Four years earlier in Mexico it had been Argentina who had claimed their second World Cup – against who else but Germany. That was Diego Armando Maradona's World Cup, just as 2014 had been touted as Lionel Messi's World Cup.

The Barcelona player has been carrying the hopes and dreams of an anxious country on his shoulders, in the hope of repeating their 1978 and 1986 successes. He had one mission: to lead the national team to triumph just as the Pelusa did in his day. They are the two best players in the history of Argentine football. But they are separated by almost 30 years, and an enormous imbalance in terms of luck. Brazil has not gone as Leo hoped. For someone who always wins, coming second is a bitter failure, which is why the prize for player of the tournament is as good as meaningless. He doesn't even make the slightest effort to smile when he goes up to collect it.

It has been mere minutes since referee Nicola Rizzoli blew the final whistle. Head bowed, Messi is trying to make sense of what has just happened at the Maracaná stadium in Rio de Janeiro. He is barely even able to look Golden Glove (outstanding goalkeeper) winner Manuel Neuer in the eye when they shake hands before posing for the obligatory photographs. It makes for an interesting visual: eyes glued to the ground, Leo seems smaller than ever next to the Germany goalie. He also looks distinctly uncomfortable, not to mention lost in his thoughts.

'It's been a long time since Argentina made it past the quarter-finals. At last, we were in the final,' he explains after leaving the dressing room, after the defeat has begun to sink in. 'We will always carry the disappointment of not being able to seal the deal. We were so close. Losing in the last few moments of extra time is gutting, but I think we can leave with our heads held high.'

That's Messi's final word on the World Cup, but it is just the beginning of the debate for the rest of the world. In particular, there is plenty of speculation about whether the Argentine deserved the Golden Ball. Some feel that the thirteen wise men of FIFA entrusted with making the

decision have opted for publicity over quality. One such person is Maradona himself: 'I would give Leo the moon, but when the marketing gurus want him to win something he didn't win, it's not fair. To me he looked like he didn't even want to go up there and get it,' he says on his World Cup television programme *De Zurda* ('From the left' – a play on both Maradona's famous left foot and the show's ideological bent). Meanwhile, football fans take to social media to accuse Adidas of pressuring FIFA to give the award to its biggest ambassador. Even FIFA president Joseph Blatter seems surprised by the decision reached by his expert committee of former players and coaches.

But in fairness, this particular honour has been steeped in controversy at every World Cup. Diego Forlán won it in South Africa even though Uruguay were knocked out in the semi-finals, and Zinedine Zidane won it in 2006 despite his unbelievable headbutt on Marco Materazzi. Choosing a World Cup Golden Ball is not an exact science. It's not based solely on the Castrol Performance Index, which measures individual performance by a strict set of parameters, and which doesn't give an accurate picture of what happens on the pitch. If that were the case, Leo wouldn't even figure in FIFA's World Cup top eleven, and yet he has won its top individual prize.

Ex-Liverpool coach Gerard Houllier, one of the panellists who picked Leo, explains his decision to *Le Monde* newspaper: 'I understand it was a surprise because people only remember the second half of Messi's final. We watched every single match and decided he was the decisive player on his team. And they made it to the final, which was one of the conditions for the award.' Another point in his favour is the fact that he 'captained a united squad, something Argentina has not had for a while', Houllier adds. Even so, it's a close call between Leo and Germany's Thomas Müller,

although the latter does not seem the slightest bit bothered to miss out on the individual prize. Still euphoric about his country's victory, he leaves a journalist speechless when he responds to a question about the Golden Ball with a comment along the lines of 'I couldn't give a shit'.

Back to Messi: the FIFA committee is right to point out that he has been decisive for the Albiceleste in the first four matches of the competition. And coach Alejandro Sabella certainly built his team around his number 10. In theory he had some of the best forwards of the tournament at his disposal – Kun Agüero, Gonzalo Higuaín and the Flea – and his team hadn't conceded a single goal in any of its four pre-tournament friendlies against Ecuador, Bosnia-Herzegovina, Romania and Trinidad and Tobago. As if that's not enough, Sabella had only chalked up two defeats in competitive matches in nearly three years leading up to Brazil 2014. Leo had arrived at the Albiceleste's World Cup headquarters conscious that his team were among the top four favourites for the trophy.

'Cidade do Galo' is the sporting complex in Belo Horizonte that is home to Atlético Mineiro, until recently the club of Messi's good friend Ronaldinho. On arrival Leo was greeted by a huge picture of the Argentine national team with Pope Francis, who is one of their most loyal fans. The photo was taken in 2013 during a visit to the Vatican just before a friendly against Italy. This was not the only detail reflecting the Albiceleste's faith in a higher power to help them win the World Cup. There were no rooms at Cidade do Galo with the numbers thirteen or sixteen, because these have long been considered bad luck for the team.

Now that he is in Brazil, Messi can put aside one of his worst seasons at Barça, along with the memory of the 2010 World Cup, where he arrived as Argentina's greatest hope

and didn't even manage to score a single goal. He has not been on his best form in Spain, but now that he is back on his home continent he hopes to turn things around. Unlike in previous years, no one is in any doubt about his 'Argentine-ness' and his loyalty to his national team. He is now their revered captain and everything is built around him. He knows what is expected of him, but he seems calm and confident that he won't be repeating the errors of the past. 'I hope it will be the reverse of when I was doing badly with Argentina and well with Barcelona,' he notes.

His debut in Brazil is on 15 June at the Maracanã, on the very same pitch where he will play in the final just a month later. Argentina are playing Bosnia-Herzegovina, their most dangerous Group F rival, who will make them sweat it out for their first victory, despite putting them ahead with an own goal in the third minute. Sabella surprises with an even more defensive strategy than usual, which does nothing to diminish Bosnia's hunger for goals. The Albiceleste look uncomfortable, and the fact that they are one of the favourites doesn't seem to bother their opponents.

The Argentine coach changes tack in the second half, reverting to a 4-3-3 formation that is much more familiar for the Flea. Nonetheless, Bosnia are taking better advantage of their possession, until finally Messi decides enough is enough. The number 10 steals the ball, pushes the play forward with Higuaín and dodges past two defenders to make it 2-0 in the 65th minute and banish all thoughts of South Africa once and for all. There is nothing shy about his celebration, as he screams with joy and runs towards the corner flag to dedicate his goal to the fans. Just before the final whistle, Vedad Ibišević scores for Bosnia, but it's not enough to deny Argentina their three points.

Mission accomplished, although the Albiceleste players have their doubts. 'Anxiety and nerves are par for the

course in the first match. But the main thing was to get a win under our belts,' assures the captain. 'In the second half we had more chances, and of course there are things we need to work on, but we got the three points, which is what matters. It was an important goal for me, but more because it ensured we got the result. The reception we've had from the fans has been incredible, I wasn't expecting there to be so many Argentinians here.'

He admits that the first-half strategy perhaps wasn't the best: 'In the first half we let them get possession, we gave the ball away and they made it difficult to get it back.' Without a hint of annoyance, Sabella accepts the criticism and acknowledges that the events of the first half are down to his errors – a *mea culpa* that reveals just how much power Leo has in the dressing room. And in case there was still any doubt, Mascherano conveys to the press just how important it is for the team that their captain is feeling good: 'He lives for the goals, that's his ammunition and that's why it's important that he scores and is happy.' Gago concurs, noting that everyone is happy when Leo is happy.

Next up, Iran. On 21 June, Carlos Queiroz's team go out onto the Mineirão pitch in Belo Horizonte with all the odds stacked against them. Fifty thousand Argentina fans and a team led by the best player in the world await them. No one is expecting what follows: a tortuous match for the Albiceleste, and a lesson in courage by the Iranians. Argentina dominate the possession from the start, but they are unable to break through their opponents' defensive line. Iran, for their part, manage a couple of attempts on Sergio Romero's goal. But Messi seems impassive, the match is boring, and even Maradona, watching from the stands, decides to leave before the final whistle. Leo perks up for long enough to score one good goal and make it 1-0 at the close. Referring to Diego's departure, the late

Julio Grondona, then president of the Argentine Football Association, who did not have the best relationship with the Pelusa, tweets: 'Our bad luck charm left and we won!' As far as Queiroz is concerned, the ones who made the difference were 'the referee and Messi'. He claims his team deserved a penalty that would have altered the result.

On 24 June Leo celebrates his 27th birthday with Antonella and Thiago. Twenty-four hours later, with their place in the last sixteen already sealed, Argentina face Nigeria. The Albiceleste put on a better performance than in their first two matches, moving more quickly and passing the ball a lot more freely. With his team playing well, Messi is on fire. He seems a lot more inspired and scores two beautiful goals, the first in the third minute and the second on the stroke of half-time. At 3-2 and with things already sewn up, Sabella decides to rest his number 10 in preparation for the knockout stages. The cameras zoom in to gauge Leo's reaction, but he comes off without a complaint, and is even smiling. After the match, his satisfaction with the team's best performance so far is evident. 'The reaction we have had from everyone has been incredible. We are chasing a dream that everyone wants really badly,' he says. Nigeria coach Stephen Keshi is blunt in his account of what went wrong for his team at the Mineirão. 'We lost because we played with too much respect for Argentina in the first half. By the second, we were able to get into our game, we were more attacking, had more possession and played better. But Argentina are a great team. And Messi is a great player, he is blessed, you can't get by him. Messi is from Jupiter.'

On 29 June Leo has another important date to celebrate: his tenth anniversary with the Albiceleste. A World Cup trophy would be the icing on the cake of the past decade. But first he has to face Switzerland in the last sixteen

at the Arena de São Paulo on 1 July. The fans are looking forward to what they are sure will be another masterful lesson in footballing excellence, but they will be bitterly disappointed. Argentina win, but it's a struggle. Sabella's men seem inert, out of ideas. With the score still 0-0 after 90 minutes, the match goes to extra time. Messi looks worn out, and takes the opportunity to put his feet up during the break. In the 118th minute he initiates a move, sees Ángel Di María to his right, and serves up the ball for the winning goal. 'At first I thought I'd run with it, then I saw Fideo [Di María], and I decided to give it to him,' he would say later. 'That's football, luck was on our side today; you just have to take advantage of it and move forward.'

It's the latest Argentina have scored a winner in a World Cup, but it's enough to send them through to the quarter-finals – the 'cursed' round that has been their downfall since their last final at Italia '90. On Saturday 5 July at the Mané Garrincha National Stadium in Brasília they are up against Belgium – a well-organised team with strong players. But this time they are up to the challenge. Before even ten minutes have passed, Higuaín scores what will be his only goal of the tournament. For the second consecutive match Messi will be heading back to the dressing room without having scored, although he initiated the move that led to the goal. The bad news of the day is that Di María will miss the rest of the tournament due to injury. For Sabella, this has been the Albiceleste's 'most balanced' match in Brazil so far. He feels the players showed they were 'willing to sacrifice themselves for each other'. But Belgium coach Marc Wilmots' opinion is more in line with that of the general public: 'We weren't that impressed. They seemed like a fairly ordinary team.'

Oblivious to all the criticism, Leo only cares that his team is in the semi-finals for the first time in 24 years. The

Albiceleste are facing the Netherlands, just two days after the death of Alfredo Di Stéfano, the Argentine football legend who immigrated to Spain like Messi. They are all too aware of what a historic moment they are about to experience. So far Lionel has played 453 minutes in five games. He has scored four goals – two fewer than Colombia's James Rodríguez – and has had nine shots on target. Everyone expects more from him, but the match on 9 July at the Arena de São Paulo ends with neither pain nor glory. Neither team creates particularly dangerous chances, and it's only set pieces that cause any upset. No one seems prepared to risk any counterattacks that could knock them out of the tournament. Leo hardly seems like a number 10, although to be fair the Dutch players don't leave him much room to manoeuvre.

The match goes to penalties. Ron Vlaar is first up for the Netherlands … and Romero clears it. Next it's Messi's turn, and he sends the ball zooming into Jasper Cillessen's net. The Flea has taken the first step towards the final, and the rest of the team follow his lead. After the victory they have to undergo anti-doping checks, and then it's back to Cidade do Galo to prepare for the ultimate clash with Germany. Messi goes online to share his excitement at making it to the most important match of his life – and such a historic duel. 'I had to go through the doping checks so I didn't get to enjoy that moment in the dressing room,' he posts. 'I feel proud to be part of this squad! What an amazing team we have, what an incredible game they played. It's crazy! We're in the final! We have to enjoy it. We are so close …'

But as we all know, the outcome on 13 July is not the one the captain had envisioned. When the big day comes, Messi plays an uneven game, and although he shoots a handful of times, it's Higuaín who really deserves the goal. Leo's performance is reminiscent of this past season with Barça

– a few flashes of brilliance, but no real magic. And he has another vomiting episode.

After such a promising start to the 2014 World Cup, Messi leaves Brazil empty-handed. His expression as he goes up to collect the Golden Ball says it all.

Career record

Personal summary

Full name: Lionel Andrés Messi

Place and Date of Birth: Rosario, Santa Fe, Argentina, 24 June 1987

Parents: Jorge and Celia

Brothers: Matías and Rodrigo

Sister: María Sol

Wife: Antonella Roccuzzo

Son: Thiago

Position: striker

Shirt number: 10

Height: 169 cm

Weight: 67 kg

Clubs

Grandoli – 1992–1994

Club Atlético Newell's Old Boys – 1994–2001

FC Barcelona – 2001–present

Barcelona

First team debut: 16 November 2003 v FC Porto (away)

La Liga debut: 16 October 2004 v RCD Espanyol (away)

First goal: 1 May 2005 v Albacete (home)

Appearances (up to 28 July 2014)
Liga 277 Goals 243
Copa del Rey 44 Goals 29
Champions League 86 Goals 67
Spanish Supercup 11 Goals 10
European Super Cup 3 Goals 1
World Club Cup 4 Goals 4
Total matches played 425 Goals 354

Argentina

Debut: 17 August 2005 v Hungary (away)
First goal: 1 March 2006 v Croatia (away)
Caps 93 Goals 42 (up to 28 July 2014)

Appearances
Under 20 World Cup 2005
World Cup 2006
World Cup 2010
World Cup 2014
Copa América 2007
Copa América 2011
Summer Olympics 2008

Honours won

Barcelona

Liga: 6
2004–05, 2005–06, 2008–09, 2009–10, 2010–11, 2012–13
Copa del Rey: 2
2008–09, 2011–12
Supercopa de Espana: 5
2005, 2006, 2009, 2010, 2011
UEFA Champions League: 3
2005–06, 2008–09, 2010–11

UEFA Super Cup: 2
2009, 2011
FIFA Club World Cup: 1
2009

Argentina
Under 20 World Cup 2005
Olympic gold medal, Beijing 2008

Individual honours
Golden Ball (player of the tournament), FIFA World Cup 2014
FIFA Ballon d'Or 2012
Golden Boot 2012
FIFA Ballon d'Or 2011
FIFA Ballon d'Or 2010
Golden Boot 2010
Ballon d'Or (European Player of the Year) 2009
FIFA World Player of the Year 2009
Onze d'Or 2009
Alfredo Di Stéfano trophy 2008–09
UEFA Champions League Top Scorer 2008–09
UEFA Club Forward of the Year 2008–09
UEFA Club Footballer of the Year 2008–09
LFP Best Player 2008–09
European Player of the Year (second place) 2008
FIFA World Player of the Year (second place) 2008
Under 21 European Footballer of the Year 2007
European Player of the Year (third place) 2007
FIFA World Player (second place) 2007
European FIFA Under 20 World Cup Top Scorer 2005
FIFA Under 20 World Cup Player of the Tournament 2005
Copa América Young Player of the Tournament 2007
Player of the Year, Argentina 2005, 2007

FIFPro Special Young Player of the Year 2006–07, 2007–08

FIFPro World Young Player of the Year 2005–06, 2006–07, 2007–08

World Soccer Young Player of the Year 2005–06, 2006–07, 2007–08

Premio Don Balón (Best Foreign Player in La Liga) 2006–07, 2008–09

EFE Trophy (Best Ibero-American Player in La Liga) 2006–07, 2008–09

FIFPro World XI 2006–07, 2007–08, 2008–09

Bibliography

Apo, Alejandro, *Y el fútbol contó un cuento* (Buenos Aires: Alfaguara, 2007)

Beha, Oliviero and Di Caro, Andrea, *Indagine sul calcio* (Milan: Bur, 2006)

Brera, Gianni, *Incontri e invettive* (Milan: Longanesi, 1974)

Fontanarrosa, Roberto, *Puro fútbol* (Buenos Aires: Ediciones de la Flor, 2000)

Frieros, Toni, *Leo Messi, el tesoro del Barça* (Barcelona: Edecasa, 2006)

Galdeano, Arnau, *Estimat Messi* (Barcelona: Empúries, 2007)

Galeano, Eduardo, *El fútbol a sol y sombra* (Madrid: Siglo XXI de España Editores, 1995)

Grosso, Cristian, *Futbolistas con historia(s)* (Buenos Aires: Ediciones Al Arco, 2007)

Hugo, Víctor and Perfumo, Roberto, *Hablemos de fútbol* (Buenos Aires: Planeta, 2006)

Luque, Xavier and Finestres, Jordi, *El caso Di Stéfano* (Barcelona: Península, 2006)

Maradona, Diego Armando, *Yo soy el Diego* (Barcelona: Planeta, 2001)

Sebreli, Juan José, *La era del fútbol* (Buenos Aires: Debolsillo, 2005)

Toro, Carlos, *Anécdotas del fútbol* (Madrid: La Esfera de los Libros, 2004)

Valdano, Jorge, *El miedo escénico y otras hierbas* (Madrid: Aguilar, 2002)

Vargas, Walter, *Fútbol Delivery* (Buenos Aires: Ediciones Al Arco, 2007)

Magazines

El Gráfico, Buenos Aires

Don Balón, Barcelona

Newspapers

Spain

El País

El Mundo

La Vanguardia

El Periódico de Catalunya

Marca

As

Sport

Mundo Deportivo

Argentina

La Nación

Clarín

Época

Olé

La Capital

UK

The Times

Guardian

Italy

Corriere della Sera

Gazzetta dello Sport

Corriere dello Sport

Yearbooks

Guía de la Liga 2005 (*Marca* Magazines)
Guía de la Liga 2006 (*Marca* Magazines)
Guía de la Liga 2007 (*Marca* Magazines)
Guía de la Liga 2008 (*Marca* Magazines)
Guía de la Liga 2009 (*Marca* Magazines)
Guía de la Liga 2010 (*Marca* Magazines)

TV channels

Canal +
TyC
Fox TV
TV3

Websites

www.fifa.com
www.uefa.com
www.afa.com.ar
www.gloriosonewells.com.ar
www.nob.com.ar
www.rosariocentral.com
www.fcbarcelona.com
www.youtube.com
www.lionelmessi.org
www.liomessi.wordpress.com
www.messiadictos.com

Acknowledgements

Thanks to Leo Messi and to his family: Jorge, Celia, Rodrigo and Marcela.

And, in order of appearance, thanks to Laure Merle d'Aubigné, Bernat Puigtobella, Fèlix Riera, Montserrat Molons, Marcela Martínez, Claudio Martínez, Julio Lagos, Diego Torres, Fernando Solanas, Asier del Horno, Pablo Zabaleta, Hugo Tocalli, Pancho Ferraro, Carlos Garaycochea, Carlos Bilardo, Manuel Giménez, Dolores García, Fernando Niembro, Claudio Codina, Mariano Bereznicki, Diego Schwarzstein, Cintia Arellano, Salvador Aparicio, Ernesto Vecchio, Adrián Coria, Horacio del Prado, Roberto Perfumo, Alfio Basile, Santiago Segurola, Cristina Cubero, José Miguel Terés, Gianluca Zambrotta, Alex García, Charly Rexach, Josep Maria Minguella, Horacio Gaggioli, Frank Rijkaard, Jorge Valdano, Ton Vilalta Seco, Albert Torrescasana, Ignacio Iraola, Analía Romano, Oliver Pugh, Simon Flynn, Andrew Furlow, Nick Sidwell, Sarah Higgins, Najma Finlay and Sheli Rodney.

Dedicated to Elvira, for everything she has done and continues to do. To Lorenzo, Olmo, Alda and Tullio.